The Political
Science Toolbox

The Political Science Toolbox

A Research Companion to American Government

STEPHEN E. FRANTZICH AND
HOWARD R. ERNST

ROWMAN & LITTLEFIELD PUBLISHERS, INC.
Lanham • Boulder • New York • Toronto • Plymouth, UK

ROWMAN & LITTLEFIELD PUBLISHERS, INC.

Published in the United States of America
by Rowman & Littlefield Publishers, Inc.
A wholly owned subsidary of The Rowman & Littlefield Publishing Group, Inc.
4501 Forbes Boulevard, Suite 200, Lanham, Maryland 20706
www.rowmanlittlefield.com

Estover Road
Plymouth PL6 7PY
United Kingdom

British Library Cataloguing in Publication Information Available

Library of Congress Cataloging-in-Publication Data

Frantzich, Stephen E.
    The political science toolbox : a research companion to American government /
Stephen E. Frantzich and Howard R. Ernst.
        p. cm.
    Includes index.
    ISBN-13: 978-0-7425-4761-2 (cloth : alk. paper)
    ISBN-10: 0-7425-4761-2 (cloth : alk. paper)
    ISBN-13: 978-0-7425-4762-9 (pbk. : alk. paper)
    ISBN-10: 0-7425-4762-0 (pbk. : alk. paper)
    eISBN-13: 978-0-7425-6456-5
    eISBN-10: 0-7425-6456-8
    1. United States—Politics and government. I. Ernst, Howard R., 1970– II. Frantzich,
Stephen E. American government. III. Title.
JK276.F73 2009 Suppl.
320.473—dc22   2008004237

Printed in the United States of America

∞™ The paper used in this publication meets the minimum requirements of American
National Standard for Information Sciences—Permanence of Paper for Printed Library
Materials, ANSI/NISO Z39.48-1992.

To our lifelong research partners—Jane and Tracey

Contents

Chapter 3: The Presidency and the Bureaucracy   95

List of Skill Boxes

The skill boxes are designed as stand-alone guidance for particular research methods. While the skill boxes are located within specific substantive realms of the text, the appropriate applications of the methodologies involved are much broader, and you should consider using them in the area you decide to research.

Preface

Few people have strong opinions regarding the key controversies of molecular biology or astrophysics, though almost all Americans have deeply held beliefs regarding the political world. From the workplace watercooler to the halls of Congress and every cocktail party in between, citizens discuss and debate topics of concern that are central to the study of American government—presidential elections, governmental corruption, immigration reform, environmental protection, Supreme Court decisions, media bias, public safety, and scores of other political issues.

While all active citizens are amateur political scientists, not all citizens are *good* political scientists. Some see the political world through ideological lenses that color their judgments and distort their ability to make objective observations. Others are overwhelmed by the 24-hour news cycle that inundates them with information about the political world but provides little of the political context that is necessary for understanding the news and none of the analytical tools that are needed to meaningfully process the information. Citizens can generally remember taking an American-government class in high school, but they have long since forgotten the most basic information regarding the political process. They are left with their beliefs intact, but they are hard-pressed to explain the sources of their political preferences.

Students of American government also struggle with similar issues. They come to their studies with their own political biases in hand, varying levels of basic knowledge, and virtually no understanding of the practice of political science. Undergraduates often struggle to make sense of the complex political world in which they live, while at the same time attempting to understand the nature of political science inquiry. The research topics that are assigned in their "substantive" classes often appear to have little to do with the research methods they acquire in their research classes. And the material covered in their much-dreaded research-methods classes—the penance they pay for majoring in an otherwise interesting topic—often appears to have little, if anything, to do with their other courses of study.

Given our experiences teaching the substance and methods of political science to undergraduate students, we understand the dilemmas facing political science majors *and the dilemmas facing political science instructors*. Students yearn for a trusted guide to help them cope with the political science experience—a single reference work that contains the basic tools that a political science major needs to succeed. And instructors desire to help students ask meaningful political science questions, but are concerned about sacrificing valuable class time to "reteach" basic research concepts. In other words, instructors desire a reference work containing the basic tools that they hope their students bring to each class but that experience tells them their students are unlikely to possess.

This book is intended as a reliable companion to students of American government as they navigate their undergraduate programs. Its basic function is similar to that of the popular writing guides that students typically receive upon arrival at college. Instead of covering the style of writing, this book addresses the basic elements of American government and political inquiry. The book serves as a bridge between research-methods classes and student research, making it a valuable supplement for an applied-research-methods class, as well as a useful supplement for introductory American-government courses or introductory political science courses. Moreover, students completing honors papers, capstone assignments, or any substantial research projects in the field of American government will find the ideas and guidance in this work invaluable.

We have intentionally omitted the narratives and glossy pictures that fill the pages of standard American-government textbooks and replaced them with material that students can use. The no-nonsense approach includes references to key primary sources in political science, as well as lists of the most authoritative works in American-government subfields. The book helps students navigate the minefield of the Internet by identifying the highest-quality Internet sources. It provides information about key political actors and important political events, research tips, ideas for future research, and a comprehensive glossary of terms. It also includes practical material concerning plagiarism, citing sources, interpreting tables, and thinking about hypotheses.

If you are looking for shortcuts to take in the research process, or for a spoon-fed approach to research, this is not the book for you. But if you desire a sturdy toolbox filled with ideas that can help you organize and explore your own unique political questions, this book will serve you well. It will help you identify meaningful political science questions and think about political issues like a social scientist, and it will guide you toward quality information. The work is designed to help students of American government transition from interested bystanders of the political world into active participants in the discipline of political science—to join the dialogue of the discipline.

We would like to thank our colleague Priscilla Zotti for reviewing the judiciary chapter, and the numerous anonymous reviewers of the text who also provided valuable feedback. At Rowman & Littlefield, we would like to thank Niels Aaboe, who saw the value of this project even before we could clearly articulate its scope; Lynn Weber, who painstakingly edited our work; and Jonathan Sisk, who has supported our many projects with Rowman & Littlefield. We would like to thank the library staff at the United States Naval Academy, in particular Barbara Breeden for her many years of dedication to faculty and student research at the Naval Academy. We would also like to acknowledge our students, who taught us how to teach political science and who continue to inspire us. And lastly, we would like to thank our spouses, Jane and Tracey, to whom this book is dedicated.

Introduction: Thinking Like a Political Scientist

In our more than forty years of combined teaching experience, we have assigned, guided, and, most importantly, read thousands of student papers. Some were disasters; most showed promise but could have been improved; and a few were truly inspired. We designed this book thinking about the tools that undergraduates need to succeed as students of American government. In the pages that follow you will find essential information about the political world, as well as information about framing research questions, collecting appropriate data, identifying important political science literature, and writing research papers. Our goal is to help you pursue your academic interests while meeting the expectations of your instructors.

As authors, we would like you to read every word in every chapter. But as teachers, we realize that is not the way that undergraduate scholars operate, and it is not the way that this book is designed. The following sections are largely self-contained and designed for "just in time" usage. When you are assigned a paper or are looking for essential information about the political process, we hope that you will go to the relevant chapter, review the material, consider our guidance, and tap the identified resources. We hope that this is a book that will remain with you for years to come, a trusted companion that helps you understand American government by teaching you to think like a political scientist.

1. The Science of Political Analysis

You are entering the world of social analysis. It is not rocket science—in many ways it is much harder. The rocket scientists consider force and thrust to determine distance and trajectory. The rocket reacts uniformly according to fixed physical rules. The social scientist also considers cause-and-effect relationships—for example, how exposure to a news story might influence a person's political opinions or voting behavior. The complicating trick for the social scientist is that this research is not subject to the same timeless generalizations that guide much of the natural sciences—social scientists seek reliable trends, but they do not have the luxury of natural laws.

The causes of political behavior are complex and inherently difficult to understand. Not all people are influenced the same way by the same stimuli; people are exposed to countless stimuli that are difficult to control and measure; and stimuli often interact with each other in unpredictable ways. Unlike rockets, our subjects can intentionally mislead us, or may simply not understand the true motivations of their political behavior. Our subjects are influenced by a unique set of ever-changing circumstances. They have the capacity to learn, and they possess free will and imagination. Humans are not slaves to circumstances, and they have the ability to envision a world that does not yet exist and take steps to achieve it. Rocket science is a simple science; ours is complex.

In over a hundred years of social science research, political analysts have not identified a single law of social science, nor are they likely to in the future. This does not make social science inferior to natural sciences, but it is indicative of the complexity of our task. Social scientists operate in the "real world," not the sterile environment of the lab. We desire to understand causal relationships *and* the motivations of political actors. No one would ever ask, "What motivates a rocket to lift?" But they would ask, "What motivates a political actor to launch an intercontinental ballistic missile?" Like the natural scientist, we seek relationships and rule out false assumptions, but the nature of our subject requires that we go one step further. We ask, "Why?"

A. WHAT MAKES POLITICAL SCIENCE A "SCIENCE"?

Some people consider the term *political science* an arrogant claim, retaining the term *science* for the limited number of subjects that have known laws, or at least reliable outcomes (e.g., chemistry, biology, physics). Science, however, is an approach to understanding rather than a list of natural laws. Any topic, including political science, can be studied scientifically. Some of the basic characteristics of scientific inquiry include

- *objective analysis*, that is, conducting an inquiry with an open mind and retaining neutrality throughout a study;
- *measurable data*, which means making use of hard evidence that can be observed and measured;

- *replicable findings*, which requires the use of research methods that enable other researchers to replicate your results; and
- *falsifiable hypotheses*, which means testing claims in such a manner that if they are inaccurate you can reject them.

B. COUNT IT, INTERPRET IT, AND FEEL IT

Political science research uses a wide variety of data. **Empirical analysis** emphasizes the collection of hard evidence of observable events (e.g., votes in Congress, dollars spent in campaigns, opinions collected from a survey, decisions made by judges). While hard data has the advantage of looking precise and indisputable, it is not always as concrete as it appears at first glance. Researchers must be careful that their empirical data truly measures the concepts in question—that is, that the data have **validity**. For example it would be invalid to make use of someone's shoe size to measure their support for capital punishment, but you could make use of polling information to garner this information. Researchers must also be careful that their empirical data yields the same results if collected on separate occasions or by different observers—that is, the data have **reliability**. For example, if two different researchers are tasked with counting the number of "negative advertisements" run during a single political campaign and produce substantially different results, their data would be said to be unreliable.

Impressionistic research uses the arguments and interpretations of others to interpret the political world. These impressions are known as **qualitative data** and may or may not be based on direct observations. Experts use a rich variety of information to make conclusions. The student researcher takes on the task of determining whose arguments make the most sense and explaining why. This type of analysis often involves looking for a "consensus of experts" or simply rejecting weak arguments. **Experiential research** involves working in the political realm, keeping close track of one's experiences, and attempting to develop generalizations based on those experiences. Formal internships are an example of experiential learning.[1] While impressionistic research and experiential research fall short of the characteristics of formal scientific inquiry, they are meaningful ways for students to become acquainted with a research topic and to form meaningful assessments about the political world.

As you read through the upcoming chapters, you will see a tendency to suggest empirical measures. In modern social analysis, empirical data tends to trump qualitative evaluations, assuming of course that legitimate empirical data is available. Using empirical data leaves less room for interpretation and tends to close the argument more effectively than qualitative data. If high-quality empirical data is available, do not ignore it—even if you are doing a largely qualitative study. For example, it is much more powerful to say, "According to a recent Gallup Poll 70 percent of Americans support a woman's right to choose," than to say "The public seems to be pro-choice."

In many realms, however, qualitative data is the only data available. For example, if someone desired to study Internet strategies of candidates in the current campaign season, qualitative data might be the preferred choice. Meaningful empirical data is unlikely to exist for something that is currently taking place, and using data from a previous campaign would be invalid given the high rate of change in this area. In this case, a researcher might choose to interview a candidate, a candidate's campaign consultants, or members of the media. This type of soft data might be less useful than hard data in establishing causal relationships, but it also might be the most useful in understanding the topic.

C. THINKING IN TERMS OF VARIABLES AND CAUSAL RELATIONSHIPS

Social analysts look at relationships between **variables** (i.e., characteristics of people and phenomena that vary). For example, one might want to test whether a representative's party identification is related to his or her vote on a gun-control bill. In this example, there are two variables: the member's party (Democratic or Republican) and the member's vote (for or against a specific gun-control bill). If all Republicans voted against gun control and all Democrats voted for gun control, it is a pretty good bet that party has some effect on the vote. In the language of science, the **independent variable** (in this example, party) is presumed to affect the **dependent variable** (in this example, preference for gun control). Stated more precisely, if changes in the independent variable are known to cause changes in the dependent variable, you have established a **causal relationship**.

While establishing a causal relationship appears to be a straightforward task, it is not. There are three criteria that must be met before establishing causality:

- *Temporal order:* The cause must precede the effect.
- *Observable relationship:* The variables must be related in an observable manner.
- *No third factors:* A third factor cannot explain the apparent relationship.

The first criterion is often relatively easy to establish. In our example, members of Congress are party members *before* they vote on an issue; they don't become members of a party because of a floor vote. The second criterion also poses no special obstacles. If all, or most, Republicans voted one way and Democrats voted another way, you would have satisfied this requirement. The third criterion, however, possess a unique challenge. For example, what if ideology (i.e., the elected official's belief system) explains both the differences in party affiliation and the specific vote? Perhaps conservatives are more likely to be Republicans and more likely to oppose gun control. In this case, the member's ideology, not the member's party, explains the variation in the two variables.

The case discussed here is an example of an **antecedent variable**—a third factor that comes prior to the independent and dependent variables and is responsible for the fluctuations in both variables. An **intervening variable** is a third variable that comes between the independent variable and dependent variable and is responsible for fluctuations in the dependent variable. For example, a researcher might claim that the independent variable "race" is related to the dependent variable "support for Democratic candidates," asserting that minority groups are more likely to support Democrats. It might, however, be that race is related to income, which in turn is related to support for Democratic candidates. In this case, race is only indirectly related to support for Democratic candidates. The failure to rule out antecedent variables can lead to **spurious claims**, that is, claiming a causal relationship exists when in fact one does not exist. The failure to rule out intervening variables can lead a researcher to mistake indirect relationships for direct causal relationships.

Since there are an infinite number of third factors to consider, it is never possible to entirely satisfy the third criterion of causality. This is why it has been said that scientists never prove causal relationships; at best they reject false claims. The problem of third variables in not unique to political science or the social sciences; it is a problem of all scientific inquiry. What makes social science different from many of the natural sciences is the sheer number of likely third variables. While researchers in the natural sciences typically control for the influence of a small number of third variables (e.g., weight, speed, temperature), researchers in the social sciences generally have many more factors to consider (e.g., race, age, ideology, gender, education, income). This is one reason social scientists always understate the certainty of their findings and never claim to have "proved" a relationship.

D. STANDING ON THE SHOULDERS OF OTHERS: THE LITERATURE REVIEW

Few research projects are entirely novel. Even the term *research* implies "search again." You will undoubtedly begin your analysis by conducting a **literature review**, analyzing the existing body of knowledge on a certain topic. In analyzing the literature it is important to assess the quality of previous studies. Research in **academic journals** (scholarly journals published by professional associations and usually affiliated with major universities) is generally the highest quality. These essays tend to be methodologically sophisticated and to have undergone a rigorous review process by experts. Books by **academic presses** (publishers that are associated with universities and that publish scholarly works) are also good bets. A good strategy to employ when writing a literature review is to locate a few high-quality journal articles and books that were recently published on your topic. These works will have literature reviews of their own and will help you identify **seminal works**—that is, leading works—on the topic and help you identify how research in the area has developed over time.

Be wary of relying on works published by **trade presses** (i.e., publications that are written for the general public and that often lack the rigor of academic studies). The line between academic presses and trade presses is not always clear, as a growing number of **crossover presses** attempt to achieve the rigor of academic presses but market their books to a wider audience. These types of books are often written by leading scholars and are well suited for guiding undergraduate research. Popular magazines and the Internet are a mix of high-quality analysis and foolish speculation. These sources should be used sparingly, or not at all. In evaluating such sources, one should see if the author is from a credible institution and whether the conclusions match those of other researchers. While a "consensus of experts" can be wrong, the individual proposing a completely different take on reality must bear the burden of proof.

E. THINKING IN TERMS OF HYPOTHESES

There is a temptation to jump into academic research and "just do it." This often leads to a scattered collection of data and incoherent results. Stating hypotheses forces precision in data collection and narrows the scope of analysis. A **hypothesis** is an estimation of how variables are related to each other. Think of it as a formal statement about which intelligent and informed people could disagree.

One useful format for a hypothesis is an "if-then statement." For example, when driving down the highway we think, "*If* I go 66 miles per hour in a 65-mile-per-hour zone, *then* I am unlikely to receive a speeding ticket." However, "*If* I go 85 miles per hour in a 65-miles-per-hour zone, *then* I am likely to receive a speeding ticket." We look around us to see what other cars are doing, we scan for police cars, and we draw on our own experience in similar situations. We are not particularly interested in counting the number of blue cars, checking license-plate numbers, or seeing whether more drivers are men or women.

In political analysis, we seek if-then statements that help explain a political phenomenon. Our *if* is our implied cause, and *then* is the implied effect. For example, we might test the hypothesis that "if a president is in the first year of his or her term, then the president will have more success with Congress than if president in a later year." Once stated, our hypotheses require fine-tuning. In the above hypothesis, "success" has to be clearly defined. We refine our hypotheses by giving our variables **operational definitions**, that is, statements expressing the manner in which variables are measured.

Some students hesitate to work from a hypothesis for fear of conducting an extensive research project only to have their key hypotheses rejected. There is nothing wrong with disproving a reasonable hypothesis; in fact, this is an important way in which knowledge progresses. If you had reason to believe that conditions would yield one set of results and they yield a different set of results, then you have learned something of great value. *Also remember that the failure to reject your hypotheses does not prove your hypotheses.* Since there are an infinite number of third factors to consider before unconditionally accepting a hypothesis, you will never be able to prove your causal claims. Rejecting a likely hypothesis might actually prove more valuable than finding conditional support for a hypothesis. In other words, there are no bad findings!

2. Types of Academic Assignments

There are numerous types of undergraduate academic writing assignments. Before starting an assignment, always make sure that you know what your instructor has in mind. When in doubt, ask; when you have no doubt about an assignment, ask anyway. While seeking knowledge is nice, meeting the instructor's expectations is what will determine your grade on any given assignment.

Listed below are a few general types of assignments.

- *Opinion piece:* An **opinion piece** is generally a short critical-thinking assignment (usually no more than five to seven pages) rather than a formal research paper. Typically, the instructor wants to know that you have considered several sides of an argument and that your opinions are based on informed logic. You are unlikely to state formal hypotheses in this type of paper. When writing an opinion piece, always make sure that you have a "worthy opponent." Start by asking yourself, "What am I arguing against?" Make sure that you understand your opponent's argument and the assumptions on which your opponent's argument rest. When you discuss your opponent's case, portray it fairly and make sure that it is believable. You want to establish that you have the best argument, not a weak opponent.
- *Descriptive analysis:* A **descriptive analysis** generally attempts to explain a specific event or phenomenon, rather than explore more general causal relationships. For example, an instructor might ask students to explain a specific presidential election by considering the key contextual factors (e.g., state of the

economy, public opinion about the parties, opinions about national security), personal factors (e.g., the personalities of the people running for office and influencing the race), and legal factors (e.g., the laws and norms that constrain legal political action). You are unlikely to state formal hypotheses in this type of paper. In descriptive analysis, the researcher takes on the role of investigative reporter rather than "scientist." Be careful not to make bold claims that cannot be supported by your limited findings.

- *Literature reviews:* A **literature review** is a summary and analysis of the existing knowledge on a certain topic. Literature reviews are often part of a larger research paper but can serve as stand-alone paper assignments in undergraduate courses. Do not think of a literature review as a series of mini book reports, but instead consider it a formal analysis of all the important research on a topic. In analyzing the literature, it is important to stress high-quality studies and how they changed the way scholars think about a topic. It is also useful to discuss how knowledge has progressed on a topic and to identify current controversies that remain in the literature. As we discussed earlier, a good strategy for writing a successful literature review is to find a few high-quality journal articles and books that were recently published on the topic and to allow the literature reviews that are contained in these works to guide your assessment. As always, be sure to cite your sources appropriately.
- *Empirical analysis:* **Empirical analysis** emphasizes hard data collected from observable events. The researcher can use data that was collected specifically for a particular study, referred to as **primary data,** or data that is adapted from a different study, referred to as **secondary data.** The data can come from several different sources—governmental records, interviews, surveys, document analysis, and other sources. Empirical analysis can also be conducted using various research designs: a **single case study,** that is, an in-depth analysis of a specific case that yields a great deal of detail but few general trends; **comparative analysis,** that is, an in-depth analysis of a small number of cases that can yield rich details and can be used to begin to explore causal relationships; or **quantitative analysis,** that is, an analysis that makes use of a large number of cases and statistical procedures that are specifically designed for testing causal claims. Empirical studies take a tremendous amount of time and are usually best suited for a semester-long honors project or capstone assignment. It is important to start this type of assignment early and to make steady progress.

3. Writing a Major Research Paper

The typical academic research paper follows a fairly standard argument structure. The initial section of the work explains why the topic is important and what others have written about the subject (introductory discussion and literature review). The second section explains the author's perspective on the topic and explains how the author plans to analyze the subject (theory section and methods section). The third section contains the researcher's results (findings, analysis, and conclusions). When you put the pieces together, the typical academic research paper explains (1) what others say about the topic; (2) what the researcher says about the topic; and (3) what the findings say about the topic.

When writing an academic paper it is important to focus on two essential factors: your audience and your topic. Generally speaking, your audience is your instructor. Know the instructor's specific expectations. While many instructors offer open-ended topics, instructors all have expectations regarding the design of the paper, even if they do not clearly express their expectations. Remember, political science professors are generally experts in a specific topic of political science, not in the art of teaching political science writing. Instructors often have difficulty expressing what they desire from a student paper, but know good writing when they see it. Ask your instructor for specific instructions and if the instructions are unclear, ask your instructor for examples of the type of essay he or she desires.

Moreover, understand your topic and the nature of the relationships that you are considering. Are you studying how one independent variable (e.g., gender) influences numerous dependent variables (e.g., attitudes about war, politics, and welfare)? Or are you interested in how numerous independent variables influence a single dependent variable (e.g., the various factors that explain congressional voting behavior on a specific bill)? Once you know specifically what you are studying, you can make sure that every word of every section relates to the topic in a logical manner. You will avoid the cardinal sin of undergraduate research—papers that wander aimlessly from issue to issue.

There are eight sections of a typical research paper:

1. *Title:* A title should capture the readers interest and describe the topic. Most academic titles are divided by a colon: the title preceding the colon tends to be catchy and is intended to grab the reader's attention, whereas the title following the colon (the subtitle) is generally more descriptive and explains the topic of the paper—for example, "Behind the Veil: The Role of Supreme Court Clerks in the Modern Court." Avoid revealing your argument in the title. Having read the title, the reader should understand what the topic is and desire to read more, but the reader should not know your perspective on the topic.

2. *Introduction:* Like the title, an introductory section should capture the reader's attention and explain the importance of the topic. Avoid making controversial claims in the introduction. Do not show your cards just yet; you

will have plenty of time to articulate your argument in the theory section. Also, avoid making unsubstantiated claims. Every bit of information that you present as fact in this section should be supported with authoritative references.

3. *Literature review:* The function of the literature review is to establish your credibility with the reader (i.e., establish that you understand the major works on the topic), "remind" the reader of the state of the literature, and prepare the reader for your argument that follows. Avoid expressing your perspective in this section. This section prepares the reader for your ideas that will be presented in the next section, but its focus should be on what *others* have said on the topic. By showing that you understand what experts have said on the topic, you are building your credibility.

4. *Theory:* The purpose of the theory section is to explicitly state the assumptions on which your hypotheses are based and to state your hypotheses. This is your opportunity to take a side in the debate. Generally, researchers enter the debate in one of the following ways: (1) by favoring one side of an ongoing debate found in the literature; (2) by arguing that the literature has omitted an important piece of information that you are going to consider; or (3) by showing how a different way of looking at the subject can solve an inconsistency found in the literature. Avoid stating hypotheses that cannot be tested with your findings or hypotheses that do not directly relate to your theoretical perspective.

5. *Methods:* The function of this section is to explain why you chose your specific research design (case study, comparative analysis, or quantitative analysis), the strengths and weakness of your design, how you collected your data, and how you operationally defined your key variables. Avoid being defensive in this section or omitting information that reveals weaknesses in your approach. Every study has flaws, but very few are fatal. It is important that you recognize the shortcomings in your study and that you present them to the reader.

6. *Findings:* Present the findings of your study and relate them to your hypotheses and ultimately to your theoretical claims. This is the section in which to present your summary tables and figures. Each table and graph should be completely self-sufficient (i.e., a reader should be able to understand the summary material without reading the analysis that accompanies the graphic). Make certain that each table has a meaningful title, that it is obvious which variable is the independent variable and which is the dependent variable, and that you provide source information for the data. In the analysis of your findings, resist the urge to overstate the significance of your findings and to claim that you have "proven a relationship." Consider the possibility of third variables and how weaknesses in your research design or data might have skewed the results.

7. *Conclusion:* The purpose of the conclusion is to relate your findings to the existing literature and make suggestions for further research. The conclusion section is not simply a restatement of your findings. This section should lead the reader in a certain direction; it should suggest what questions your study raises, as much as what questions it answers.

8. *References:* The purpose of the references section is to give a full citation for each of the works referenced in the essay. The reader should be able to locate all the information you used in writing your essay. Make sure to ask your instructor which reference format he or she prefers.

4. Making Use of Summary Tables

Most research papers make use of some sort of summary table, and at the very least you need to understand how to interpret tables in order to understand the academic literature. Summary tables can be broken down into two broad categories: tables that make use of **descriptive analysis**, that is, information that describes the characteristics of individual variables, and tables that make use of **explanatory analysis**, that is, analysis that describes relationships between variables and that tends to make use of explanatory statistics.

The simplest kind of descriptive table is a **frequency distribution**, which lists the values of a variable along with the number of cases or the percentage of cases for each value (see table I.1 for an example of a frequency distribution). Other common statistical measures used in constructing descriptive tables include the **mode**, the most frequently occurring value for a variable; the **median**, the value below which 50 percent of the cases fall and above which 50 percent of the cases fall; and the **mean** (or average), a simple statistical measure calculated by summing the values of a variable and dividing by the total number of cases (see table I.2).

The simplest kind of explanatory table is the **contingency table**, also known as a cross-tabulation (see tables I.2 and I.3). A contingency table is a straightforward mechanism for assessing whether changes in an independent variable (gen-

Table I.1.   Presidential Job-Approval Ratings

	Rating (%)
Strongly approve	5
Approve	10
Neutral	20
Disapprove	40
Strongly disapprove	25
Total	100

Table I.2.   Average Presidential Job-Approval Ratings by Group

	Rating (%)
Men	41
Women	30
Whites	40
African Americans	10
Hispanics	35
Protestants	45
Catholics	30

der, race, and religion in table 1.2) have an observable impact on a dependent variable (presidential approval). A contingency table is typically constructed by calculating the percentage of cases that satisfy the criteria of both the independent variable and the dependent variable. In table I.3, the independent variable (region) is represented by the columns in the table, and the dependent variable (party identification) is represented by the rows. In this table, substantial variation across columns would provide support for the claim of a regional influence on party identification. If the percentages across the columns are identical, or nearly identical, it would suggest the absence of a relationship. (See box 2.4, in chapter 2, on creating and analyzing contingency tables.)

Beyond the simple contingency table listed here, political scientists also make use of sophisticated statistical procedures to independently gauge the strength of relationships—**measures of association**. The primary benefits of measures of association are that they objectively estimate the strength of relationships and the likelihood that relationships have occurred by chance. **Multivariate statistical analysis**, like multivariate regression analysis, enables a researcher to estimate the combined influence of several independent variables on a single dependent variable. This type of analysis also enables the researcher to estimate the individual impact of each independent variable while controlling for the impact of the other independent variables.

While multivariate statistical analysis is well beyond the scope of most undergraduate research projects, with some assistance from your professor you

Table I.3.   Party Identification by Region

Party Identification	Northeast (%)	Southeast (%)	Midwest (%)	West (%)
Democrat	60	40	48	55
Republican	39	59	51	42
Other	1	1	1	3
Total	100	100	100	100

should be able to interpret tables that make use of multivariate analysis in the political science literature. The R^2 statistic of a regression model estimates the combined influence of the independent variables on the dependent variable. An R^2 score of 1 suggests that the independent variables explain all the fluctuation of the dependent variable (this never happens in social science). An R^2 score of 0 suggests that together the independent variables explain none of the fluctuation of the dependent variable. Typically, political science models produce R^2 scores in the 0.5 range or lower, though there is no standard.

In multivariate regression analysis, each independent variable is assigned a coefficient that estimates its individual impact on the dependent variable. For standardized coefficients, the higher the number (on a 0 to 1 scale), the greater the estimated impact of the independent variable. Most researchers also make use of a star system to indicate the likelihood that the estimated impact is attributable to chance. One star (*) next to an independent variable suggests that it is unlikely that the independent variable's effect on the dependent variable is happening by chance. Two stars (**) suggest that it is highly unlikely that an independent variable's effect on the dependent variable is happening by chance. No stars suggest that it is likely that whatever relationship has been observed between an independent variable and the dependent variable is attributable to chance.

5. Giving Credit Where Credit Is Due

A key component of building on existing knowledge lies in the careful citation of sources. Academic writing is generally enhanced with ideas, facts, direct quotations, and visual representations of others. Each of these components is the intellectual property of the creator. **Plagiarism** is making use of someone else's words or ideas without clear and complete credit being given to the original source. In short, it is academic theft. It can happen accidentally because of sloppy citations or ignorance, and it can occur intentionally in the case of flagrant fraud. In either case, it is plagiarism and should be avoided at all costs.

The lack of a citation is an implied fraudulent claim that the work of someone else is yours. Citations should be clearly linked to the material in question (as opposed to all-encompassing citations at the end of a paragraph or paper). Direct quotes always require quotation marks and a citation to identify the source. Paraphrasing does not abrogate your responsibility to cite ideas that are not your own, and mentioning the source in the text does not mitigate the need for citations. Alternative formats such as pictures, graphics, music, and personal interviews also require citations. The type of source material—whether a book, a magazine, a radio program, a television show, the Internet—has no effect on the need to cite the source.

A. TYPES OF PLAGIARISM

1. ***Intentional and flagrant:*** Turning in a paper written largely or wholly by someone else is unacceptable. Submitting a paper of another student or purchasing a paper online and submitting it under your name is pure fraud, deserving the harshest penalties. Beware, Internet search software enables instructors to track down intentional plagiarism with remarkable ease. Also note that some institutions consider it intentional plagiarism to submit your own work to two different instructors without gaining prior approval from the instructors. Make sure that you know your institution's rules on this subject.

2. ***Unintentional or misleading:*** Sporadic misuse of the intellectual property of others may stem from disorganization, laziness, or ignorance—none of which excuses the misdeed. Some common errors include:
   - using the exact words of another without using quotation marks or citing the source;
   - using someone else's original ideas, data, or visual representations (images, graphs, charts, etc.) without a full citation;
   - paraphrasing another's words while retaining the basic idea without citing the original source; and
   - misrepresenting the words or ideas of others through edits or other distortions.[2]

The best protection against plagiarism is to fully and accurately cite all sources using one of the standard citation formats. It is better to err on the side of caution.

B. THE CASE AGAINST PLAGIARIZING

Arguments against plagiarism tend to take on a very legalistic tone. While the value of following rules is one component of the argument, the following discussion attempts to broaden the rationale for avoiding plagiarism.

- In the real world, plagiarism has severe consequences. Numerous famous authors in recent years have been forced to pay monetary penalties for using uncited material in their work. Others have had their books removed from store shelves at great expense and have had their reputations tarnished and careers sidetracked. For students, plagiarism can result in receiving a failing grade for the project, a failing grade for the course, or expulsion from the institution.
- Plagiarism *weakens your argument*. Citing sources for your work is not a sign of weakness but a powerful way to increase the legitimacy of your paper in

the eyes of the reader. Citations show that you have consulted the existing literature and have attempted to expand on it. Citations are a sign of academic rigor that instructors will look for when forming initial impressions of your work.

- Plagiarism can *hurt your intellectual development*. Too much borrowing of the work of others limits the degree to which you engage yourself in the analytical process of making an argument and supporting it. Moreover, in a future paper you might want to further develop a portion of a paper you wrote in the past. Insufficient citations will make it more difficult for you to find the sources you worked from.
- In a competitive academic environment, plagiarism as a shortcut is *unfair to students who created their papers properly*. It is not just stealing from the original source; it is also cheating your fellow students. The advantage that plagiarism gives one student comes at the expense of other students.

6. Sources That Will Help You Understand the Research Process

Babbie, Earl R. *The Basics of Social Research*. Belmont, Calif.: Thomson Wadsworth, 2007.

Johnson, Janet Buttolph, and H. T. Reynolds. *Political Science Research Methods*. 5th ed. Washington, D.C.: CQ Press, 2005.

King, Gary, Robert O. Keohane, and Sidney Verba. *Designing Social Research*. Princeton, N.J.: Princeton University Press, 1994.

Kranzler, Gerald, Janet Moursund, and John H. Kranzler. *Statistics for the Terrified*. 4th ed. Englewood Cliffs, N.J.: Prentice Hall, 2006.

Le Roy, Michael K., and Michael Corbett. *Research Methods in Political Science: An Introduction Using MicroCase*. 6th ed. Belmont, Calif.: Thomson Wadsworth, 2006.

7. Resources for Citing Sources and Avoiding Plagiarism

Where can I find information about different types of citation styles?
A good book to use is Julia Johns and Sara Keller, *Cite It Right: The SourceAid Guide to Citation, Research, and Avoiding Plagiarism*, 2nd ed. (Osterville, Mass.: SourceAid, 2005). Cornell University Library also provides a useful summary of various citation styles, at http://www.library.cornell.edu/newhelp/res_strategy/citing/index.html.

Where can I find information about the American Psychological Association (APA) style of citations?
See *Publication Manual of the American Psychological Association*, 5th ed. (Washington, D.C.: American Psychological Association. 2001) and Ohio State University Library, "APA Citation Guide," http://library.osu.edu/sites/guides/apagd.php.

Where can I find information about the Chicago style of citations?
See *The Chicago Manual of Style*, 15th ed. (Chicago: University of Chicago Press, 2003) and Ohio State University Library, "Chicago Manual of Style Citation Guide," http://library.osu.edu/sites/guides/chicagogd.php.

Where can I find information about the Modern Language Association (MLA) style of citations?
See Joseph Gibaldi, *MLA Handbook for Writers of Research Papers*, 6th ed. (New York: MLA, 2003) and Ohio State University Library, "MLA Citation Guide," http://library.osu.edu/sites/guides/mlagd.php.

Where can I find information about the Turabian style of citations?
See Kate L. Turabian, *A Manual for Writers of Term Papers, Theses, and Dissertations*, 6th ed. (Chicago: University of Chicago Press, 1996) and Ohio State University Library, "Turabian Citation Guide," http://library.osu.edu/sites/guides/turabiangd.php.

Notes

1. See Stephen Frantzich, *Studying in Washington* (Washington, D.C.: American Political Science Association, 2002).
2. In developing the list of examples, a number of ideas were drawn from the North Carolina State University Library website, at http://www.lib.ncsu.edu.lobo2/using/plagiarism.

CHAPTER 1

The Founding Era

The period of time between the conclusion of the **French and Indian War** (a costly seven-year global struggle that lasted from 1756 to 1763 and in which Britain and its North American colonists defeated France and its Native American allies) and the ratification of the **Bill of Rights** (the first ten amendments to the U.S. Constitution) is generally considered the **founding era** (1763–1791). During this period, the founders declared their independence from England, defeated the most powerful military force of the day, wrote state constitutions, established and reestablished a national governing arrangement, and adopted the Bill of Rights. Ultimately, the founders' many accomplishments not only would inspire a nation but also would set off a wave of democratic fervor that continues to spread around the globe to this day.

1. The Structure of the U.S. Constitution and the Intentions of the Founders

A. THE BASIC STRUCTURE OF THE U.S. CONSTITUTION

Constitutions are documents that define the structure and legal authority of a government. The U.S. Constitution is divided into seven separate articles. The first three articles establish the institutional structure of the new government: Article I establishes Congress; Article II establishes the presidency; and Article III establishes the federal court system. Article IV outlines state relations; Article V addresses constitutional change; Article VI defines national authority; and Article VII describes the ratification process for the Constitution. The first ten amendments to the Constitution, known as the Bill of Rights, were adopted in

1791 and enumerate many of the basic civil liberties that Americans have come to enjoy (e.g., freedom of assembly, press, religion, speech) as well as the procedural due process rights of those accused of a crime. Including the Bill of Rights, there have been twenty-seven amendments to the U.S. Constitution.

Outline of the Constitution:[1]

Preamble
Article I (The Legislative Branch):
    Section 1 (Legislative Power Vested)
    Section 2 (House of Representatives)
    Section 3 (Senate)
    Section 4 (Elections of Senators and Representatives)
    Section 5 (Rules of House and Senate)
    Section 6 (Compensation and Privileges of Members)
    Section 7 (Passage of Bills)
    Section 8 (Scope of Legislative Power)
    Section 9 (Limits on Legislative Power)
    Section 10 (Limits on States)
Article II (The Presidency):
    Section 1 (Election, Installation, Removal)
    Section 2 (Presidential Power)
    Section 3 (State of the Union, Reception of Ambassadors, Faithful Execution of the Law, Commissioning of Officers)
    Section 4 (Impeachment)
Article III (The Judiciary):
    Section 1 (Judicial Power Vested)
    Section 2 (Scope of Judicial Power)
    Section 3 (Treason)
Article IV (The States):
    Section 1 (Full Faith and Credit)
    Section 2 (Privileges and Immunities, Extradition, Fugitive Slaves)
    Section 3 (Admission of States)
    Section 4 (Guarantees to States)
Article V (The Amendment Process)
Article VI (Legal Status of the Constitution)
Article VII (Ratification)
Bill of Rights:
    Amendment I (Freedom of Religion, Speech, Press, Assembly, Petition), 1791
    Amendment II (Right to Bear Arms), 1791
    Amendment III (Quartering of Troops), 1791
    Amendment IV (Search and Seizure), 1791

Amendment V (Grand Jury, Double Jeopardy, Self-Incrimination, Due Process), 1791

Amendment VI (Criminal Prosecutions—Jury Trial, Right to Confront and to Counsel), 1791

Amendment VII (Common-Law Suits—Jury Trial), 1791

Amendment VIII (Excess Bail or Fines, Cruel and Unusual Punishment), 1791

Amendment IX (Nonenumerated Rights), 1791

Amendment X (Rights Reserved to the States and the People), 1791

Additional Amendments:

Amendment XI (Suits against a State), 1795

Amendment XII (Election of President and Vice President), 1804

Amendment XIII (Abolition of Slavery), 1865

Amendment XIV (Privileges and Immunities, Due Process, Equal Protection, Apportionment of Representatives, Civil War Disqualification and Debt), 1868

Amendment XV (Rights Not to Be Denied on Account of Race), 1870

Amendment XVI (Income Tax), 1913

Amendment XVII (Election of Senators), 1913

Amendment XVIII (Prohibition), 1919

Amendment XIX (Women's Right to Vote), 1920

Amendment XX (Presidential Term and Succession), 1933

Amendment XXI (Repeal of Prohibition), 1933

Amendment XXII (Two-Term Limit on President), 1951

Amendment XXIII (Presidential Vote in D.C.), 1961

Amendment XXIV (Ban on Poll Tax), 1964

Amendment XXV (Presidential Succession), 1967

Amendment XXVI (Right to Vote at Age 18), 1971

Amendment XXVII (Compensation of Members of Congress), 1992

B. THE CONSTITUTIONAL AMENDMENT PROCESS

Proposing an Amendment:

Option One: Two-thirds vote of both branches of Congress

Option Two: Two-thirds of state legislatures call for a national convention (this method has never been used)

Adopting an Amendment:

Option One: Three-fourths vote of state legislature (twenty-six amendments have been ratified this way)

Option Two: Constitutional conventions in three-fourths of the states (only the
Twenty-first Amendment, the repeal of prohibition, was ratified this way)

C. COMPOSITION OF THE NATIONAL GOVERNMENT

The Constitution outlines three major groups of participants in the federal government: the executive branch (headed by the president), the legislative branch
(composed of members of the U.S. House and the U.S. Senate), and the judicial
branch (composed of the U.S. Supreme Court and lower federal courts). How
the members of the federal government were to be selected and the conditions
for their removal from office were carefully considered. These important issues
influenced not only who would hold positions of authority but also the nature
of the key institutions. (See table 1.1.)

D. KEY GOVERNING PRINCIPLES EMBODIED IN
THE U.S. CONSTITUTION

Popular Sovereignty

Popular sovereignty is the governing principle that all legitimate governmental
authority is derived from the consent of the governed. The concept is based on
social contract theory, a theory put forward by John Locke that claims legitimate government authority must be derived from the consent of free people. It
is a rejection of the ancient tradition of **divine right**, the governing principle that
political leaders receive their authority from a divine source. Unlike political systems based on divine right, popular sovereignty requires a clear link between the
citizens and the leaders who represent them. While popular sovereignty does not
necessarily require that average citizens have direct control over government institutions, it does require popular checks on government authority and mecha-
nisms for holding public officials accountable to the general public.

Representative Democracy

Representative democracy is a form of government that is tied to public opinion but that also aims to "refine and enlarge" the will of the people. Elections are
intended to select the most knowledgeable and responsible leaders, and political
institutions are designed to promote deliberation. Representative democracy differs from **direct democracy** (a political system in which government actions are
directly controlled by the people), in that it attempts to refine the will of the majority.

Table 1.1. Composition of the National Government under the U.S. Constitution

	Executive	Legislative		Judicial
	President	House of Representatives	Senate	Supreme Court
Selection	Selected by electors in the Electoral College "in such a manner as the (state) Legislature may direct" (modified by the Twelfth Amendment, which separated presidential selection from vice-presidential selection	Elected by the eligible voters of each state	Initially selected by the state legislature, but following adoption of the Seventeenth Amendment in 1913, directly elected by eligible voters	Appointed by the president "with the Advice and Consent of the Senate"
Number	Single person	Apportioned to states according to population	Two per state	No size limit (tradition of nine justices)
Term	Four-year term (Twentieth Amendment limits the president to two terms)	Two-year term (no term limits)	Six-year term (no term limits)	Life term

Separation of Powers

Separation of powers refers to the creation of separate political institutions with overlapping powers for the purpose of fostering competition among political actors and reducing the chance of tyranny. The overlap of powers pits the ambition of one political actor against the ambition of other political actors, causing each political actor to check the ambition of the others. The concept is distinct from the notion of "**checks and balances**," in that the founders never intended the system to possess an equal balance of power. The founders believed that the legislative branch (i.e., the lawmaking branch) would be the most powerful branch and consequently divided the Congress into two separate institutions.

American Federalism

American federalism is a division of power between the federal government and state governments in which each derives power directly from the people and each level of government retains sovereignty in its separate sphere. American federalism differs from **unitary federalism**, in which a strong national government has sovereignty over the lower levels of government in a country. It is also different from **confederated systems**, in which strong state governments have sovereignty over the federal government.

Rule of Law

Rule of law refers to the concept that no person or groups of people are above the law. In the American political system, the Constitution represents the highest law of the land.

Civil Rights

Civil rights are protections from arbitrary discrimination based on classifications such as race, sex, national origin, age, or sexual orientation. While the concept of civil rights is a cornerstone of the Constitution, the notion of what constitutes arbitrary discrimination has changed over time.

Civil Liberties

Civil liberties are a special category of personal freedoms that governments should not abridge without a compelling government interest. Civil liberties are freedoms from the government. Many of the nation's well-known civil liberties are enshrined in the Bill of Rights (e.g., freedom of speech, freedom of religion, freedom from cruel and unusual punishment, freedom from self-incrimination).

E. BASIC GOALS OF THE CONSTITUTION

Encourage Responsive and Responsible Governance

In the *Federalist* No. 10, James Madison expresses one of the key goals of the founders—the desire to achieve a system of government that is tied to the will of the governed but is more stable and responsible than a pure democracy. Madison argues that pure democracies, which he defines as "societ[ies] consisting of a small number of citizens, who assemble and administer the government in person," are inherently unstable. He goes so far as to state that pure democracies "have in general been as short in their lives as they have been violent in their deaths." Madison argues that the founders' system, with its numerous checks and protections, guards against the mischief of factions and improves on pure democracy.

Control the Government

In the *Federalist* No. 51, Madison explains the need to control government. Madison famously argues that "if men were angels, no government would be necessary. If angels were to govern men, neither external nor internal controls on government would be necessary." And since men are not angels, one of the primary functions of government is to devise a series of checks to ensure that government will control itself. The primary check on government authority is a reliance on the voters. Auxiliary checks are derived from the system of separation of powers, which serves to "pit ambition against ambition" and to constrain government actions. Toward this end, the government is divided between federal and state levels; the federal government is divided into three separate branches; and the most powerful institution, Congress, is divided into two separate chambers.

Give Government Energy without Creating Tyranny

The Constitution not only created a new form of government; it was a rejection of the **Articles of Confederation** (the first governing document of the United States). One of the primary flaws of the Articles of Confederation was that the government lacked an independent executive and the power to govern effectively. With this in mind, the founders sought to give the new government sufficient "energy" while not re-creating a monarchy. In the *Federalist* Nos. 67–77, Alexander Hamilton explains the nature of the new executive branch. In the *Federalist* No. 70, Hamilton writes, "A feeble Executive implies a feeble execution of the government. A feeble execution is but another phrase for a bad execution; and a government ill executed, whatever it may be in theory, must be, in practice, a bad government."

F. KEY CONSTITUTIONAL COMPROMISES

Representation in Congress

The **Virginia Plan**, also known as the "large-state plan" or Randolph Plan, was written primarily by James Madison, though it was submitted at the Constitutional Convention by Edmund Randolph, a fellow Virginian. The Virginia Plan became the primary basis for discussion at the convention. The plan called for three branches of government (executive, legislative, and judicial) and a **bicameral legislature**, that is, a legislature that is divided into two separate chambers. The plan was known as the "large-state plan" because it allocated congressional representation in both chambers of Congress according to each state's population, which would have given large states like Virginia greater political representation than they enjoyed under the Articles of Confederation, which gave each state equal representation regardless of population. The Virginia Plan would have also given Congress veto power over laws passed by state legislatures as well as the power to choose the president and national judiciary.

The **New Jersey Plan**, also known as the "small-state plan" or the Paterson Plan (named after its chief author, William Paterson), was introduced at the Constitutional Convention as a reaction to the Virginia Plan. Representatives from states with relatively small populations, which included New Jersey in 1787, opposed Madison's proposal to base congressional representation on state population. Their plan called for a **unicameral legislature**, that is, a legislative body that is not divided into separate chambers, and allocated congressional representation equally to each state. This plan, though far different from the plan that was eventually accepted at the convention, was the most similar to the arrangement that existed under the Articles of Confederation. It called for a multiperson executive, elected by the legislature and removable by a majority vote of state governors, and a Supreme Court with members appointed for life terms by the executive committee.

The **Connecticut Compromise** (also known as the Great Compromise), was drafted primarily by Roger Sherman from Connecticut. The compromise combined key elements of the Virginia Plan and the New Jersey Plan. Like Madison's Virginia Plan, Sherman's compromise called for a divided legislature, which was the norm for all the state legislatures of the time except Pennsylvania's. In a concession to the small states, the Connecticut Compromise allocated political representation in the lower chamber (the House) according to population and allocated political representation in the upper chamber (the Senate) equally to all states.

Three-Fifths Compromise

The **three-fifths compromise** addressed the issue of political representation and slavery. Southern states, with their large slave populations, wanted slaves included in their population totals, a situation that would have given slave states greater representation in the House and in the presidential selection process and protected the slave trade. Northern states wanted only free inhabitants counted in a state's population. Under the three-fifths compromise, which resolved the issue—at least temporarily—each slave was counted as three-fifths of a person.

Voting Rights Compromise

Article I, Section 2 of the U.S. Constitution reads, "The House of Representatives shall be composed of members chosen every second Year by the People of the several States, and the Electors in each State shall have the Qualifications requisite for Electors of the most numerous Branch of the State Legislature." In short, the Constitution initially did not establish voting rights but instead left it up to each state to decide who could vote in U.S. House contests—the only branch of the federal government that was originally selected by the people. The Constitution's silence regarding voter qualifications does not mean that the issue was of little importance or that it was not debated at the Constitutional Convention. On the contrary, conservatives argued that voting rights should be reserved for a privileged few. Their argument was based on the aristocratic ideal that those with the most at stake in society (i.e., those who had achieved an elevated standing in society) were best qualified to hold public office and to participate in elections. Opponents of a restrictive national standard for voting argued that such restrictions would weaken support for the Constitution, as it would inevitably restrict suffrage in states in which the right to vote was already widely enjoyed. They also argued that popular sovereignty necessitated active participation in the political process. In the end, the issue proved too prickly to be resolved at the Constitutional Convention, and the founders deferred to the states.

G. COMPARATIVE PERSPECTIVE

It has been argued that the Articles of Confederation were less a product of a thoughtful governing philosophy than a reaction to rule under the British Crown. Having struggled with an overbearing monarchy, the former colonists created a system of government that was as different from the British system as they could envision. It contained no independent executive branch; it allowed the states to retain their autonomy; it made it difficult to declare war, impose taxes, or make any important decisions or alterations to the federal system. Table 1.2 provides a list of some of the key differences between the Constitution and the Articles of Confederation.

Table 1.2.   Key Differences between the Constitution and the Articles of Confederation

	U.S. Constitution	Articles of Confederation
Federalism	American federalism	Confederation system
Checks and balances	Separate institutions with overlapping powers	Single legislative branch
Source of authority	Popular sovereignty	State sovereignty
Legislative body	Bicameral legislature	Unicameral legislature
Term of office (legislature)	House: two-year term Senate: six-year term	One-year term
Term limits	None	No person permitted to serve in Congress more than three out of every six years
Congressional representation	House: based on state's population Senate: equal representation for each state	Equal representation for each state (i.e., each state delegation, regardless of its size, is given one vote)
Congressional pay	Paid by the federal government	Paid by the states
Decision making	Majority rule	Supermajority for important issues (approval by nine out of thirteen states)
Constitutional amendment process	A two-step process that does not require unanimous support of all states	Requires unanimous approval by all states

Box 1.1.   Skill Box: Analyzing Tables

Look at table 1.2. Do the differences between the Articles of Confederation and the Constitution suggest that they were based on different political philosophies? Was one form of government more democratic in nature than the other, or do the differences between the two documents reflect the different problems that the nation faced when the documents were drafted (e.g., the Articles were drafted during the Revolutionary period and reflect the states' fear of a strong central government, whereas the Constitution was drafted during a later period when the nation was suffering under a weak central government)?

H. ENDURING STRUCTURAL QUESTIONS AND HOW TO RESEARCH THEM

American Federalism

One of the key structural controversies surrounding the U.S. Constitution concerned the relationship between the federal government and the state governments. The founders rejected both unitary federalism and confederated systems, instead hoping to create a hybrid known as American federalism. Over time, the practice of American federalism has evolved, generally delivering increased authority to the federal government.

Sample Hypothesis

If the state governments have retained their independence from the federal government, then they should be able to provide the basic functions of state government without federal involvement.

Hints for Accomplishment

The federal-state relationship that James Madison describes in the *Federalist* Nos. 45 and 46 only vaguely resembles the relationship that exists in practice today. One way to investigate the changing nature of American federalism is to explore how the federal government influences state governments in specific policy areas. For example, you could explore how federal education spending and programs like "No Child Left Behind" changed state and federal relations in the area of education policy. Similar analysis can be conducted in the areas of environmental policy, transportation policy, police protection, and agricultural policy.

Suffrage and Voter Choice

One of the most dramatic structural changes to the U.S. Constitution has been the expansion of suffrage and voter choice. Through the constitutional amendment process, voting rights have been extended to African Americans and other racial minorities, women, and eighteen-year-olds. Voter choices have also been expanded to include nomination contests and the direct election of U.S. senators, while other reforms have given voters greater control over the presidential selection process. Prior to the adoption of national voting rules, many states granted voting rights to previously disenfranchised groups. The historical evolution of suffrage at the state level can foster several interesting research topics.

Sample Hypothesis

a. If a state had a low female population (like many Western states during the nineteenth century), then the state would be more likely to grant women voting rights.
b. If a state had a low African American population (like many northeastern states in the nineteenth century), then the state would be more likely to grant African Americans voting rights.
c. If a state had a small immigrant population, then the state would be more likely to do away with the landowning requirement for voting.
d. If a State had a small number of religious minorities, then the state would be more likely to do away with religious barriers to voting.

Hints for Accomplishment

The central assumption behind each of the hypotheses is that states are more likely to expand voting rights to a disenfranchised group if the size of the disenfranchised group does not threaten the established authority. As the hypotheses suggest, this could be explored from a number of angles: (1) gender-based voting rules; (2) race-based voting rules; (3) property-based voting requirements; and (4) religious restrictions. A simple timeline that illustrates when states granted a specific disenfranchised group voting rights and the relative size of the group in the state (expressed as a percentage of the total state population) would be sufficient to meaningfully explore the issue. An alternative research approach would be to compare two states that granted a specific group (e.g., women) voting rights at different times.

I. IDEA GENERATOR: A SAMPLE OF STRUCTURAL QUESTIONS RELATED TO THE CONSTITUTION

The following chart provides some general guidelines for developing a research plan.

Specific Issue	Hypotheses	Hints

Judicial Review

The constitutional basis for judicial review (i.e., the power of the Supreme Court to rule actions of the other branches of government unconstitutional)	a. If the framers intended the Supreme Court to exercise the power of judicial review, then it should have been widely discussed in the *Federalist Papers*. b. If the framers intended the Supreme Court to exercise the power of judicial review, then it should have been debated at the Constitutional Convention. c. If the framers intended the Supreme Court to exercise the power of judicial review, then it should have been mentioned in Article III of the Constitution.	Of the three branches of government, the federal court system received the least attention at the Constitutional Convention. Alexander Hamilton argued that the courts lacked the power "of the purse" (i.e., the power to tax) and the power of the "sword" (i.e., coercive powers) and consequently would be little threat to the liberties of the citizens or the balance of power in the federal government. Starting with the Marshall Court, the role of the Supreme Court has been vastly expanded to include the power of judicial review; the Supreme Court is the final arbiter of all things constitutional. See the *Federalist* Nos. 78–83 for a glimpse into the founders' thinking regarding the proper role of the Supreme Court.

Bill of Rights

Why did the Constitution, as originally ratified, lack a bill of rights?	a. If a state's constitution contained a bill of rights, then the state would be slow to ratify the U.S. Constitution. b. If a state's constitution contained a bill of rights, then the state would not ratify the U.S. Constitution until receiving a promise for a federal bill of rights.	The strongest objection to the U.S. Constitution was based on the absence of a bill of rights. This particularly offended George Mason, who had drafted the Virginia Declaration of Rights in 1776 and who thought that such a list of inalienable rights was essential to the protection

(*continued*)

Specific Issue	Hypotheses	Hints
		the people against an overbearing government. James Madison and others disagreed with Mason, arguing that a bill of rights was unnecessary since the federal government was not empowered to infringe on individual rights, and that any list of rights would be incomplete and consequently would misrepresent the entire scope of freedoms that the people retained. The disagreement over the Bill of Rights led to countless debates during the founding period and nearly sidetracked the ratification process.

Three-fifths Compromise

Specific Issue	Hypotheses	Hints
The electoral consequences of the three-fifths compromise	a. If the three-fifths compromise created a political bias in favor of southern interests, then most early American presidents should have come from the South. b. If the three-fifths compromise created a political bias in favor of southern interests, then most early American presidents should have owned slaves. c. If the three-fifths compromise created a political bias in favor of southern interests, then southerners in the House should have been able to block the	Since the three-fifths compromise gave more political representation (i.e., more seats in the U.S. House and more votes in the Electoral College) than southern states would have been granted if representation was based on the free population, it helped turn the balance of federal power in favor of southern slave states. A few worthwhile ways to track the consequences of this structural compromise is to analyze the number of early presidents that came from the South, the number who were slave

Specific Issue	Hypotheses	Hints
	consideration of antislavery legislation.	owners, and the influence that southerners possessed in the House.

The Virginia Plan versus the New Jersey Plan

Specific Issue	Hypotheses	Hints
What if the New Jersey Plan had been adopted at the Constitutional Convention?	a. If representation in the U.S. Congress had been based on the New Jersey Plan, then the landmark civil rights legislation of the 1960s would not have passed Congress. b. If representation in the U.S. Congress had been based on the New Jersey Plan, then the federal government would not have adopted a progressive federal income tax. c. If representation in the U.S. Congress were based on the New Jersey Plan, then there would be greater oversight of Congress and less political corruption.	The New Jersey Plan, favored by states with relatively small populations, proposed a single legislative body that allocated political representation equitably to each state. An interesting research exercise, one that illustrates the importance of political institutions in determining policy outcomes, would be to apply the rules of the New Jersey Plan to recent policy battles. Looking at roll-call votes in the Senate should provide a meaningful glimpse into what life might have been like if the framers had adopted the system of representation presented in the New Jersey Plan. This type of counterfactual analysis depends on realistic logical claims (i.e., identifying your assumptions and explaining them) and a thorough knowledge of the policy issue under consideration. Be careful not to overstate the importance of structural changes or downplay the importance of the social and economic climate in which policies are made.

2. Participants

A. WHO WERE THE FRAMERS OF THE U.S. CONSTITUTION?

Seventy delegates were selected to participate in the Constitutional Convention, with only Rhode Island choosing not to send any representatives to the convention. Only fifty-five of the delegates actually attended the convention. Notable absentees included Thomas Jefferson, Patrick Henry, John Adams, Samuel Adams, and John Hancock. Of the fifty-five delegates who made the trip to Philadelphia—the **framers** of the Constitution—only thirty-nine signed the final document. Those who attended the convention had extensive political experience: forty-one of the framers had been elected to the Continental Congress, eight had signed the Declaration of Independence, six had signed the Articles of Confederation, and eight had been governors. (See table 1.3 for selected biographies of the framers.)

Table 1.3.   Selected Biographical Summaries of Key Framers of the U.S. Constitution

Elbridge Gerry, Massachusetts (1744–1814)
Gerry was one of the most vocal delegates at the Constitutional Convention of 1787. He presided as chairman of the committee that produced the Great Compromise but disliked the compromise itself. He antagonized nearly everyone by his inconsistency. At first an advocate of a strong central government, Gerry ultimately rejected and refused to sign the Constitution because it lacked a bill of rights and because he deemed it a threat to republicanism. He led the drive against ratification in Massachusetts and denounced the document as "full of vices." Among the vices, he listed inadequate representation of the people, dangerously ambiguous legislative powers, the blending of the executive and the legislative, and the danger of an oppressive judiciary. Gerry saw some merit in the Constitution and believed that its flaws could be remedied through amendments. In 1789, after he announced his intention to support the Constitution, he was elected to the First Congress.

James Madison, Virginia (1751–1836)
Madison was a guiding force behind the Mount Vernon Conference (1785), attended the Annapolis Convention (1786), and was instrumental in the convening of the Constitutional Convention. Madison, who was rarely absent from the convention and whose Virginia Plan was in large part the basis of the Constitution, advocated a strong government. Despite his poor speaking abilities, he took the floor more than 150 times, third only after Gouverneur Morris and James Wilson. His journal of the convention is the single best record of the event. He also played a key part in guiding the Constitution through the Continental Congress and played a lead in the ratification process in Virginia. Madison defended the document against such powerful opponents as Patrick Henry, George Mason, and Richard Henry Lee. Madison collaborated

with Alexander Hamilton and John Jay in writing the influential *Federalist Papers*.

George Mason, Virginia (1725–1792)
Mason was one of the five most frequent speakers at the Constitutional Convention. He exerted great influence at the convention, though he ultimately decided not to sign the document. He explained his reasons at length, citing the absence of a declaration of rights as his primary concern. He then discussed the provisions of the Constitution point by point, beginning with the House of Representatives. The House he criticized as not truly representative of the nation, the Senate as too powerful. He also claimed that the power of the federal judiciary would destroy the state judiciaries and render justice unattainable. These fears led Mason to conclude that the new government was destined to either become a monarchy or fall into the hands of a corrupt, oppressive aristocracy. Two of Mason's greatest concerns were ultimately addressed in the Constitution: the Bill of Rights answered his primary objection, and the Eleventh Amendment addressed his call for strictures on the judiciary.

Gouverneur Morris, Pennsylvania (1752–1816)
Morris emerged as one of the leading figures at the Constitutional Convention. His speeches, more frequent than those by anyone else, numbered 173. Although sometimes presented in a light vein, they were usually substantive. A strong advocate of nationalism and aristocratic rule, he served on many committees, including those on postponed matters and style, and stood in the thick of the decision-making process. It was Morris who apparently drafted the Constitution.

William Paterson, New Jersey (1745–1806)
Paterson attended the convention until late July. During his time in Philadelphia, he took notes of the proceedings and coauthored the New Jersey Plan, also known as the Paterson Plan. In his plan, which was ultimately rejected, he asserted the rights of the small states against the large. He returned to the convention in time to sign the final document and went on to serve a career in the new government.

Roger Sherman, Connecticut (1721–1793)
Sherman attended practically every session of the convention. Not only did he sit on the Committee on Postponed Matters, but he also probably helped draft the New Jersey Plan and was a prime mover behind the Great Compromise, also known as the Connecticut Compromise. This compromise broke the deadlock between the large and small states over representation. He was also instrumental in Connecticut's ratification of the Constitution.

George Washington, Virginia (1732–1799)
Dissatisfied with national progress under the Articles of Confederation, Washington was convinced of the need for a stronger central government. He hosted the Mount Vernon Conference (1785), though he did not attend the Annapolis Convention (1786). In 1787, he was chosen by his colleague to preside over the Constitutional Convention in Philadelphia. Following ratification of the Constitution, the Electoral College unanimously chose him as the nation's first president.

(continued)

Table 1.3.   (*continued*)

James Wilson, Pennsylvania (1741-1797)
Wilson reached the apex of his career at the Constitutional Convention, where his influence was probably second only to that of Madison. Rarely missing a session, he sat on the Committee of Detail and in many other ways applied his excellent knowledge of political theory to convention problems. Only Gouverneur Morris delivered more speeches. That same year, overcoming powerful opposition, Wilson led the drive for ratification in Pennsylvania, the second state to endorse the Constitution.

Robert Yates, New York (1738-1801)
In the 1780s Yates led the charge against ratification of the Constitution. When he traveled to Philadelphia in May 1787 for the federal convention, he expected that the delegates would simply discuss revising the existing Articles of Confederation. It soon became apparent to Yates that the convention intended much more than modification of the current plan. On July 5, Yates and John Lansing (to whom Yates was related by marriage) left the proceedings. In a joint letter to Governor George Clinton of New York, they spelled out the reasons for their early departure. They warned against the dangers of centralizing power and urged opposition to the Constitution. Yates continued to attack the Constitution in a series of letters signed "Brutus" and "Sydney" and voted against ratification at the Poughkeepsie convention.

Source: National Archives, "America's Founding Fathers: Delegates to the Constitutional Convention," http://www.archives.gov/exhibits/charters/charters.html.

B. COMPARATIVE PERSPECTIVE: FEDERALISTS VERSUS ANTI-FEDERALISTS

The Federalists

The **Federalists** were those people who favored ratification of the Constitution. They believed that the Articles of Confederation were fatally flawed and that they needed to be replaced with a more effective constitution. The Federalists argued that a stronger central government would help foster economic growth, promote national security, and resolve competition between the states. The bulk of their support came from landowners, merchants, and creditors, who stood to benefit from commercial development.

The Anti-Federalists

The **Anti-Federalists** opposed the adoption of the Constitution. While most Anti-Federalists agreed that some changes to the Articles of Confederation were warranted, they did not believe that the deficiencies within the Articles of Confederation warranted an entirely new form of government. Some of the most prominent Anti-Federalists included Patrick Henry, Robert Yates, Samuel Bryan, George Clinton, Melancton Smith, and Richard Henry Lee. The Anti-Federalists feared centralized government at the federal level, favored states' rights, supported a bill of rights, and generally favored government at the state and local level because they thought it would be more closely tied to the will of farmers and the middle class.

C. THE *FEDERALIST PAPERS*

The *Federalist Papers* consist of eighty-five essays written in support of ratification of the Constitution. Though the essays were published anonymously, it is now known that they were written by Alexander Hamilton, James Madison, and John Jay. The essays are considered the nation's most thoughtful and thorough defense of the Constitution. To this day, the *Federalist Papers* are widely considered the single best guide to understanding the desires and hopes of the nation's founders. (See table 1.4 for an outline of the topics covered by the *Federalist Papers*.)

Table 1.4. Outline of the *Federalist Papers*

No.	Topic and Author
1	Introduction (Hamilton)
2–5	Dangers from foreign influence (Jay)
6–7	Dangers from dissensions between the states (Hamilton)
8	Hostilities between the states (Hamilton)
9	Safeguards against factions (Hamilton)
10	Safeguards against factions (continued) (Madison)
11	Commercial relations and a navy (Hamilton)
12	Revenue (Hamilton)
13	Economy in government (Hamilton)
14	Addressing objections to the proposed Constitution (Madison)
15–17	Weakness of the present confederation (Hamilton)
18–20	Weakness of the present confederation (continued) (Hamilton or Madison)
21–22	Defects of the present confederation (Hamilton)
23	The necessity of an energetic union (Hamilton)
24–25	The common defense further considered (Hamilton)
26–28	Legislative authority and the common defense (Hamilton)
29	The militia (Hamilton)
30–36	Power of taxation (Hamilton)
37–38	Difficulty of devising a proper form of government (Madison)
39	Conformity of the plan to republican principles (Madison)
40	Powers of the convention to form a government (Madison)

(continued)

Table 1.4. *(continued)*

No.	Topic and Author
41	Powers conferred by the Constitution (Madison)
42–43	The powers conferred by the Constitution further considered (Madison)
44	Restrictions on the authority of the several states (Madison)
45	Preserving powers of the state governments (Madison)
46	Influence of the state and federal governments compared (Madison)
47	Structure of the new government (Madison)
48	Separation of powers (Madison)
49	Appealing to the people through a convention (Hamilton or Madison)
50	Appeals to the people (Hamilton or Madison)
51	Checks and balances (Madison)
52–53	The House of Representatives (Hamilton or Madison)
54	The apportionment of members among the states (Hamilton or Madison)
55–56	Size of the House of Representatives (Hamilton or Madison)
57	Powers of the few versus powers of the many (Hamilton or Madison)
58	Political representation in a growing nation (Madison)
59–61	Power of Congress to regulate the election of members (Hamilton)
62–3	The Senate (Hamilton or Madison)
64	The powers of the Senate (Jay)
65	The powers of the Senate (continued) (Hamilton)
66	Objections to the power of the Senate (Hamilton)
67	The executive branch (Hamilton)
68	The mode of electing the president (Hamilton)
69	The real character of the executive (Hamilton)
70	The executive branch further considered (Hamilton)
71	The duration in office of the executive (Hamilton)
72	The duration in office of the executive (Hamilton)
73	Presidential power and the veto Power (Hamilton)
74	Presidential power: military power and the power to pardon (Hamilton)
75	Treaty-making power of the executive (Hamilton)
76	Appointing power of the executive (Hamilton)
77	Appointing power (continued) (Hamilton)
78–79	The judiciary (Hamilton)
80	Powers of the judiciary (Hamilton)
81–82	The judiciary (continued) (Hamilton)
83	The judiciary in relation to trial by jury (Hamilton)
84	Miscellaneous objections to the Constitution (Hamilton)
85	Concluding remarks (Hamilton)

Source: Compiled by the authors from the Avalon Project at Yale Law School, http://www.yale.edu/lawweb/avalon/federal/fed.htm.

D. ENDURING QUESTIONS ABOUT THE FRAMERS AND HOW TO RESEARCH THEM

Even before the new constitution was ratified, critics were claiming that the arrangement benefited the wealthy at the expense of the poor (see the *Federalist* No. 57). Charles Beard's seminal work, *An Economic Interpretation of the Constitution of the United States* (1913), breathed new life into this perennial controversy. Beard argues that the nation's founders represented an elite class that was primarily interested in protecting property rights and promoting their own financial well-being. Beard's controversial work caused a reappraisal of the founders and the government that they created. Today, some scholars agree with Beard's basic thesis, while others hold that the founders were motivated by a genuine desire to set the nation on a more secure and prosperous course.

Sample Hypothesis

a. If the founders represented an elite class, then they should have possessed far more wealth than the average person in their states.
b. If the founders were motivated by economic interest, then their wealth should have increased following ratification of the Constitution.

Hints for Accomplishment

Two excellent works that refute Beard's claims include John Patrick Diggins's "Power and Authority in American History: The Case of Charles A. Beard and His Critics," *American Historical Review* 86 (1981): 701–730, and Robert Brown's book *Charles Beard and the Constitution: A Critical Analysis of "An Economic Interpretation of the Constitution"* (Princeton, N.J.: Princeton University Press, 1956). Two important works that are more sympathetic to Beard's perspective include Jackson Turner Main's book *The Social Structure of the American Revolution* (Princeton, N.J.: Princeton University Press, 1965) and Woody Holton's recent work *Unruly Americans and the Origins of the Constitution* (New York: Hill and Wang, 2007). A manageable undergraduate research project might involve writing a literature review (i.e., an analysis of the existing scholarly works) on the topic. Does the balance of scholarship today support or refute Beard's claims about the founders?

Anti-Federalism and the Bill of Rights

The Anti-Federalists' primary objection to the Constitution was based on its lack of a bill of rights. This particularly offended George Mason, who had drafted the Virginia Declaration of Rights in 1776 and who thought that such a list of inalienable rights was essential for the protection of the people against an overbearing government. Fellow Virginian James Madison disagreed with Mason, arguing that a bill of rights was unnecessary since the federal government was not empowered to infringe on individual rights, and that any list of rights would be incomplete and consequently would misrepresent the entire scope of freedoms that the people retained. The disagreement between the Federalists and the Anti-Federalists over a bill of rights led to countless conflicts during the founding period.

Sample Hypothesis

a. If the lack of a bill of rights was the Anti-Federalists' chief concern, then Anti-Federalist opposition to the new government should have waned once the Bill of Rights was promised.
b. If the lack of a bill of rights was the Anti-Federalists' chief concern, then they should have played an active role in the process of drafting the Bill of Rights.

Hints for Accomplishment

The fact that the Anti-Federalists faulted the Constitution for not containing a bill of rights is clear. However, it is less clear whether the Anti-Federalists made use of the issue because it was popular and promoted their larger opposition to the creation of a more powerful federal authority, or if it was truly a major concern. In other words, did the Anti-Federalists oppose the entire idea of creating a stronger federal government, or did they simply desire to address a few of the problems they identified with the proposed Constitution? If Anti-Federalist opposition to the Constitution was based on broader concerns regarding federal power, then they should have continued to oppose the Constitution even after the Bill of Rights was promised. It might also be interesting to explore whether opposition to the federal government was greater in states that possessed a state bill of rights. This type of research requires careful historical analysis of state constitutions and Anti-Federalist writings. A good source for the primary documents needed for this type of research is Yale Law School's Avalon Project, http://www.yale.edu/lawweb/avalon.

E. IDEA GENERATOR: A SAMPLE OF ADDITIONAL QUESTIONS RELATED TO THE FRAMERS

The following chart provides some general guidelines for developing a research plan.

Specific Issue	Hypotheses	Hints

Political Experience and Support for the Constitution

How did the Federalists' and the Anti-Federalists' political experiences influence their support for or opposition to the Constitution?	a. If a person had served in the Confederation Congress, then he would be more likely to support the proposed Constitution. b. If a person had served only in state government, then he would be likely to oppose the Constitution.	The framers were quintessential political insiders—active participants in state and national government. It is worth exploring whether there are identifiable differences in the political experiences of those who favored the Constitution and those who opposed it. Did the Federalists tend to have more experience at the national level and the Anti-Federalists more experience at the state level? A review of the biographies of the Federalists and the Anti-Federalists should provide insights into this line of questioning.

The Anti-Federalists after Ratification

Following ratification of the U.S. Constitution, did Federalists attempt to reduce Anti-Federalist opposition by offering Anti-Federalists key positions within the new government, and did the Anti-Federalists express their preference for states' rights by choosing to	a. If Federalists reached out to Anti-Federalists following ratification of the Constitution, then a large number of Anti-Federalists should have been offered positions of authority in the new government. b. If Anti-Federalists favored strong state governments over the federal government, then the Anti-Federalists should have returned to the state office following ratification.	Several interesting trends could have materialized after ratification of the Constitution. The Anti-Federalists could have shown their disdain for the new system by retiring from national politics and focusing on state issues. Or the Anti-Federalists could have run for national office to ensure that the new government would adopt a bill of rights and govern in a restrained manner. Moreover, the Federalists could have offered Anti-Federalists positions in the new government to assuage

(continued)

Specific Issue	Hypotheses	Hints
serve in state governments following ratification?		the Anti-Federalists' concerns about the new system. One interesting approach might be to research the postconvention career of a staunch Anti-Federalist like Patrick Henry, who turned down a seat in the U.S. Senate, an opportunity to serve as secretary of state, and a chance to serve as the chief justice of the Supreme Court. Widely available biographies for many of the Anti-Federalists make this type of historical analysis relatively straightforward. Key Anti-Federalists worth investigating include Patrick Henry, Robert Yates, Samuel Bryan, George Clinton, George Mason, James Monroe, Melancton Smith, and Richard Henry Lee.

Religion and the Framers

To what extent did religious beliefs influence the founders?	a. If the founders were highly influenced by organized religion, then they should have played active roles in their respective churches. b. If the founders were highly influenced by organized religion, then they would have sought the advice and consent of religious leaders when drafting the Constitution. c. If the founders were highly influenced by	It has often been argued that the founders were guided primarily by the ideals of the Enlightenment rather than organized religion. The founders' religious beliefs, when they were mentioned at all, often reflected a type of deism (i.e., a religious philosophy based on reason and observation rather than divine revelation). More recent scholarship challenges the notion of the founders as primarily

Specific Issue	Hypotheses	Hints
	organized religion, then they would have referred to God in the Constitution.	deists, and argues that they held diverse religious views (deism being one of them) and that religion played a larger role in their thinking than previously credited. For two thoughtful works on the subject, see David L. Holmes, *The Faiths of the Founding Fathers* (New York: Oxford University Press, 2006) and Jon Meacham, *American Gospel: God, the Founding Fathers, and the Making of a Nation* (New York: Random House, 2006). One manageable way to address the topic would be to address the religious beliefs of a single founder.

America's Second Revolution?

Was the adoption of the U.S. Constitution a rejection of the ideals embodied in the Declaration of Independence?	a. If the founders favored a Hobbesian philosophy, then the *Federalist Papers* should have explained their beliefs. b. If the founders favored a Hobbesian philosophy, then the Anti-Federalists should have made this point and argued from a Lockean perspective.	The view of human nature embodied in the Declaration of Independence and put into practice in the Articles of Confederation was clearly influenced by John Locke. The Lockean view argues in favor of limited government, that people are created equal, that they possess rights independent of those granted by government, and that citizens are more likely to endure political ills than to rise up in rebellion. The Hobbesian view, made popular by Thomas

(*continued*)

Specific Issue	Hypotheses	Hints
		Hobbes, argues that people are prone to violence, are self-interested, and require a strong central government to secure peace. An interesting research project is to compare and contrast the views of human nature described in the Declaration of Independence with the views embodied in the Constitution and discussed in the *Federalist Papers* (see the *Federalist* Nos. 10 and 51). This analysis allows you to assess the extent to which the Constitution was a rejection of Lockean ideals in favor of a system more in line with Hobbesian thinking.

Signers of the U.S. Constitution

Specific Issue	Hypotheses	Hints
The differences between those who attended the Constitutional Convention but chose not to sign the document and those who signed the Constitution	a. If a delegate had served as a state governor prior to the Constitutional Convention, then he would be less likely to sign the Constitution. b. If a delegate had been influential in the drafting of a state's bill of rights prior to the Constitutional Convention, then he would be less likely to sign the Constitution. c. If a delegate made his living from agricultural production, then he would be less likely to sign the Constitution.	Of the fifty-five delegates who attended the Constitutional Convention in the summer of 1787, only thirty-nine signed the document. Compare the biographies of the delegates who signed the Constitution with those who left the convention. See the National Archives website, http://www .archives.gov/exhibits/ charters/charters.html, for brief biographical sketches.

Specific Issue	Hypotheses	Hints

The Reputation of the Founders (The Case of Thomas Jefferson)

Specific Issue	Hypotheses	Hints
Man of virtue or hypocrite?	a. If Jefferson was troubled about the morality of slavery, then he would have treated his slaves better than other slave owners treated their slaves. b. If Jefferson was troubled about the morality of slavery, then he would have freed some or all of his slaves upon his death. c. If Jefferson was troubled about the morality of slavery, then he would have refrained from engaging in sexual relations with his slaves.	Historians have long debated the character of the founders and what motivated their behavior. While much of the early work praised the founders as men of unquestionable ideas and virtue, over time others have found serious fault with the founders. Critical works include John Bach McMaster's classic work, *The Political Depravity of the Founding Fathers* (1896) and Charles Beard's seminal work, *An Economic Interpretation of the Constitution of the United States* (1913). There are numerous ways to address these issues. For undergraduate research, it is advisable to limit this type of analysis to a specific founding personality and to a specific issue of concern. Topics might include exploring conflicts between what a founder said about slavery and what he did to end the slave trade, or how a founder's financial status colored his perspective on economic matters. Remember, this line of inquiry is about investigating whether a founder's words matched his actions. It is not about applying current moral standards to previous generations.

3. Context and Performance

A. IMPORTANT ANTECEDENTS TO THE U.S. CONSTITUTION

The Magna Carta (1215)

Sometimes referred to as the "Great Charter of Freedoms," the **Magna Carta** was imposed on King John of England by disgruntled English barons. It forced the king to accept legal procedures and to acknowledge that even the king was subject to the law. It was one of the earliest examples of a written document that was created to constrain the actions of government officials.

The Virginia Charter (1606) and the Mayflower Compact (1620)

Colonists in the New World created legal procedures for governing themselves. Some of the procedures were granted by the king in the form of governing charters, while others were created by the colonists themselves, like the Mayflower Compact. In either case, the documents served as the highest law of the land and essentially established the first written constitutions in the New World.

British Bill of Rights (1689)

Following the Glorious Revolution of 1688–1689, in which King James II was forced from the throne and British parliamentary democracy was established, the British parliament passed a proclamation of basic political rights. The British Bill of Rights established the freedom to petition the government, the freedom from a standing army, the freedom to elect members of Parliament, the freedom from cruel and unusual punishment, and the right of habeas corpus.

The French and Indian War (1756–1763)

The French and Indian War was part of a global struggle between Britain and France more broadly known as the Seven Years' War. In North America, the war was fought over control of western lands and pitted the British and their North American colonists against the French and their Native American allies.

The End of Salutary Neglect (the Sugar Act of 1764, the Stamp Act of 1765, and the Quartering Act of 1765)

The conclusion of the French and Indian War brought an end to an extended period of **salutary neglect** in North America—the period in which Parliament chose not to strictly enforce British authority in the New World. With a large war debt to pay, Parliament passed a series of unpopular taxes, including the **Sugar Act** and the **Stamp Act**. Parliament also sent additional troops to North America and passed the Quartering Act of 1765, which required colonists to provide living quarters for British troops.

The Stamp Act Congress (1765)

The **Stamp Act Congress** was the first national meeting of colonial leaders in the New World. The meeting took place in New York and was attended by delegates from nine of the thirteen colonies. The purpose of the meeting was to formally petition the British authorities with colonial grievances—the chief grievance being taxation without representation in Parliament.

The Townshend Acts (1767)

Following the Stamp Act Congress, British authorities repealed the Stamp Act and modified the Sugar Act. The colonists' victory was short-lived, however, as Parliament passed a new round of taxes in 1767 known as the **Townshend Acts**.

The Boston Massacre (1770)

Passage of the unpopular Townshend Acts led to a boycott of British tea, which was taxed under the new acts, and to a dramatic escalation of tensions. British authorities sent additional troops to patrol Boston Harbor, and colonists in New England organized a resistance group known as the **Sons of Liberty**. On March 5, 1770, British troops fired on a group of colonists, killing five in what became known as the **Boston Massacre**.

Committees of Correspondence (1772)

Initiated under the leadership of Samuel Adams in Boston—one of the leading figures among the Sons of Liberty—**Committees of Correspondence** were created to establish channels of communication between colonial leaders, particularly leaders who were growing increasingly discontent with British rule. In less than three years, committees were established in twelve of the thirteen colonies.

The Tea Act (1773)

The colonists' boycott of British tea led to a surplus of this important commodity and a subsequent decline in price. To address the problem, Parliament passed another round of taxes on tea and granted the East India Company a monopoly on the colonial tea trade.

The Boston Tea Party (1773)

Protesting the Tea Act and the more general concept of taxation without representation, the Sons of Liberty, dressed as Mohawk Indians, seized the British tea being held in Boston and dumped it into Boston Harbor.

The Coercive Acts (1774)

King George III's response to the Boston Tea Party was swift and severe. Four thousand additional troops were sent to the New World, a blockade was imposed on Boston Harbor, and the Quartering Act was strengthened. The **Coercive Acts**, as they were called in Britain, were referred to by the colonists as the Intolerable Acts.

The First Continental Congress (1774)

The **First Continental Congress** met in Philadelphia for the purpose of communicating to the king the colonists' grievances. Every colony except Georgia sent representatives to the congress, which produced a statement called the Declaration of Rights and Resolves.

Shots Fired at Lexington and Concord (April 19, 1775)

On the morning of April 19, 1775, tensions turned to violence as armed conflicts took place in Lexington and Concord, Massachusetts.

Second Continental Congress (1775)

At the **Second Continental Congress**, also held in Philadelphia, delegates produced the Olive Branch Petition, which, among other things, requested a cessation to the violence. Instead of withdrawing troops, King George responded by sending an additional twenty thousand troops to quell the colonial uprising.

Thomas Paine Publishes Common Sense (1776)

The most widely read and influential political pamphlet of its time, Thomas Paine's **Common Sense** helped transform colonial thinking. Not only did he assert that the time had come for colonists to sever their ties to the Crown, but he also argued that all forms of monarchical rule were unjust.

The Declaration of Independence (1776)

The **Declaration of Independence**, while not a constitution itself, was written in the tradition of constitutional law. It served as a formal declaration that the British government had violated its responsibilities to British subjects and that the states had officially severed their ties to England. The document reflected the ideas of John Locke and other Enlightenment thinkers. Thomas Jefferson is often credited with authoring the Declaration of Independence, as he in fact penned the first draft of the document. Jefferson, however, was but one member of a five-person committee that was responsible for creating the document. Other members of the committee included John Adams, Benjamin Franklin, Robert R. Livingston, and Roger Sherman. On July 4, 1776, the Declaration of Independence was accepted by the Second Continental Congress.

State Constitutions (1776)

Having broken their ties with England, most of the colonies drafted new state constitutions to replace their royal charters. A notable exception was the tiny state of Rhode Island, which chose to remain governed by its original royal charter until the mid-nineteenth century.

The Articles of Confederation (1781–1788)

In the summer of 1776, a committee of the Continental Congress was formed to draft the nation's first governing document. It took over a year for Congress to approve the Articles of Confederation and another four years for the Articles of Confederation to be ratified by the final state. As each of the state's retained their sovereignty under the new compact, the Articles of Confederation were more similar to a treaty between sovereign nations than a traditional constitution.

Mount Vernon Conference (1785)

Virginia and Maryland had long disputed control of the Potomac River. One such dispute led to a conference in Mount Vernon, Virginia, presided over by George Washington. While the conference failed to resolve the differences between the two states, it led to an invitation to all states to meet in Annapolis, Maryland, to discuss weaknesses in the Articles of Confederation.

Shays' Rebellion (1786)

Rule under the Articles of Confederation was rife with problems. Important legislative action under the articles required approval from nine of the thirteen states, and amending the Articles of Confederation required unanimous consent of the thirteen states, making governmental action difficult and structural reform almost impossible. Congress lacked the power to impose taxes or to enforce its rules. There was a need for executive power and a national judiciary to resolve interstate disputes. Moreover, British troops remained on western lands, Spanish troops threatened the Mississippi, and the national economy was floundering. The crisis came to a head in 1786 when Daniel Shays and his relatively small band of supporters attempted to forcibly halt foreclosures on farms by closing the state courts in Massachusetts. **Shays' Rebellion** shocked the nation into action and provided the proponents of a strong national government with the evidence they needed to fuel a full-fledged constitutional movement.

The Annapolis Convention (1786)

With the failed rebellion as it primary catalyst, five states sent delegates to the **Annapolis Convention** (1786) to discuss ways to strengthen the national political system. The Annapolis Convention led to a larger convention held in 1787 in Philadelphia (the Constitutional Convention), which was attended by delegates from every state except Rhode Island.

The Philadelphia Convention (1787)

The **Philadelphia Convention** (also known as the Constitutional Convention) was authorized by Congress to meet "for the sole and express purpose of revising the Articles of Confederation and reporting to Congress and the several legislatures such alterations and provisions therein as shall, when agreed to in Congress and confirmed by the states, render the federal constitution adequate to the exigencies of Government & the preservation of the Union." Not only did the delegates overreach the authority granted to them by Congress when they created an entirely new constitution, but they also ignored the instruction to submit their proposal to the state legislatures through Congress. Instead, the delegates chose to submit the Constitution to special ratification conventions within each state. Moreover, they called for the Constitution to go into effect after being approved by only three-fourths of the states (i.e., nine), rejecting the requirement of unanimity specified by the Articles of Confederation.

Ratification of the Constitution (1787–1791)

The Constitution was adopted by delegates at the Constitutional Convention in Philadelphia on September 17, 1787, and sent to the various states for ratification. Delaware became the first state to ratify the Constitution (December 7, 1787), followed by Pennsylvania (December 12, 1787), New Jersey (December 18, 1787), Georgia (January 2, 1788), Connecticut (January 9, 1788), Massachusetts (February 6, 1788), Maryland (April 28, 1788), South Carolina (May 23, 1788), and New Hampshire (June 21, 1788). With ratification by the ninth state, New Hampshire, the Constitution was enacted. The remaining states joined the Union in the following order: Virginia (June 25, 1788), New York (July 26, 1788), North Carolina (November 21, 1789), and Rhode Island (May 29, 1790).

B. HISTORICAL DEVELOPMENT OF THE CONSTITUTION

Adoption of the Bill of Rights

Before the ratification of the Constitution and before the colonists declared their independence from Britain, the European settlers in North America had already established a rich tradition of written political rights. The Virginia House of Burgesses passed laws regarding citizens' rights, and responsibilities, as early as 1624. Maryland passed its Act for the Liberties of the People in 1639. The British Bill of Rights was established in 1689, striking a blow to the Crown's unlimited political power and formally granting British citizens certain rights. The Continental Congress passed the Declaration of Rights in 1774, in the lead up to the Revolutionary War. Virginia passed its own Declaration of Rights in June of 1776, and by 1783, eight states had attached declarations of rights to their state constitutions. While neither the Articles of Confederation nor the original Constitution contained a bill of rights, a bill of rights was promised as a consequence of the constitutional ratification process and opposition by the Anti-Federalists. In 1791, two years after the Constitution was ratified, the promise was fulfilled and the Bill of Rights was ratified as the first ten amendments to the Constitution.

The Expansion of Voter Choice and Suffrage Rights

The Constitution that was ratified in 1789 created a severely limited democracy. The only branch of government that was directly selected by the voters was the House of Representatives; the Senate was selected by the various state legislatures, the president was selected through the Electoral College, and members of the federal judiciary were appointed by the president. With the passage of the Seventeenth Amendment, which called for the direct election of U.S. senators, and the democratization of the presidential selection process, the scope of electoral choices at the federal level has been greatly expanded. The size of the electorate has also expanded dramatically throughout the course of American history. The Constitution originally left it entirely up to the individual states to determine voter eligibility, which in most states meant that only white property-owning males were eligible to vote. The Fifteenth Amendment granted African Americans the right to vote; the Nineteenth Amendment granted women the right to vote; the Twenty-third Amendment granted residents of Washington, D.C., the right to vote in presidential contests; the Twenty-fourth Amendment banned poll taxes; and the Twenty-sixth Amendment lowered the voting age from twenty-one to eighteen. The Voting Rights Act of 1965 was also influential in expanding voting rights for groups that had traditionally experienced significant barriers to their political participation.

C. ENDURING CONTEXTUAL QUESTIONS AND HOW TO RESEARCH THEM

The Electoral College and Representative Democracy

In light of the 2000 presidential election, in which Al Gore won a majority of the popular vote only to lose the election in the Electoral College, there has been increased attention given to the way presidents are selected in the United States. The presidential selection process, which was controversial from the outset, has evolved significantly since the founding and only vaguely resembles the original system. The founders intended that members of the Electoral College would be selected either by voters or by the state legislatures and that the electors would not be attached to any given candidate. The electors would meet in their respective state capitals and enter into deliberations regarding the candidates. Each elector would cast two votes—one would most likely go to the state's "favorite son" (i.e., a leading official in that state), and one was required to go to a candidate from another state. If a candidate won a majority of the Electoral College vote, that candidate would become president, and the runner-up would become vice president. If the Electoral College failed to yield a majority winner, the election would be determined in the House of Representatives, where each state delegation would be given one vote. In a country without mass communication, political parties, or nominating contests, the Electoral College was designed to infuse deliberation into the selection process and to narrow the field to the most qualified national figures.

Sample Hypothesis

If the framers were alive today, then they would oppose the Electoral College.

Hints for Accomplishment

The point of this counterfactual statement is to compare the Electoral College as the founders envisioned it with the Electoral College as it exists today. It could be argued that the Electoral College has evolved into something that is difficult to justify, neither adding the deliberation that the founders desired nor serving as an accurate reflection of the public will. With the exception of the Twelfth Amendment, which requires electors to cast a vote for president and vice president, the system has not been significantly reformed since the founding. While the sample hypothesis appears to be normative in nature, it necessitates an evaluation of the modern Electoral College by making use of the founders' intent. This type of analysis would benefit from a careful reading of the *Federalist* Nos. 67–70 (particularly, the *Federalist* No. 68).

Sample Hypothesis

a. If the Articles of Confederation were failing economically, then national economic conditions should have been on the decline in the late 1780s.
b. If the Articles of Confederation were failing economically, then support for the Constitution should have been greatest in poor states.
c. If the Articles of Confederation were failing militarily, then there should be evidence of foreign plots to invade the United States.
d. If the Articles of Confederation were failing to provide internal security, then Shays' Rebellion should have been difficult to suppress.

Hints for Accomplishment

The level of crisis in the 1780s can be assessed from an economic or security perspective. A straightforward way to assess the perception of crisis would be to conduct an analysis of stories running in major newspapers throughout the 1780s. If there was an increase in the number of stories about the looming economic and security crisis, then it could be assumed that the public did posses a growing concern about the utility of the Articles of Confederation. Moreover, looking at papers from different regions (e.g., industrial centers in the Northeast and agricultural centers in the South) might yield interesting results that help explain uneven support for the Constitution.

The Crisis of the Late 1780s

The level of crisis that the nation endured under the Articles of Confederation is a worthy research subject. While few doubt that the nation faced pressing economic, political, and security concerns by the late 1780s, it remains a point of controversy whether the problems facing the nation required a complete rejection of the Articles of Confederation. Opponents of the Constitution noted that under the Articles of Confederation, the states had created a powerful army and navy, defeated one of the world's great military powers, negotiated a peace, created an effective postal service, passed the Northwest Ordinance, and established a system of government that provided unprecedented individual liberties to its citizens. A close investigation of the subject yields numerous hypotheses.

D. IDEA GENERATOR: A SAMPLE OF CONTEXTUAL QUESTIONS RELATED TO THE CONSTITUTION

The following chart provides some general guidelines for developing a research plan.

Specific Issue	Hypotheses	Hints
Shays' Rebellion		
To what extent did Shays' Rebellion pose a legitimate threat to the young nation?	a. If Shays' Rebellion was a symptom of larger problems under the Articles of Confederation, then farmers in other states should have been sympathetic to the rebels. b. If Shays' Rebellion was a significant threat to the established authority in Massachusetts, then upon defeating the rebels the state authorities should have handed down harsh punishments to send a message to other potential rebels.	Conventional wisdom suggests that Shays' Rebellion (1786), in which Daniel Shays and his relatively small band of supporters attempted to forcibly halt foreclosures on their farms by closing the state courts in Massachusetts, served as the catalyst for the Constitutional Convention. But it could also be argued that the danger of the rebellion, which was short-lived, mostly peaceful, and easily suppressed, was exaggerated to justify a strong national government. A close look at the rebellion should

Specific Issue	Hypotheses	Hints
		shed light on its significance in the early republic.

Competing Interests and Support for the Articles of Confederation

| Which economic interests (New England merchants, Southern plantation owners, laborers, shopkeepers, small farmers) benefited the most, and the least, from rule under the Articles of Confederation? | a. If owners of small farms benefited from rule under the Articles of Confederation, then the *Anti-Federalist Papers* should make appeals directly to small farming interests.
b. If small farmers benefited from rule under the Articles of Confederation, then opposition to the Constitution should have been greatest in states with large numbers of small farms. | For many, the debate over the Constitution was less about who was going to govern the new nation and more about in whose interest the new nation would be governed. It pit the interests of the New England merchant class, who stood to benefit from the international trade and interstate commerce that the Federalists promised, against interests of small farmers, who relied on local markets and had less of a need for a strong federal government. A close look at the *Anti-Federalist Papers* should reveal the economic conflicts that played out in the debate over the ratification process. |

Voting Rights and the Future of Constitutional Reform

| What factors are likely to drive the next wave of voting-rights reform? | a. If the drive to increase voting rights continues in the United States, then it is likely that the country will adopt a national referendum process in the future.
b. If the drive to increase voting rights continues in the United States, then the Constitution will likely be amended to limit campaign spending. | One of the major contextual changes in American history has been the desire to expand voting rights: the Fifteenth Amendment granted voting rights to all races (1870); the Nineteenth Amendment granted voting rights to women (1920); the Twenty-third Amendment granted voting rights to residents of the District of Columbia |

(*continued*)

Specific Issue	Hypotheses	Hints
	c. If the drive to increase voting rights continues in the United States, then the Constitution will likely be amended to create a national voting system.	(1961); the Twenty-fourth Amendment abolished the use of poll taxes (1964); and the Twenty-sixth Amendment lowered the voting age to eighteen. If this trend continues in the future, where might we expect to see the next round of constitutional reforms related to voting rights? Be careful not to overstate your claims, as it is impossible to make definitive statements about future events.

4. Secondary Sources That Will Help You Get Started

Agel, Jerome B., and Mort Gerberg. *The U.S. Constitution for Everyone*. New York: Perigee Trade, 2001.

Davis, Sue. *Corwin & Peltason's Understanding the Constitution*. 17th ed. Belmont, Calif.: Thomson/Wadsworth, 2008.

JusticeLearning.org. *The United States Constitution: What It Says, What It Means: A Hip Pocket Guide*. New York: Oxford University Press, 2005.

5. Original Research That Will Impress Your Professor

Anderson, Thornton. *Creating the Constitution: The Convention of 1787 and the First Congress*. University Park: Pennsylvania State University Press, 1994.

Bailyn, Bernard. *The Ideological Origins of the American Revolution*. Cambridge, Mass.: Harvard University Press, 1967.

Beard, Charles A. *An Economic Interpretation of the Constitution of the United States*. New York: Macmillan, 1913.

Bradford, M. E. *Founding Fathers: Brief Lives of the Framers of the United States*. Lawrence: University Press of Kansas, 1994.

Brown, Robert. *Charles Beard and the Constitution: A Critical Analysis of "An Economic Interpretation of the Constitution."* Princeton, N.J.: Princeton University Press, 1956.

Cornell, Saul. *The Other Founders: Anti-Federalism and the Dissenting Tradition in America.* Chapel Hill: University of North Carolina Press, 1999.

Dahl, Robert. *Democracy and Its Critics.* New Haven, Conn.: Yale University Press, 1989.

Dahl, Robert. *How Democratic Is the American Constitution?* 2nd ed. New Haven, Conn.: Yale University Press, 2002.

Diggins, John Patrick. 1981. "Power and Authority in American History: The Case of Charles A. Beard and His Critics." *American Historical Review* 86 (1981): 701–730.

Ellis, Joseph J. *Founding Brothers: The Revolutionary Generation.* New York: Alfred A. Knopf, 2000.

Farrand, Max. *The Framing of the Constitution of the United States.* New Haven, Conn.: Yale University Press, 1962.

Holmes, David L. *The Faiths of the Founding Fathers.* Oxford: Oxford University Press, 2006.

Holton, Woody. *Unruly Americans and the Origins of the Constitution.* New York: Hill and Wang, 2007.

Levy, Leonard W., ed. *Essays on the Making of the Constitution.* New York: Oxford University Press, 1969.

Maier, Pauline. *American Scripture: Making the Declaration of Independence.* New York: Knopf, 1997.

McMaster, John Bach. *The Political Depravity of the Founding Fathers.* New York: Noonday Press, 1896.

Meacham, Jon. *American Gospel: God, the Founding Fathers, and the Making of a Nation.* New York: Random House, 2006.

Main, Jackson Turner. *The Social Structure of the American Revolution.* Princeton, N.J.: Princeton University Press, 1965.

Morgan, Edmund S. *The Birth of the Republic, 1763–1789.* 3rd ed. Chicago: University of Chicago Press, 1992.

Riker, William H. *The Strategy of Rhetoric: Campaigning for the American Constitution.* New Haven, Conn.: Yale University Press, 1996.

Rossiter, Clinton. *1787: Grand Convention.* New York: Macmillan, 1966.

Rutland, Robert Allen. *The Ordeal of the Constitution: The Anti-Federalists and the Ratification Struggle.* Norman: University of Oklahoma Press, 1966.

Sabato, Larry J. *A More Perfect Union: 23 Proposals to Revitalize Our Constitution and Make America a Fairer Country.* New York: Walker and Company, 2007.

Storing, Herbert J. *What the Anti-Federalists Were For.* Chicago: University of Chicago Press, 1981.

Wood, Gordon S. *The Creation of the American Republic, 1776–1787.* Chapel Hill: University of North Carolina Press, 1969.

Wood, Gordon S. *The Radicalism of the American Revolution.* New York: Alfred A. Knopf, 1992.

Wood, Gordon S. *Revolutionary Characters: What Made the Founders Different.* New York: Penguin, 2006.

6. In Their Own Words: Primary Sources

Farrand, Max, ed. *The Records of the Federal Convention of 1787*. 4 vols. New Haven,
    Conn.: Yale University Press, 1911.
Hamilton, Alexander, James Madison, and John Jay, *The Federalist: With Letters of Bru-
    tus*. Edited by Terence Ball. Cambridge, U.K.: Cambridge University Press, 2003.
Kammen, Michael G., ed. *The Origins of the American Constitution: A Documentary His-
    tory*. New York: Penguin, 1986.
Jefferson, Thomas. Letter to Philip Mazzei, April 24, 1796. In *The Papers of Thomas Jef-
    ferson*. Vol. 29, *March 1796 to December 1797*, edited by Barbara B. Oberg, 73–88.
    Princeton, N.J.: Princeton University Press, 2002. Available online at http://www
    .princeton.edu/~tjpapers/mazzei/index.html.
Jensen, Merrill, ed. *The Documentary History of the Ratification of the Constitution*. 21
    vols. Madison: State Historical Society of Wisconsin, 1976.
Madison, James. *Notes of the Debates in the Federal Convention of 1787*. New York: W. W.
    Norton, 1987.
Kenyon, Cecelia M., ed. *The Antifederalists*. New York: Bobbs-Merrill Company, 1966.
Ketchman, Ralph, ed. *The Anti-Federalist Papers and the Constitutional Convention De-
    bated*. New York: Mentor Books, 1996.
Marshall, John. *The Life of George Washington*. Edited by Robert Faulkner and Paul Car-
    rese. Indianapolis, Ind.: Liberty Fund, 2000.
Storing, Herbert J., ed. *The Complete Anti-Federalist*. 7 vols. Chicago: University of
    Chicago Press, 1981.
Storing, Herbert J., and Murray Dry, eds. *The Anti-Federalist*. Chicago: University of
    Chicago Press, 1985.
Tocqueville, Alexis de. *Democracy in America*. 1835. Reprint, New York: Vintage Press,
    1955.

7. Where To Find It

**Where can I find a complete set of the *Federalist Papers*, the Declaration of
Independence, the Constitution, and other primary-source materials related
to the founding?**
Yale Law School's Avalon Project has copies of major documents of importance
for the founding (including the Declaration of Independence, the Articles of
Confederation, the U.S. Constitution, original state constitutions, and a complete set of the *Federalist Papers*), at http://www.yale.edu/lawweb/avalon/18th
.htm. The University of Oklahoma College of Law also maintains an excellent
site with many original documents related to the founding, at http://www.law.ou
.edu/ushistory.

Where can I find an annotated version of the Constitution that describes each section in detail?
Congressional Research Service's annotated Constitution is available online from Cornell University Law School's Legal Information Institute, at http://www.law .cornell.edu/constitution/index.html.

Where can I find brief biographies of the delegates to the Constitutional Convention and information about the ratification process, the U.S. Constitution, the Bill of Rights, and the Declaration of Independence?
The National Archives and Records Administration, http://www.archives.gov/ exhibits/charters/charters.html, is an excellent source.

Where can I find information about different types of governments around the world?
Politicalresources.net, http://www.politicalresources.net, is a good source of information for those wishing to compare government types.

Note

1. Cornell University Law School, Legal Information Institute, http://www.law.cornell .edu/constitution/constitution.table.html.

CHAPTER 2

Congress

1. The Structure and Intention of Congress

The framers gave Congress (the law-making branch) a great deal of attention both in terms of time spent at the Constitutional Convention and in its placement and detail in the Constitution itself. Congress was designed to bring the people into the governmental process more directly than the other branches, providing the public advocates in the policy-making process.

A. CONSTITUTIONAL BASIS

Article I of the Constitution outlines the method of membership election, as well as the structure and powers of Congress, often giving rise to the characterization of Congress as the "first branch of government." Among the key provisions established by the Constitution are the following.

- *Structure:* Congress has two independent chambers (**bicameralism**).
- *Qualifications:* The number of House members from each state is based on population. House members must be at least twenty-five years of age, must be residents of the state from which they are elected, and must have been citizens of the United States for at least seven years. Senators must be at least thirty years of age, must be residents of the state from which they are elected, and must have been citizens of the United States for at least nine years.
- *Election:* House members are elected for two-year terms and senators for six-year terms. For the House, **apportionment** of seats is based on the decennial census. The number of seats for each state is established by the House of

Representatives. The drawing of district lines (**redistricting**) is the responsibility of the respective state legislatures. Initially, each state's two senators were chosen by their state legislatures. The **Seventeenth Amendment** (1913) provided for their election by statewide popular vote.

- *Internal rules:* Each chamber has the power to establish its own internal rules of procedure.
- *Powers of Congress:* Among the specific powers granted to Congress in the Constitution are those to borrow money; establish rules for **naturalization** (becoming a citizen), interstate commerce, and patents; declare war; and create government agencies such as post offices, courts, armies, and navies. The "**necessary and proper**" clause greatly increases Congress's power by granting it the right to "make all Laws which shall be necessary and proper for carrying [out] . . . all other Powers vested by this Constitution" to the national government.
- *Powers of the House or Senate:* Some powers are specifically restricted to one house of Congress. For example, all revenue (tax) bills must originate in the House, and only the House has the power to **impeach** (bring charges against) government officials for improper actions. Only the Senate has the power to *try* impeachment cases and to approve treaties and a specified list of presidential appointments (the "**advise and consent**" provision).
- *Limitations on congressional power:* Among those things Congress is specifically prohibited from doing are expending government funds without a specific appropriations law, imposing taxes or tariffs for goods crossing state lines, granting titles of nobility, and making an action punishable after it happened (enacting an **ex post facto law**).

B. GOALS AND INTENTIONS

Functions and Rules (Why Was Congress Created?)

The term *congress* means coming together. Congress was designed to collectively bring the views and interests of the public into the policymaking process. Working on the premise that "two heads are better than one," a congress brings together a large group of individuals, each responsible for expressing the preferences of an identifiable group of citizens. Legislatures (parliaments) had long histories of serving as advisers to kings and governors by the time the U.S. Congress was created. The unique nature of the U.S. Congress and its contribution to impending forms of governance lie in its independent realms of power. Each branch of Congress was granted the absolute right to express public sentiment in particular realms (the Senate was granted the right to approve treaties and presidential appointments; the House, the right to initiate legislation concerning taxation). In addition, approval of the two houses of Congress is required for passing all legislation.

The Many Faces of Representation

The key concept associated with Congress is **representation**. Ultimately, representation is a process by which the views of a group are re-presented (presented another time) to other members of a collective decision-making body. The process of representation is often facilitated by choosing representatives with demographic characteristics and political preferences that are similar to those of the citizens they purport to represent. It is not absolutely necessary to agree with, or to be like, a set of individuals to represent them, but frequently it helps. An older person potentially can look out for the interests of younger citizens (or vice versa) but often lacks the empathy or experience to represent them to the fullest extent. Representation is also facilitated by holding members of Congress accountable to a particular set of citizens through frequent elections. Citizens living in a member of Congress's district are **constituents**, whose political views must be taken into account. The United States employs a **single-member-district** system, in which each representative is elected by voters in a specific constituency and is expected both morally and politically to remain accountable to them.

Representation is difficult, since congressional districts include individuals with diverse political preferences and it is difficult to determine public preferences regarding many issues. Historical figures and contemporary legislators identify two idealized solutions for legislators forced to make a decision. **Delegates** take the requirement of representation quite literally, placing their own preferences in abeyance and responding to the expressed majority of their constituents. If few communicate appropriate information, delegates take it as a lack of interest and defer to those who do express a preference. **Trustees**, on the other hand, view their role as protecting the "interests" of their constituents, not simply their expressed preferences. Trustees believe that they were selected for their superior judgment and experience, which allows them to make wiser long-term decisions.

The eighteenth-century British parliamentarian Edmund Burke clearly outlined the trustee perspective, arguing that his behavior in Parliament should be informed by his knowledge and experience and that he should serve the public interest, not some local or narrow interest. In his words, *"[A representative's] unbiased opinion, his mature judgment, his enlightened conscience, he ought not to sacrifice to you, to any man, or to any set of men living. . . . Your representative owes you, not his industry only, but his judgment; and he betrays, instead of serving you, if he sacrifices it to your opinion."* A trustee considers an issue and, after hearing

Box 2.1. Representation in Theory and Reality

One can picture Edmund Burke, member of Parliament, facing his constituents and giving a passionate and well-argued speech in support of the grievances presented by the American colonies. It was not *what* he stood for in Parliament, though, that got him into political trouble but *how* he stood on issues. Burke is best known for his firm statements to his constituents on the role of the representative. It is hard to know for sure whether his constituents understood the deep distrust his trustee position showed for the audience he was addressing. Without mincing words, Burke argued that he would use his own judgment in Parliament, not simply answer the demands of his constituents. A few weeks later, Burke's constituents had the final say, throwing him out of office. Despite his failure, many politicians through the ages have followed his representational style, although few have been unwise enough to throw it back into the faces of their constituents.

all sides of the debate, exercises his or her own judgment in making decisions concerning an issue. *"You choose a member, indeed; but when you have chosen him, he is not member of Bristol [Burke's constituency], but he is a member of Parliament."*[1] (See box 2.1.)

In real life, the process is much more complex. While certain types of members (junior and less politically secure) are more likely to act as delegates, and while

Box 2.2. On Making Generalizations

The goal of scientific analysis is to identify broad generalizations (laws) that apply to the widest range of phenomena. For example, applying heat to pure water will have it boil at 212 degrees. If it does not boil at that temperature, the scientist must determine the impurities affecting the boiling level. The ultimate law of nature must *specify* the conditions. In social science research, it is often even more necessary to *specify* various kinds of phenomena before making generalizations. Since we cannot often determine all the unique conditions, social science "laws" usually take on the character of probabilities, where the best we can say is "usually" or "most often" something will happen. Thus we might make the generalization that members of Congress *usually* play a delegate role on domestic issues and a trustee role on those issues dealing with foreign policy.

some issues (domestic versus foreign policy) encourage a delegate strategy, the decision of how to represent is not universal but seems to follow well-established patterns that enable prediction and explanation, the ultimate goal of social science research. (See box 2.2.)

Congress's Role in the Separation of Powers

The framers of the Constitution feared concentrated power. **Separation of powers** among the three branches of government (executive, legislative, and judicial) served as one means of "**checks and balances**." The power of Congress as an institution lies in its independent ability to thwart the other branches should they overstep their bounds or act counter to Congress's expressed wishes. Congress has the right to investigate the other branches of government and to make any findings public. Presidential appointments to executive- and judicial-branch positions require Senate approval. Ultimately, Congress has the power to determine the fitness of executive- and judicial-branch personnel to serve, through the **impeachment** process, in which the House brings formal charges of wrongdoing and the Senate sits as a court determining innocence or guilt. (See box 2.3.)

Bicameralism: Congress Divided among Itself

Not satisfied with simply dividing powers among the three branches, the framers created a system of **bicameralism** (a two-branch legislature). Many political systems include a two-branch legislature, with one of those branches having few if any independent powers. The British House of Lords, for example, can delay, but not stop, a policy. But in the United States, formal approval of *both* the House and the Senate is required before a bill can become law. No monies can be expended from the U.S. treasury by other branches of the government without budgetary authority from both houses of Congress (the "**power of the purse**"). All U.S. states, except Nebraska, follow the national pattern of bicameralism.

Organizing for Action

Large organizations are difficult to move, so Congress uses a process of division of labor. Congressional committees draw together interested members who develop expertise on particular topics. One set of committees (**authorizing**), determines the desirability of new legislation, while another set (**appropriating**) determines how much funding, if any, approved programs receive. Each piece of legislation must go through numerous formal steps in each chamber of Congress to ensure that the legislation has broad support. At a minimum, most legislation

Box 2.3.   The Impeachment Box Score

Impeachment is relatively rare, and conviction even more unlikely. The House has begun proceedings sixty-two times, resulting in seventeen impeachments. Defining "high crimes and misdemeanors" (the constitutional criteria for impeachment) and proving guilt have been elusive. Throughout history, the figures look like this:

Presidents[1]	2 impeached (A. Johnson and Clinton)	neither convicted
Cabinet officers	1 impeached (William Belknap)	not convicted
Senators	1 impeached (William Blount)	not convicted
Supreme Court justices	1 impeached (Samuel Chase)	not convicted
Federal judges	12 impeached[2]	6 removed

Impeachment and conviction votes have tended to be quite partisan, laying open the question whether political advantage, rather than disdain for an official's behavior in office, motivated impeachment proceedings. In the case of President Clinton, a Democrat, the key Senate votes looked like this:

	Republicans	Democrats
Perjury:		
Guilty	45	0
Not guilty	10	45
Obstruction of justice:		
Guilty	50	0
Not guilty	5	45

1. President Richard Nixon resigned before the inevitable impeachment by the House and probable conviction by the Senate.

2. Including Alcee Hastings (D-Fla.), who was impeached and removed from office for allegedly taking a bribe as a federal judge. He went on to win a seat in Congress, deliberating with members of the Judiciary Committee and other members of the House and Senate who had supported his removal.

is looked at by two subcommittees (an authorizing subcommittee and an appropriating subcommittee) and two full committees in each house before it is submitted for a full vote on the floor of the respective chamber.

Each house is organized by the majority party in that chamber. The presiding officers (the Speaker of the House and the president pro tempore of the Senate) are chosen by their political party. All committee chairs and subcommittee chairs are members of the majority party, and the majority party retains a majority on each committee. Majority-party leaders control the agenda of each house. (See chapter 7 for a discussion of party voting in Congress.)

C. CONGRESS IN COMPARATIVE PERSPECTIVE

The U.S. Congress exists within a presidential, rather than a parliamentary, system. In a **presidential system**, the legislature is elected independently of the president and for different terms of office. In a **parliamentary system**, the chief executive (usually a prime minister) is selected by the legislative body (the parliament) and is most often a member of the parliament. Many parliamentary systems use the title "president" for the symbolic head of government, while the prime minister serves as the functional head of government, instigating policy and overseeing its administration. The prime minister serves only as long as he or she maintains support within the parliament. If the prime minister attempts to act in ways antagonistic to the parliament's wishes, the members of parliament take a **vote of no confidence**, forcing both the dissolution of the parliament and a new election for all seats in the parliament. The newly elected parliament will then have the chance to choose a new prime minister.

Given the need to maintain parliamentary support, parliamentary systems tend to be characterized by much more party loyalty, both among voters and among legislators. Voters in a parliamentary system see their vote much more clearly as support for a party team composed of their member of parliament and his or her party colleagues who wish to form a government. In presidential systems, members of the legislature see winning office as more of a personal victory. Particularly on domestic issues, they are willing to challenge presidents, even from their own party. Presidents tend to dominate foreign-policy issues, especially when they are relatively popular with the public.

The United States has experienced long periods of **divided government**, with one party controlling the presidency and the other party controlling one or both houses of Congress, a situation that would be impossible in a parliamentary system. The implications of divided government are a matter of lively debate. While some see it as a recipe for partisan gridlock where little is accomplished, David Mayhew asserts that it has little impact on the ability to process legislation.[2]

D. ENDURING STRUCTURAL QUESTIONS AND HOW TO RESEARCH THEM

What Are the Advantages and Disadvantages of Moving toward a Parliamentary System?

Many observers are frustrated with the presidential system, with its potential gridlock between the legislative and executive branches. No political structure is inherently good or bad, but rather helps approach certain goals and thwarts others. Eventually, the answer to this question requires making a choice as to what constitutes an advantage or a disadvantage.

Sample Hypothesis

a. If the United States moved to a parliamentary system, then public policy would be determined in a more efficient way.
b. If the United States moved toward a parliamentary system, then Congress would be responsive to chief executive initiatives.
c. If the United States moved to a parliamentary system, then there would be more political instability as Congress removed chief executives from office.

Hints for Accomplishment

As a "what if question," it cannot be answered with hard data, but rather one could speculate on the basis of what typically happens in other political systems. A reasonable answer to this question involves identifying the purported advantages, evaluating the arguments made for categorizing them as advantages, then justifying your personal position as to whether one system is ultimately better than the other overall. To make such a judgment, you will need a set of criteria against which to evaluate the purported advantages. For example, is the supposed efficiency of united government in a parliamentary system necessarily better than the deliberation, conflict, and compromise so often evident in a presidential system?

A number of sources on the debate are readily available. Arend Lijphart, ed., *Parliamentary versus Presidential Government* (Oxford and New York: Oxford University Press, 1992), provides a comprehensive set of readings that outline the main arguments of the long-standing presidential versus parliamentary debate. For a description of presidential and parliamentary systems, see United Nations Development Program, "Governing Systems and Executive-Legislative Relations: Presidential, Parliamentary and Hybrid Systems," http://www.undp.org/governance/docs/Parl-Pub-govern.htm. For a useful table of comparisons, see "Differences between Presidential & Parliamentary Regimes," http://professional.jodyb.net/presparl.pdf.

What Are the Different Approaches to Representation?

We normally think of House members with their short (two-year) terms and members with weak electoral margins as being forced to play more of a delegate role. Comparing the political statements of different types of members provides an opportunity to see how they view representation and to test hypotheses.

Sample Hypothesis

a. If you are a member of the Senate, then you are more likely to express trustee views than if you are a member of the House.
b. If you have a weak electoral margin, then you are more likely to express delegate views than if you have a strong electoral margin.

Hints for Accomplishment

Go to the online version of the *Congressional Record* on Thomas (http://www.thomas.gov/). Choose either the House or the Senate section, and search for the word "constituent." Select twenty or more references. Categorize each reference to constituents either as an example of the delegate view of representation (following constituents' wishes), as an example of the trustee view (looking out for constituents' interests using one's own judgment), or as not relevant. For hypothesis (a), compare responses from House and Senate members. For hypothesis (b), you will need to categorize members as electorally marginal. There is no absolute figure of electoral security. Members receiving less than 55 percent of the vote are usually considered "marginal." (See *The Almanac of American Politics,* published every two years by the National Journal Group, or *CQ's Politics in America,* published every two years by CQ Press, for electoral margins.)
   Summarize the dominant forms of representation for each chamber or electoral group.

What Factors Influence Presidential and Congressional Relations?

Congressional support for the president can be measured in several ways. Congressional Quarterly (or CQ), a private research firm providing data on Congress, creates congressional presidential-support scores based on congressional voting on legislation specifically endorsed by the president. A presidential veto represents a president's last-ditch attempt to thwart congressional action, whereas a successful veto override exemplifies Congress's ability to trump the president. A number of basic hypotheses can be readily tested.

Sample Hypothesis

a. If a member of Congress is from the president's party, then his or her presidential support will be higher than if he or she is from the opposition party.
b. If a president is in his or her first year of office, then his or her support in Congress will be higher than later years.
c. If the president's party controls both houses of Congress, then vetoes are less likely (and veto overrides are less likely).
d. If a president vetoes many items, then his or her percentage of veto overrides will be high.
e. If a president's popularity among the public is high, then his or her support in Congress will also be high.

Hints for Accomplishment

Each year, CQ creates a measure of the president's success in dealing with Congress. Analyzing speeches and presidential requests, CQ determines what the president wants from Congress. CQ then calculates the percentage of issues in which the president is largely successful. As a percentage, this measure attempts to correct for the large differences in the number of presidential initiatives requested. Another measure of presidential success is the ability to avoid vetoing legislation and the ability to prevail in Congress when vetoes are challenged. Reports are published at the end of each year in *CQ Weekly* (usually in December or January). They also are published in the yearly *CQ Almanac*. Historical data (for the last thirty or forty years) are available in Norman Ornstein et al., *Vital Statistics on Congress* (Washington, D.C.: American Enterprise Institute), and Harold W. Stanley and Richard G. Niemi, *Vital Statistics on American Politics* (Washington, D.C.: CQ Press), both of which are generally published every two years. Veto data is available in Stanley and Niemi's *Vital Statistics on American Politics*, or online from Magruder's American Government, at http://www.phschool.com/atschool/Magruders/2001/internet_updates/images/MAG05_CH14_S4_vetoes.gif. Detailed presidential popularity data is available from the American Presidency Project, at http://www.presidency.ucsb.edu/data/popularity.php.

Your first step will be to establish some categories for each of your variables. For example, in testing hypothesis (e), you will need to determine what "high" means for both popularity and support. You might simply calculate the average for each variable and categorize anything above the average as high and below the average as low.

Box 2.4.   Skill Box: Creating and Analyzing a Contingency Table

One way to discover a pattern in data involves creating a contingency table, which allows you to assess the impact of one variable on another. For simplicity, we will only use data from four years. To be more confident in your analysis, you would want to include more years, either choosing them randomly or selecting them for a particular purpose (e.g., all years with a Republican president or all years with divided partisan control between Congress and the presidency). For example, if your data on presidential support and presidential popularity for each year indicated

- high popularity and high support in Years A and C,
- high popularity and low support in Year B, and
- low popularity and low support in Year D,

then you would create a contingency table with the expected cause (in this case, level of presidential popularity) in the columns and the expected effect (presidential support) in the rows. This will later allow you to percentage down the columns of your data and compare them to each other to see if the causal variable has any impact. You would enter your data in the table contingent on the value of *both* presidential popularity and presidential support (your hypothesized cause and effect variables) as follows:

		Presidential Popularity	
		High	Low
Congressional Support	High	Year A Year C	
	Low	Year B	Year D

Note that Year A can only go in the upper-left-hand corner since it is both a high-popularity and a high-support year. We have placed popularity as our independent (proposed causal) variable in the columns.

To turn this into a percentage table, we calculate the percentage of years in each box of a given column. For example, in the first column (high popularity), two out of the three years (67%) are in the high-support box, whereas in the second column (low popularity), none of the years are in the high-support box. Though not conclusive, the table provides some support for hypothesis e (presidential support increases congression support).

		Presidential Popularity	
		High	Low
Presidential Support	High	67%	0%
	Low	33%	100%

With a table such as this you can also perform a number of statistical tests to determine the strength of the relationship. This sample table, of course, is based on too few data points to mean very much.

E. IDEA GENERATOR: UNDERSTANDING CONGRESS'S STRUCTURE

The following chart provides some general guidelines for developing a research plan.

Specific Issue	Hypotheses	Hints
Structure and composition of Congress		
Impact of selection rules on House and Senate candidates	If you are a Senator, then you enter Congress at an older age than if you are a House member.	Although the legal age for serving in the House and Senate varies by five years (twenty-five years old versus thirty years old), that may not lead to differing entrance ages. Using biographies in the *Congressional Directory* or online biographies, compare the age at election of a sample of House and Senate members.

Specific Issue	Hypotheses	Hints
Origin of Governmental Systems		
Why countries choose a presidential versus a parliamentary system	a. If a country was a colony of a country with a parliamentary system, then it is more likely to choose a parliamentary system itself. b. If a country is north of the equator, then it is more likely to choose a parliamentary system than if it is south of the equator.	Data on governmental types and colonial rules can be found in the Central Intelligence Agency, "The World Factbook," http://www.cia.gov/library/publications/the-word-factbook/. If taking the geographic approach, look beyond geography. What else ties these countries together?
Creating One's Job Description		
The freedom that members of Congress have in defining exactly how they plan to do their job	a. If you are a junior member of Congress, then you are more likely to play a delegate role, keeping close to your constituents and responding to their direction. b. If you are a politically secure member, then you are more likely to play a trustee role.	Think about what a member can do to stay close to constituents. Consider comparing different member websites to see what proportion of their staff is back in the district, the emphasis on the first page of their website on constituent services, the percentage of pictures obviously taken in the district or of constituents versus pictures of Washington activities.

2. Participants in Congress

A. WHO ARE THE PARTICIPANTS AND HOW WERE THEY ELECTED?

The framers of the Constitution intentionally created a system by which members would be elected *to* Congress *from* an identifiable constituency. The intention was to make legislators accountable to those who elected them. By the mid-nineteenth century, these constituencies were required to be based on geographical boundaries. House districts were to be drawn by state legislators every ten years (**redistricting**) on the basis of U.S. census figures. House terms were intentionally kept short and constituencies small (thirty thousand people). Senators were initially selected by state legislatures for six-year terms, which insulated them, to some degree, from constituents. Direct election of senators, provided by the Seventeenth Amendment in 1917, placed them under public control. Early members of Congress often served only a few years before voluntarily retiring or being defeated. Growing careerism in Congress was facilitated by incumbent desires, increasing congressional staffs, partisan redistricting favoring incumbents, and voter preferences.

Through much of history, political parties played a dominant role in nominating congressional candidates, providing resources, and managing their campaigns. The rise of primaries as a means for getting one's name on the ballot and the inability of the parties to take on the increasing costs of high-tech campaigns decreased their role. In recent years, congressional campaigns have become more "candidate centered," with the party playing a more supportive role. The events in Iraq led to a 2006 contest that was nationalized with clear party components. Whether it was a unique event or a new move toward party-centered campaigns is yet to be seen. Candidate-centered and party-centered campaigns differ in several important ways (see figure 2.1).

Concern over the demographics of Congress is based partially on the assumption that demographics imply particular policy perspectives. If this is the case, the gender, ethnicity, or occupation of a congressional candidate serves as a shorthand cue for voters deciding between candidates. For some observers, legislators who simply vote the self-interest of their demographic group are both selfish and unfair to the broader constituency those legislators have pledged to represent. As a predictive tool, demographics become less useful as the correlations between characteristics break down. For example, ethnic-minority legislators are often drawn to social programs designed to help ethnic minorities, who historically have had a lower level of income in the United States. On the other hand, businesspersons tend to favor caution in spending on social programs since higher expenditures lead to higher taxes. The crunch comes when minority businesspeople enter Congress. Do they take the route favorable to ethnic minorities or to business? In the words of social psychologists, they are "cross-pressured." Additional cross-pressure enters the calculation when individuals are elected from districts atypical of their personal demographics. While most ethnic-minority legislators still come from **majority-minority districts**, there has been a growth of minority legislators elected from districts where ethnic minorities do not comprise a majority of voters. For years nonminority legislators represented districts in which the minorities were in the numerical majority (see box 2.5). One of the interesting questions is how members of Congress perform their representational role in situations in which competing pressures make each decision difficult.

	Candidate Centered	Party Centered
Candidate Recruitment	Candidate Decides	Party
Campaign Management	Candidate's Paid Staff	Party
Fundraising	Candidate and Staff	Party
Polling	Candidate's Paid Staff	Party
Political Advertising	Paid Political Consultants	Party
Voter Mobilization	Candidate's Staff and Volunteers	Party
Campaign Themes	Candidate Decides	Party

Figure 2.1. Comparison of candidate-centered and party-centered campaigns.

The more than twelve thousand individuals who have served in Congress since its founding have differed on many issues but share many characteristics. Compared with the general population, they have tended to be older, more white, more male, more educated (especially in law), and wealthier. To some degree, this reflects the preferences of voters, and to some degree, the misdistribution of resources necessary to seek and win political office. For much of Congress's existence, women and minorities could neither vote nor hold office. With the legal barriers largely gone, diversity is slowly increasing, as more women, more ethnic minorities, and a broader range of occupations are now represented in Congress. Despite the change, Congress is far from mirroring the U.S. population in demographic terms (see table 2.1).

B. CONGRESSIONAL DEMOGRAPHICS IN COMPARATIVE PERSPECTIVE

The U.S. Congress has considerably fewer female members than many national parliaments (see tables 2.2 and 2.3). Until relatively recently, few women served in state legislatures, an important stepping-stone to higher office. Political parties often discouraged women from running, except in hopeless districts, for fear they

---

Box 2.5.   Majority-Minority Districts and Results, 109th Congress (2004–2006)

- Of the twenty-five districts in which the majority of the population was African American, twenty-four (96 percent) had an African American representative.
- Of the twenty-five districts in which the majority of the population was Hispanic, twenty (80 percent) had a Hispanic representative.
- The lowest percentage of African American residents electing an African American representative chose Charles Rangel (D-N.Y.) (35 percent African American and 48 percent Hispanic).
- The lowest percentage of Hispanic residents electing a Hispanic representative chose Nydia Velazquez (D-N.Y.) (49 percent Hispanic and 11 percent African American).
- Of the African American representatives, 100 percent were Democrats.
- Of the Hispanic representatives, 85 percent were Democrats.

Source: Techpolitics, "House of Representatives: Socioeconomic Data for the 109th Congress," http://www.techpolitics.org/congress/109fh7.php.

---

would lose. At the state level, conditions have improved significantly. The "bench" of women in lower office has increased dramatically.

C. ENDURING QUESTIONS ABOUT PARTICIPANTS AND HOW TO RESEARCH THEM

Where Do Congressional Candidates Obtain Campaign Funding?

Observers of American politics often suggest that we "follow the money." American political campaigns are funded largely through private donations. Federal campaign laws require candidates to disclose who has contributed to their campaigns and how much money they have received.

How Do Underrepresented Groups Move into Elected Office?

In terms of demographic characteristics, members of Congress do not mirror the population they serve, despite a presumption that it is important to move in that direction. Minority racial, gender (while women are not a numerical minority in

Table 2.1.   A Snapshot of the 110th Congress

	% of House	% of Senate	% of U.S. Population
Gender			
Male	83	84	49
Female	17	16	51
Race			
White	83	94	75
Black	10	1	12
Hispanic	6	3	14[a]
Asian	1	2	4
Occupation			
Business	38	27	n.a.
Law	37	58	n.a.
Education	20	14	n.a.
Religion			
Protestant	62	62	59
Catholic	30	25	25
Jewish	7	13	1
Other/none	2	0	15
Average age	56 years	62 years	22 years[b]
Education			
Less than bachelor's degree	8	2	73[c]
Bachelor's degree	92	98	27
Master's degree	29	19	n.a.
Law degree	41	58	n.a.
Military service	23	29	9 (18% of males)

Other background characteristics:
   19% are former congressional staff members
   51% are former state legislators
   38% list their occupation as public service/politics
   2% are medical doctors, dentists or pharmacists

Source: Congressional data are from Mildred Amer, *Membership of the 110th Congress: A Profile*, CRS Report No. RS22555 (Washington, D.C.: Congressional Research Service, 2008), http://www.senate.gov/reference/resources/pdf/RS22555.pdf. U.S. population figures are from the Census Bureau website, http://www.census.gov (under "Data Sets").
[a]There is some double counting because of identification with more than one race.
[b]Median age; half the population is above this age and half is below.
[c]Figures are for adults over twenty-five.

Table 2.2.   Women in National Parliaments by Country (Lower House)

Country	Women (%)	
Sweden	47	
Finland	42	
Denmark	38	
Spain	37	
Austria	33	
Germany	32	
Bulgaria	22	
Canada	21	
China	20	
Poland	20	
Great Britain	20	
France	18	
Italy	17	
United States (House)[a]	**16**	**Ranks 79th of 134 countries**
United States (Senate)[b]	**14**	**Ranks 45th of 72 countries**
Ireland	13	
Japan	9	
Egypt	9	

Sources: Data are as of 2007 and from U.K. Government Equalities Office, "Women's Representation in Politics," http://www.womenandequalityunit.gov.uk/public_life/parliament.htm (last accessed March 29, 2008), and Inter-Parliamentary Union, "Women in National Parliaments: World Classification," http://www.ipu.org/wmn-e/classif.htm (last accessed March 29, 2008).
[a]Rankings based on countries with parliaments and for which data was available. After the 2006 election, the percentage of women in the House increased to 17% (see table 2.1).
[b]Rankings based on countries with upper chambers and for which data was available. After the 2006 election, the percentage of women in the Senate increased to 16% (see table 2.1).

Table 2.3.   Women in National Parliaments by Region (Lower House)

Region	Women (%)
Nordic countries	41
Americas	22
Europe: OSCE member countries (including Nordic countries)	21
Europe: OSCE countries (excluding Nordic countries)	19
Asia	17
Sub-Saharan Africa	17
Pacific	13
Arab states	10

OSCE: Organization for Security and Cooperation in Europe.
Source: Data are as of 2007 and from Inter-Parliamentary Union, "Women in National Parliaments: World and Regional Averages," http://www.ipu.org/wmn-e/world.htm (last accessed March 29, 2008).

Sample Hypothesis

a. If you are an incumbent, then you are likely to raise more money than if you are a challenger.
b. If you are a member of the majority party, then you are likely to raise more money than if you are a member of the minority party.
c. If you have a significant leadership post, then you are likely to raise more money than if you do not.
e. If you are on a committee focusing on a particular industry, then you are likely to raise more money from political action committees (PACs) from that industry.
d. If you are a Democrat, then you are more likely to depend on PAC funding than if you are a Republican.

Hints for Accomplishment

Vital Statistics on Congress is the best source for summary figures comparing incumbents and challengers. Data on fund-raising by individual candidates are available from the *Almanac of American Politics*, *Politics in America*, and the Federal Election Commission, at http://www.fec.gov. The Center for Responsive Politics, through its "Open Secrets" website (http://www.opensecrets.org/index.asp), provides both individual data and aggregate comparisons of contributions to committee and party groups.

The most interesting analysis will require you to make some decisions on how to *code* different members to place them in categories relevant to your hypothesis. For example, hypothesis (c) above would require you to determine whether a person has a "significant leadership position." It is important that you justify your coding scheme to your reader. You could then compare the totals raised for all (or a sample of) leaders and non-leaders. In some cases totals are less important than percentages, since the percentages will tell you how dependent particular candidates are on different sources.

---

the population, they are a minority among elected officials), economic, and religious groups have slowly been moving into political office in percentages closer to their distribution in the population. Using newspaper articles and other commentary, you could test one of the following hypotheses.

Sample Hypothesis

If you look at a recent Congress, then it will be more representative of the U.S. population in terms of (age, gender, educational level, or occupation) than if you look at a historical Congress.

Hints for Accomplishment

Choose two or more Congresses separated by a decade or more. Recent editions of the *Congressional Directory* are available online at http://www.gpoaccess.gov/cdirectory/, and biographical data on members of earlier Congresses can be found in the online *Biographical Directory of the United States Congress*, http://bioguide.congress.gov/biosearch/biosearch.asp. Select a sample of thirty or more members from the same chamber in each Congress, read their biographies, and compile statistics for each on age, gender, occupation, education, or some other characteristic. (It would be a good idea to begin by creating a set of four or five categories for each characteristic, such as lawyer, businessperson, educator, farmer, and other, for occupation.) Make sure the categories you create are *exhaustive* (cover all the possibilities) and *mutually exclusive* (each individual will readily fall into one, and only one, of the categories). Summarize your statistics as percentages of members falling into each category and prepare a chart comparing the general characteristics of the two sets of members. A bar graph would make your findings easier to understand. Where possible, look for U.S. census data on the distribution of that characteristic in the general population. Your paper should indicate whether you believe that your data suggests that Congress is becoming more or less representative and what the consequences of your findings might be. Raw data seldom speaks for itself. At some point in your paper you should discuss the implications of your findings.

Sample Hypothesis

If you are a (specific minority) running in a majority white district, then the current environment allows you to use traditional techniques to be elected to office.

Hints for Accomplishment

Choose one or more minority candidates for case studies. Assess the degree to which the minority characteristic was an issue in the campaign. Did it help or hurt?

Did the candidate run as a minority member? If so, how did he or she attempt to capitalize on it?

> To what degree did the political and social context of the district help or hurt the minority candidate?
>
> To add an international comparison, look at the campaign strategies of one or more of the minority candidates in another country.

D. IDEA GENERATOR: THE CAUSES AND CONSEQUENCES OF CONGRESS'S DEMOGRAPHIC MIX

The following chart provides some general guidelines for developing a research plan.

Specific Issue	Hypotheses	Hints
Congressional Demographics		
Disadvantages of under-represented groups	a. If you are a female candidate, then you can raise less money than if you are a male candidate. b. If you are a female candidate, then you are less likely to be able to run in a district that is secure for your party than if you are a male candidate.	Compare the fund-raising capabilities of a sample of winning and losing men and women candidates. Compare the "normal" vote for a district (the average party vote for the last three or four election cycles) for men and women candidates. Similar analyses could be done for African American or Hispanic candidates. (See *The Almanac of American Politics* or *CQ's Politics in America* for data.)
Causes of Political Behavior		
Are demographics destiny? To what degree do the personal characteristics of members of	a. If you are a businessperson, then you are more likely to support pro-business legislation than if you are not a	Using the *Congressional Record* or *CQ Almanac*, identify votes with particular relevance to specific demographic groups. Compare the

(continued)

Specific Issue	Hypotheses	Hints
Congress determine their votes?	businessperson. b. If you are a woman, then you are more likely to support reproductive rights than if you are a man.	votes of each group on the issue with the overall vote. Make sure you consider factors other than demographics that might explain the difference.

The Representational Role

How should a legislator represent his or her constituents?	If you are a delegate, then you better serve your constituents than if you are a trustee.	Edmund Burke makes the classic case supporting the trustee approach (see section 1). Look for competing arguments from philosophers and legislators themselves supporting the delegate perspective.

The Degree to Which Legislators Are Beholden to Campaign Contributors

Do political action committee (PAC) contributions lead to "the best Congress money can buy"?	a. If you run a PAC, then you will give your money strategically to members on committees that oversee your interests. b. If a legislator gets money from a PAC, then he or she will vote in its interests.	Using data from the Federal Election Commission or the Center for Responsive Politics, compare the contributions made to relevant committee members with those for other members. Find key votes of interest to particular interest groups and determine whether members receiving large contributions are more likely to support the groups' preferred positions.

3. Congressional Context and Performance

The test of an institution is not in its legal basis or membership but in its performance. Institutions like Congress do not act on their own. Their successes or failures are based on the collective commitment, motivations, and actions of their membership.

A. HISTORICAL DEVELOPMENT

Early Congresses were filled with many more short-term members who came to Washington for a few months each year and who operated in a much less institutionalized setting. Members served for a few years and then moved on to other endeavors. Permanent committees did not develop in either house until after the Civil War. Up until that time, bill drafting was done by ad hoc committees or on the floor. Members of Congress operated with a handful of personal and committee staff members until after World War II. The distribution of power in Congress has also shifted over time. The Speaker of the House gained considerable power by the early 1900s, only to face a revolt by the membership. This began a long ascendancy in the power of committee chairmen and the development of a virtually automatic method of choosing chairmen according to time in office (**seniority**).

By the 1980s, careerism was the norm in Congress, with most members choosing to run for reelection and few suffering electoral defeat. Campaigns became more candidate centered as political parties proved unable to raise the necessary funds and to provide the communications tools successful campaigns needed. Each member was forced to create his or her own campaign organization and run the campaign in a manner that benefited him or her. Loyalty once directed at the party was greatly diminished. Service in Congress clearly became a full-time job as Congress operated nearly year-round. Offices of individual members and committees became well staffed, and the number and variety of research-support agencies responsible to Congress grew. By weakening the seniority system, party leaders gained some power through their ability to influence committee leadership positions. The traditional pattern of processing legislation through established committees was augmented with the increased use of short-term task forces and policy summits.

The Republican takeover of the House in 1994, after forty years of Democratic Party control, was accompanied by an increased concentration of power in the hands of party leaders. For example, the Speaker regained a much larger role in appointing committee members. As the twenty-first century dawned, partisan polarization had become the norm for both parties. Partisan redistricting and the concentration of power of party leaders decreased the number of moderates in each party, making bipartisan compromise less common.

In 2006, voters expressed a desire for change both in terms of congressional policy (especially in foreign policy) and in how Congress operates. Tightened ethics rules were an early agenda item. (See box 2.6.)

B. PUBLIC SUPPORT AND EXPECTATIONS— WHAT DOES THE PUBLIC WANT CONGRESS TO DO?

Public support for Congress as an institution is relatively low, yet voters strongly support their individual members, as evidenced by public-opinion

Box 2.6. The Public Speaks at the Polls

Most citizens never contact their member of Congress directly. Only about half go to the polls in presidential election years, when all members of the House and a third of the Senate also runs for office. In off-year elections, when all members of the House and a third of the Senate runs for office, only about a third of eligible voters show up to vote. Most elections fail to send a clear signal about a policy, party, or institution. At times, though, the signal is clear, as the following figures show:

1994:

Republican House members losing[1]	0
Democratic House members losing	34
House reelection rate	90%
Republican Senators losing	0
Democratic Senators losing	2
Senate reelection rate	92%

*Result: Republicans took over the House and the Senate for the first time in forty years.

2006:

Republican House members losing	23
Democratic House members losing	0
House reelection rate	94.3%
Republican Senators losing	5
Democratic Senators losing	0[2]
Senate reelection rate	81.5%

*Result: Democrats took over the House and Senate.

1. Loss figures apply only to general-election losses by incumbents. Each year a few members lose in primaries.
2. Democrat Joseph Lieberman of Connecticut lost in the primary but won in the general election as an Independent.

polls and reelection rates for incumbents over the last twenty years. The public seems uncomfortable with Congress's partisanship, conflict, and seeming inefficiency. While there is always room for improvement, much of the dissatisfaction with the institution stems from the fact that Congress is tasked with universal "right" answers to most issues brought before it. The public seems not only to want Congress to deal with big issues of national concern but also to want their individual members of Congress to look out for parochial constituency interests.

C. CONGRESS AT WORK

Managing 535 Independent Legislators (Mr. Roberts Meets Mr. Jefferson— Rules of Order and Their Purpose)

While *Robert's Rules of Order* serves as the preeminent guide for running a meeting, the U.S. House and Senate each have their own unique set of rules that determine who can speak, what they can speak about, and what constitutes winning and losing. What is allowable in one chamber or for one type of action may not be appropriate in the other chamber or in relation to other official actions. A few examples:

- Amendments in the House must be related to the issue at hand (germane), but that is not the case in the Senate.
- Only members voting with the majority can ask for a vote to be reconsidered in his or her respective chamber.
- Some legislative actions require a simple majority, some a three-fifths vote, and some a two-thirds vote in both chambers.
- The House must take up revenue (taxation) bills first; only Senate approval is needed for treaties and presidential nominations.

While the specific rules are more important to the practitioner than to the student, it is important to realize that knowledge of the rules is a power resource. Thomas Jefferson wrote the first set of precedents by which congressional rules were interpreted. Each chamber employs a parliamentarian to interpret the rules and to keep track of precedents.[3]

Congressional Workloads—What Congress Can and Must Do

Each year members of Congress introduce four thousand to five thousand bills, of which an average of five hundred are adopted.[4] Congressional committees serve as the main tool for sorting through legislative proposals. The key piece of legislation that must be passed each year is the federal budget, which must be approved before the president (through the executive agencies) can spend government funds. Each year some legislation passed in previous years expires (because its original passage included a **sunset provision**), and there is usually pressure to

---

Box 2.7.   It Is Not Just about the Feds

While Congress is important, federalism means that there are fifty unique
state legislatures whose structure, composition, and makeup are worthy of
analysis. Many questions also apply to state legislative data. The National
Conference of State Legislatures (NCSL) provides easy access to relevant
facts and figures. Election data is available at http://www.ncsl.org/programs/
legismgt/elect/analysis.htm.

---

renew it. In the process of considering legislation, Congress carries out oversight
hearings in which it analyzes and critiques previous government behavior.

D. ENDURING CONTEXTUAL AND PERFORMANCE
QUESTIONS AND HOW TO RESEARCH THEM

How Do the House and Senate Differ in Terms of Partisanship?

It makes both logical and political sense that House districts would be more politically homogeneous than complete states represented by members of the Senate. But states themselves vary in their political homogeneity.

Sample Hypothesis

If a state is more politically homogeneous, then its senators will reflect
more politically extreme voting patterns.

Hints for Accomplishment

There are several ways to measure political homogeneity. In recent elections, analysts have characterized states as "red" (Republican), "blue" (Democratic), or "purple" (toss-up). The lists of states in each category can be
found in chapter 7. Using average presidential- or party-support scores, calculate the average support for the senators from each state in each category for one or more years. Party-support scores calculated by CQ measure
the percentage of times a member votes with his or her party on those
votes that split the parties. Remember to use the presidential-opposition
score for senators not from the president's party. Alternatively, categorize
states according to the composition of their House delegation, defining
"red" states as those in which Republicans make up at least 70 percent of
the delegation, "blue" states as those in which Democrats make up at least
70 percent of the delegation, and "purple" states as the remaining states.

How Does Legislation Flow through the Legislative Process?

One way to understand congressional behavior is to do a case study of a particular congressional decision. Case studies are powerful tools for understanding the intricacies of a specific decision. They may or may not reflect a general pattern that applies to all decisions. You will want to discover the *nature* of the **natural coalition** (those supporting the proposal because of constituency needs or personal preferences) and the bargaining chips involved in creating a **bought coalition** (encouraging members to support the bill through amendments or political promises).

Sample Hypothesis

a. If you are a Democrat in Congress, then you will vote differently than if you are a Republican.
b. If you receive campaign funds from one of the protagonists in a legislative battle, then you are likely to support their position on that legislation.
c. If you are a male member of Congress, then you will vote differently than if you are a female.

Hints for Accomplishment

Pick a policy that has progressed far enough through the legislative process to have had some votes on the floor. The *CQ Almanac* outlines key policy decisions in various issue areas each year.

Many policies are subject to a series of votes. The amendment process is a way in which coalitions are expanded through additions and revisions. Members of Congress who support winning amendments can often be counted on to approve the final bill. Discussion about the politics associated with each bill and individual votes are available in *CQ Weekly*. Additional voting information is available on the congressional website, at http://www.thomas.gov. Analyze the final voting blocks and discuss the nature of the policy cleavage (partisan, ideological, geographic, etc.). Your paper could be a broad overview looking at the vote division by party (often listed in *CQ Weekly*) or a more detailed analysis in which you code members on other characteristics (gender, region, committee membership, campaign contributions, etc.) and compare typical voting for each group. Such detailed information on members is available in the *Almanac of American Politics* and *CQ's Politics in America*.

You might want to do a sub-case study to determine the voting record of the member of Congress representing you in the House or of one of the two senators representing your state on the issue you have chosen and indicate why you think he or she voted in that way.

Don't be afraid to point out the difficulty of discovering the more private deals in the coalition-building process.

E. IDEA GENERATOR: CONGRESS AT WORK

The following chart provides some general guidelines for developing a research plan.

Specific Issue	Hypotheses	Hints
Public Expectations of Congress		
Competing expectations	If a member of Congress attempts to please all the people while performing his or her job, then he or she will face an impossible task.	Look at polls about the public's expectations of members of Congress and of Congress as a whole. To what degree are the expectations contradictory?
Rules and Procedures		
Uniqueness of congressional rules	a. Even if you have mastered *Robert's Rules of Order*, then you still will not have mastered Congress's procedures. b. Even if you have mastered the rules of the House, then you still will have a lot to learn about the Senate's procedures.	Compare the House or Senate rules with those in *Robert's Rules of Order*. Consider the consequences of the differences. Do the same in comparing the House and Senate rules.
The Importance of Structure		
The value of the bicameral system	If legislation goes through a two-chamber legislature then it is improved because it is subject to the differing interests of legislators serving different constituencies.	Search for the changes made in legislation by either the House or the Senate. Consider the degree to which the needs of different constituent interests encourages members to look at legislation from various perspectives and, in the process, to improve it.

4. Major Data Sources on Congress

The "trade magazine" of Congress is the privately published *CQ Weekly*. Extensively used by both congressional insiders and outside observers, this weekly periodical contains member profiles, analyses of key policy battles, voting statistics, and a chronicle of each week's major happenings. The *National Journal* focuses more on the executive branch but does include relevant information on Congress.

Two roughly comparable almanacs of Congress, *CQ's Politics in America* (Washington, D.C.: CQ Press) and *The Almanac of American Politics* (Washington, D.C.: National Journal), provide an in-depth look at every member of Congress and the members' districts. Both contain election statistics, information on campaign contributions, demographic profiles of each member's district, voting patterns in Congress, and a political profile of each member.

The *Congressional Directory* is the official guide to Congress. It provides biographies supplied by the members as well as committee listings. It can be accessed at http://www.gpoaccess.gov/cdirectory. CQ's *Guide to Congress* is published regularly with comprehensive information on Congress and its members.

For a quantitative, historical look at the nature of Congress and its members, see *Vital Statistics on Congress* (Washington, D.C.: American Enterprise Institute). Issued every two years, this volume summarizes overall election statistics, the congressional workload, and voting patterns. It also includes data going back to the First Congress on many items.

5. Original Research That Will Impress Your Professor

General
Quirk, Paul J., and Sarah A. Binder, eds. *The Legislative Branch.* Institutions of American Democracy series. New York: Oxford University Press, 2005. This volume provides rich historical and contemporary information on Congress.

Congressional Elections and Constituent Relations
Cooper, Joseph, ed. *Congress and the Decline of Public Trust.* Boulder, Colo.: Westview Press, 1999.
Fenno, Richard F., Jr. *Home Style: House Members in the Districts.* Boston: Little, Brown, 1978.
Herrnson, Paul. *Congressional Elections: Campaigning at Home and in Washington.* Washington, D.C.: CQ Press, 2000.
Hibbing, John, and Elizabeth Theiss-Morse. *Congress as Public Enemy: Public Attitudes Toward American Political Institutions.* New York: Cambridge University Press, 1995.
Jacobson, Gary. *The Politics of Congressional Elections.* New York: Longman, 2004.
Mayhew, David. *Congress: The Electoral Connection.* New Haven, Conn.: Yale University Press, 1974.

Congress in Action
Bond, Jon R., and Richard Fleisher, eds. *Polarized Politics: Congress and the President in a Partisan Era.* Washington, D.C.: CQ Press, 2000.

Deering, Christopher, and Steven S. Smith. *Committees in Congress*. Washington, D.C.: CQ Press, 1997.

Kingdon, John. *Congressmen's Voting Decisions*. Ann Arbor: University of Michigan Press, 1989.

Oleszek, Walter. *Congressional Procedures and the Policy Process*. Washington, D.C.: CQ Press, 2001.

Sinclair, Barbara. *Unorthodox Lawmaking: New Legislative Processes in the U.S. Congress*. Washington, D.C.: CQ Press, 2000.

6. Where to Find It

A number of sources provide unique access to information relevant to Congress. The following discussion focuses on free Internet sources, or those available in most public libraries. You may also want to see if your campus has access to one of the fee-based sources such as Lexis-Nexis's "Congressional Universe" or Congressional Quarterly's CQ.com.

Who are my members of Congress?

This is not a silly question. People move around so often and congressional district lines change so often that it may be hard to keep up with who represents you in Congress. A number of Internet sites allow you to find your House and Senate members by entering your zip code. For the House, go to: http://www.house.gov; for the Senate, http://www.senate.gov/.

Where can I get a biography of my senators and representative?

The official biographies submitted by members are available in the *Congressional Directory*, either in hard copy or online, at http://www.gpoaccess.gov/cdirectory/index.html. Browse by your state.

Many individual member's webpages provide additional biographical information. They can be accessed from the main House (http://www.house.gov) or Senate (http://www.senate.gov) pages.

Historical biographies of members since the First Congress are in the *Biographical Directory of the United States Congress*. The online version, at http://bioguide.congress.gov/biosearch/biosearch.asp, is searchable by individual, state, party, or individual Congress.

More detailed (and objective) biographies that go beyond basic facts and are written by outsiders are available in *The Almanac of American Politics* or *CQ's Politics in America*.

Brief basic biographical information on the current Congress is available from Project Vote Smart, at http://www.vote-smart.org, or from Congress.org, at http://www.congress.org/congressorg/home/ (under "Officials").

How did my Senators or House member fund his or her campaign?
For detailed listings of who contributed to a particular candidate's campaign, go to the Federal Election Commission's website, at http://www.fec.gov/finance/disclosure/norcansea.shtml.

Contributions to candidates by categories are available at C-SPAN's website, at http://www.c-span.org (go to "Resources," then "Congress/Legislative" and "Campaign Finance Database") or from the Center for Responsive Politics through its "Open Secrets" website, at http://www.opensecrets.org/politicians/index.asp.

Where can I find election results for congressional races?
Complete results by state for current and past elections are available from the website of the clerk of the House, at http://clerk.house.gov/member_info/election.html. C-SPAN's website often provides information on upcoming races.

How can I find out who serves on which committees?
Member biographies list their current committee memberships (see above). The full membership of each committee is available from Congress.org, at https://ssl.capwiz.com/congressorg/directory/congdir.tt, or on Congress's official website, Thomas, at http://www.thomas.gov (under "Government Resources" and then "Committee Home Pages").

How can I find out the status of legislation in Congress?
The congressional website, http://www.thomas.gov, enables you to search for legislation by word or phrase, bill number, or sponsor. Bills introduced by a senator have a number starting with "S" (such as S. 1776), and those introduced by a House member begin with "H.R." (such as H.R. 2001). Members seek cosponsors for their bills to show support and allow other members to take some credit. Both the House and the Senate can choose to take up a bill from the other chamber. In many cases the same bill is introduced under two different numbers, one in each chamber. Eventually, one of the bills becomes the lead bill for both chambers. The final bill must be passed in identical form by both chambers before it can be sent to the president for approval or rejection.

What is my member of Congress saying in public?
The *Congressional Record* is the official record of what was said on the House and Senate floors. Members have the right to "revise and extend" their remarks to make sure what they said was what they actually meant to say. A searchable version of the *Congressional Record*, beginning with the 101st Congress, is available on Thomas, at http://www.thomas.gov/home/r110query.html.

Project Vote Smart provides access to a wide variety of public statements of members at http://www.vote-smart.org/index.htm.

How can I determine the public's evaluation of Congress and its members?
Polls on the public's general support for Congress are posted regularly at PollingReport.com, at http://www.pollingreport.com (under "State of the Union" and "Congress").

Interest groups rate individual members of Congress on issues of particular importance to them. Ratings can be found from Project Vote Smart, at http://www.vote-smart.org/index.htm (go to "Interest Group Ratings" and then choose a state and member). Ratings indicate the percentage of times a member supported the organization's preferences on chosen bills in a particular year. Except at the extremes of support and opposition, the figures are best interpreted relative to the average for that chamber in a specific year.

Where can I find data to analyze votes in Congress?
Voting in Congress is the most common measure of a member's influence and activity. Recorded votes are very important, but a number of caveats are in order. Many actions in Congress are not taken by recorded vote. Votes are not always what they seem. **Omnibus legislation** includes a wide variety of topics, and it is not always clear which sections of a bill a member supports or opposes. When votes are recorded, members are careful that they are able to explain their votes to their constituents.

The official record of roll-call votes can be found on Thomas, at http://www.thomas.gov. If you know the roll-call number and the session of Congress, choose "Roll Call Votes." Then choose the session of Congress and the particular roll-call vote. The chart will provide the partisan breakdown and individual supporters. To find the roll-call vote number, use the search function of Thomas. Once you have found the bill in which you are interested, choose "Bill Summary and Status," and then "Major Congressional Action." That will take you directly to a chart of the vote and individual voting.

Congress.org allows you to search for votes in the current Congress by subject matter, at http://www.congress.org/congressorg/issuesaction/vote.

How can I tap into Congress's own research resources?
The Congressional Research Service (CRS) is Congress's in-house research arm. It collects, synthesizes, and distributes hundreds of different research papers (usually called "issue briefs"). Members of Congress usually willingly share these reports with their constituents. Congressional member offices can search a full database of CRS products and order copies for constituents. Do not hesitate to contact your congressional office for help in securing CRS reports. CRS products serve members of Congress whose political views vary widely. CRS analysts seek to present a balanced discussion of policy issues, providing extensive background and competing perspectives.

A number of Internet sites provide selected CRS reports in full text. The Law Librarians' Society of Washington, D.C., provides an extensive list of reports focusing on Congress and its procedures at http://www.llsdc.org/crs-congress, as does the House Rules Committee, at http://www.rules.house.gov/CRS_Rpt/index.html.

Where can I find the rules of the House and Senate?
Floor procedures for the House are outlined on the House Rules Committee page, at http://www.rules.house.gov. Rules of the Senate are at http://rules .senate.gov/senaterules.

How do I determine the activity levels of various Congresses?
Senate statistics for the last twenty years are available at http://www.senate.gov/ reference/resources/pdf/yearlycomparison.pdf. Similar data for both the House and Senate is available in *Vital Statistics on Congress* (see above).

Where can I find out about the impeachment process?
The Library of Congress American Memory Project provides extensive access to print and electronic materials on impeachment, at http://memory.loc.gov/ ammem/amlaw/Impeachment-Guide.html.

Where can I find more opinionated views of Congress and the legislation it deals with?
Most interest groups have websites that provide their perspectives on impending legislation. Publications such as the *New Republic* (liberal), available online at http://www.tnr.com, and the *National Review* (conservative), available online at http://www.nationalreview.com, as well as the online magazine *Slate* (liberal), http://www.slate.com, take clear policy positions.

Where can I find the religious affiliations of members of Congress?
Look at the survey done by Americans for Religious Liberty, available at http://arlinc.org/pdf/110thCongressReligiousAffiliation.pdf.

Where can I find statistics about women serving in office?
The Center for American Women and Politics gathers both contemporary and historical data about women officeholders on a state-by-state basis, at http:// www.cawp.rutgers.edu.

What if I can't find what I need?
Check out the C-SPAN website for dozens of other sources of congressional data and information, at http://www.c-span.org/resources/congress.asp, or Congress-pedia, at http://www.sourcewatch.org/index.php?title=Congresspedia.

7. Taking Action—
Contacting and Influencing Congress

Tips for Writing Congress:

- Legitimize the rationale for contacting a particular member (i.e., "as your con-stituent," "recognizing your role on the XYZ Committee"). In most cases members will show little interest in communications from nonconstituents.
- Show some effort in your communication. While e-mail is widely used in Congress, the ease of its use sends the message that the issue is of relatively lit-tle importance. A well-researched and written letter will carry a great deal more weight.
- State your purpose for writing in the first sentence of the letter; for example, "As your constituent, I am writing to urge your support for increased funding for health care."
- If your letter pertains to a specific piece of legislation, identify it. And make sure that you are referencing the correct legislation to the correct body of Con-gress. House bills are designated H.R.____; Senate bills, S.____. It is also im-portant to know the status of the bill.
- Be courteous. An attack does little but turn off the recipient.
- If appropriate, include personal information about why the issue matters to you. "Cold sweat" letters legitimately implying that the author woke up in the middle of the night with great concern about an issue carry more weight than lukewarm "it would be kind of nice" requests.
- Address only one issue in each letter.
- Close your letter with a restatement of your purpose and indicate the response that you expect.

Addressing Your Correspondence to a Senator:

> The Honorable [Abraham Lincoln]
> [room number] [name of] Senate Office Building (optional)
> United States Senate
> Washington, D.C. 20510
>
> Dear Senator [Lincoln]:

Addressing Your Correspondence to a Representative:

> The Honorable [Theodore Roosevelt]
> [room number] [name of] House Office Building (optional)

United States House of Representatives
Washington, D.C. 20515

Dear Representative [Roosevelt]:

Notes

1. Edmund Burke, "Speech to the Electors of Bristol" (November 3, 1774). The text of the speech is available online at The Founder's Constitution, http://press-pubs.uchicago.edu/founders/documents/v1ch13s7.html.
2. David Mayhew, *Divided We Govern* (New Haven, Conn.: Yale University Press, 1991).
3. For the House, see "Rules and Precedents that Govern the U.S. House of Representatives," http://www.gpoaccess.gov/precedents. For the Senate, see "Riddick's Senate Procedure," http://www.gpoaccess.gov/riddick/index.html.
4. See Jennifer E. Manning, *Congressional Statistics: Bills Introduced and Laws Enacted, 1947–2003*, CRS Report No. 96-727 (Washington, D.C.: Congressional Research Service, 2004).

CHAPTER 3

The Presidency and the Bureaucracy

The president of the United States is the most visible of national leaders. Elected with a national mandate, the president is the spokesperson for and symbol of American national government. Modern presidents have used their constitutional powers and extraconstitutional privileges to dominate the policymaking process, especially in the realm of foreign policy. Unable to carry out most policies on their own, both the president and Congress depend on a large federal bureaucracy to carry out the laws.

1. The Structure and Intention of the Presidency and the Bureaucracy

A. CONSTITUTIONAL BASIS AND EXTRACONSTITUTIONAL ROLES

Article II of the Constitution outlines the general responsibilities of the president, the requirements for serving as president, the method of selecting the president, procedures for removing the president, and relationships between the president and the other branches of government. As the American republic developed, presidents have taken on additional duties not specified or anticipated by the framers. Among the key provisions established by the Constitution are the following.

- ***Qualifications:*** Legally, presidents must be natural-born citizens (not naturalized immigrants from another nation) and at least thirty-five years of age. The political requirements for acquiring the party nomination and eventual election revolve around issues of experience, visibility, and communications skills.

- *Election:* Not fully confident in the general public, the framers created an indirect method of election by establishing the **Electoral College**. Under this system, a plurality (the greatest number) of voters in a state chooses a slate of electors committed to one of the presidential candidates. The number of electoral votes is based roughly on the state's population: it is equal to the number of House and Senate members. Each individual elector is chosen as a part of a slate proposed by the competing presidential candidates. The winning slate casts its ballots for the candidates who placed them on the ballot.[1] In a few cases "unfaithful electors" have refused to vote for the presidential candidate on whose slate they ran, but their duplicity has not affected the outcome. As was the case in 2000, the winner of the national popular vote does not necessarily receive a majority in the Electoral College. (See chapter 8 for additional discussion of the presidential election process.)

- *Constitutional powers of the president:* Among the powers granted to the president are the power to serve as **chief executive**, overseeing executive agencies and appointing ambassadors, judges, and other governmental officials, and the power to act as **commander in chief** of the armed forces. The president's ability to perform as military strategist and tactician is not without constraint, however. Congress still retains the power to declare war and power over funding executive initiatives (the "power of the purse"). **The War Powers Resolution** (1973) was designed to limit military actions initiated by the president. It requires consultation with Congress and congressional approval for sending troops into hostile areas. Under the resolution, presidents receive a sixty- to ninety-day window for unilateral action, justified on the basis of the speed of modern threats. This allowance has the result of legitimizing military action without a congressionally approved declaration of war. The president also has the power to function as the **chief diplomat**, speaking for the country and making treaties (with the advice and consent of the Senate). Modern presidents also often serve as creators of international coalitions to challenge threats to freedom, democracy, or American interests.

- *Extraconstitutional powers of the president:* Although these powers are not specified in the Constitution, tradition and necessity have granted the president the power to act as **chief legislator**, dominating the legislative agenda by proposing a presidential program of new and revised legislation; serve as **national party leader**; operate as **chief of state**, the ceremonial head of government who greets foreign dignitaries, bestows honors, and expresses national sentiment; and manage the economy as the nation's **chief economist**. Through his direct influence over budgets, taxes, and spending and his more indirect ability to influence economic players through public pronouncements and the appointment of officials such as members of the **Federal Reserve Board**, the modern president is expected to ensure a strong economy with limited inflation and high levels of employment.

B. GOALS AND INTENTIONS

The Presidency

The Framers were of mixed mind about the presidency. On the one hand, they had a healthy distrust of concentrated power after their experience as colonists. On the other hand, their experience under the Articles of Confederation convinced them of the need for enhanced executive power. Throughout history, presidents have varied in the aggressiveness with which they used and expanded their power. (See box 3.1 for a discussion of the problems of comparing presidents.) A classic comparison exists between two presidents who served back-to-back. Theodore Roosevelt promoted a "stewardship theory" in which an activist president is responsible for doing everything he can to solve problems, only avoiding those

---

Box 3.1.   Skill Box: The N=1 Problem

One of the difficulties of analyzing the presidency with hard data lies in the fact that we have only one president at a time. It is more difficult to develop clear and isolated variables for presidents than it is for members of Congress, for judges, or for other offices with multiple members. The social, economic, and historical contexts under which individual presidents operate are so different that it may not be valid to compare one president with the next. We could simply throw up our hands and eschew analysis, but that would not further our understanding. Instead, we do the best we can, always recognizing with modesty the limits on our endeavors. Some ways of getting around the "n=1 problem" include

- comparing the same president over time doing repetitive tasks;
- comparing presidents doing similar tasks, recognizing that the comparisons will not be perfect; and
- capitalizing on the possibility of doing a detailed analysis, viewing each presidential act as a case study whose richness adds understanding that more empirical comparisons may miss.

actions clearly forbidden by the Constitution. His successor, William Howard Taft, took a much more restrictive "clerkship" view of the presidential role, arguing that presidents could take only those actions that could be specifically traced back to a constitutional grant of power. Public expectations and personal inclinations have forced all modern presidents to be activists. The difference lies in whether they attempt to move the country in a liberal or conservative direction.

The presidency created by the framers stands not as an independent institution but part of the **separation of powers** model. The framers anticipated that the legislative, executive, and judicial branches would monitor and check each other, thereby tempering the threat that any one branch, or the government in general, would amass too much power.

The Bureaucracy

Presidents can do little on their own and must count on the federal bureaucracy to carry out most tasks of government. Almost 2 million civilian government employees (along with 1.4 million members of the active-duty military) administer the policies of government.[2] Members of the bureaucracy must act in accordance with laws passed by Congress and signed by the president. In reality, no law can anticipate every potential situation, so bureaucrats are given some **discretion** to administer laws in accordance with the spirit of the laws, if not in explicit accordance with the words. Bureaucrats report to the president through a chain of command, which typically ends with a cabinet secretary. Thus a tax collector at the Internal Revenue Service would report to his or her superior in a local office, who would report to his or her superior in a regional office, who would report to his or her superior in Washington, before the communication might be passed on to the secretary of the treasury.

C. COMPARATIVE PERSPECTIVE: PRESIDENTS VERSUS PRIME MINISTERS

From the outside, presidents and prime ministers, as chief executives of their nations, may look very similar. The differences, however, are basic and fundamental. Although presidents are elected independently, prime ministers are elected by the majority party (or coalition of parties) in the parliament. Members of the winning party coalition in the parliament have a direct stake in the prime minister's success and usually support him or her on legislation. Prime ministers do not face a national electorate directly as do presidents. Presidents can serve with legislative majorities of the opposing parties (**divided government**) and have no guarantee of legislative support. Presidents serve a fixed term in office (in the United States, four years with one possible reelection). Prime ministers generally have a maximum term (often five years), but seldom serve that full period. If their policies prove popular, they often call an election earlier, at which time every member of parliament must run for reelection or retire. If a prime minister loses the support of his or her party, a **vote of no confidence** may take place, dissolving the government and forcing all parliamentarians back into the electoral arena.

U.S. presidents serve as both head of state and head of government. Prime ministers are head of government, but not the symbolic head of state. As members of parliament and chosen by it, prime ministers have a much closer relationship with their legislatures than do presidents. While U.S. presidents usually give only one speech a year to Congress (the **State of the Union address**), prime ministers in many parliamentary systems face their legislatures in a regular **question time**, where they are grilled on their legislative intentions and governmental performance.

D. ENDURING STRUCTURAL QUESTIONS AND HOW TO RESEARCH THEM

Is the Presidency Strong Enough for the Job?

Considerable debate, especially in the last four decades, has emerged over the desirability of growing presidential power. Those fearful of presidential power (often coming from the party out of power) raise the specter of the "imperial presidency,"

Sample Hypothesis

a. If a president supports congressional action, then it will be forthcoming.
b. If a president is in the early years of his or her first term, then the president's support will be higher.

Hints for Accomplishment

Presidential power is hard to measure. One concrete way to measure a portion of it is to look at the president's success with Congress. Each year, the *CQ Almanac* publishes average presidential-support scores for the president and individual presidential-support scores for each member of Congress. The American Presidency Project makes historical data available online, at http://www.presidency.ucsb.edu/data/concurrence.php. The average House and Senate presidential-support scores are also shown in figure 3.1.

Look at these scores over several years. Do they show an unchecked president or one who must find common ground with Congress? (See box 3.2.)

Box 3.2.   Skill Box:
Understanding Presidential-Support Scores

Numerous journalistic and political organizations evaluate congressional voting. Each takes a subset of votes of interest to that organization. The choice of votes to evaluate has a significant effect on the analysis. CQ, unlike many interest groups doing ratings, has no particular agenda. It chooses votes on the basis of clear and public criteria. According to CQ, support scores reflect the "percentage of recorded votes in a year on which the President took a position and on which a representative voted 'yea' or 'nay' to agreement with the president's position. Failures to vote lower support scores."

AVERAGE PRESIDENTIAL VOTING SUPPORT IN THE HOUSE

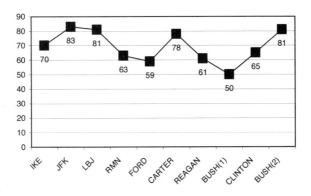

AVERAGE PRESIDENTIAL VOTING SUPPORT IN THE SENATE

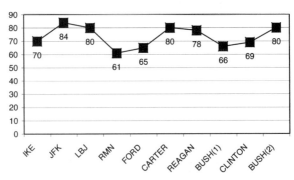

Figure 3.1.   House and Senate average concurrence with presidents.
Source: Reprinted from the American Presidency Project, http://www.presidency.ucsb
.edu/images/datacharts/concurrence.php, with additional data from *CQ Almanac*.

unchecked and uncontrolled. Specific reforms such as the **War Powers Resolution** have focused on the second portion of the equation and attempted to constrain the president's ability to wage war by requiring congressional involvement.

Does the Bureaucracy Serve as an Extension of the President, or
Do We Regularly Face the Danger of a "Rogue" Bureaucracy Pursuing
Its Own Interests?

Presidents can appoint only a small percentage of the bureaucracy and have virtually no power to remove or punish members of the civil service.

Sample Hypothesis

If the president had more power to hire and fire bureaucrats, then democracy would be better served.

Hints for Accomplishment

Consider the arguments for and against giving the president more control of the bureaucracy. Consider the responsible-party model,[3] which argues that electoral victory gives the president the right to move government policy in the direction promised during the campaign. Balance that against the assertion that bureaucrats are experts with special knowledge and should remain independent from partisan politics.

What Would We Gain (and Lose) by Adopting a Parliamentary System?

Create a list of what you see as the advantages and disadvantages of a parliamentary system. Make sure you indicate your rationale for listing a characteristic as an advantage or a disadvantage. Which criteria of good government does the parliamentary system promote, and which does it undermine?

Sample Hypothesis

If we had a parliamentary system, then . . . (specify an advantage or disadvantage).

Hints for Accomplishment

For some ideas, see United Nations Development Program, "Governing Systems and Executive-Legislative Relations: Presidential, Parliamentary and Hybrid Systems," http://www.undp.org/governance/docs/Parl-Pub-govern.htm; and George Thomas Kurian, ed., *World Encyclopedia of Parliaments and Legislatures*, vol. 2 (Washington, D.C., Congressional Quarterly, 1998).

Is Divided Government a Threat to Effective Democracy?

Some analysts argue that divided government leads to ineffective government. Over sixty years ago, a committee of the American Political Science Association asserted that politics would be better if two widely divergent parties competed in elections and that after the election it would be better to have one party control both the legislative and executive branches. Once in office, the victorious party should, under this view, follow through on campaign promises. See American Political Science Association, *Toward a More Responsible Two-Party System*, available at http://www.apsanet.org/~pop/APSA_Report.htm. More recently, political scientist David Mayhew has questioned the negative consequences of divided government. See David Mayhew, *Divided We Govern: Party Control, Lawmaking, and Investigations, 1946–2002* (New Haven, Conn.: Yale University Press, 2005).

Sample Hypothesis

If there is divided government, then the president will have less success steering his legislative agenda through Congress.

Hints for Accomplishment

For a qualitative paper, consider the arguments in each source. Which seem to make the most sense?

To do a quantitative analysis, use the yearly measures of presidential support published in the *CQ Almanac*. Compare the success rates for presidents whose party controlled Congress with those for presidents who operated under a divided government. See box 3.3 for suggestions on analyzing data regarding divided government.

Box 3.3.   Skill Box: Summarizing Data

Long lists of data are difficult to interpret in their raw form. The following listing indicates whether the president's party also controlled both branches of Congress (unified government) or the opposition party controlled one or both congressional houses (divided government). Create percentages based on the number of years with divided government compared with the total number of two-year congressional sessions in the specified category; that is, create one or more of the following percentages:

- the percentage of sessions with divided government in various eras (e.g., 1824–1900, 1902–1974, 1976–present, or some other period)
- the percentage of sessions with divided government for each party
- the percentage of sessions with divided government in various eras for each party

Alternatively, compare the average percentage of House seats for the president's party by era or party.

Year	President's Party	% of Seats Won by President's Party	Unified or Divided Government
1824	DR	58	U
1826	DR	61	D
1828	D	44	U
1830	D	53	U
1832	D	55	U
1834	D	54	U
1836	D	52	U
1838	D	54	U
1840	W	54	U
1842	W	45	D-h
1844	D	51	U
1846	D	53	D-h
1848	W	48	D
1850	W	45	D
1852	D	54	U
1854	D	80	D-h
1856	D	70	U
1858	D	69	D-h
1860	R	57	U
1862	R	63	U
1864	R	64	U
1866	D	59	U
1868	R	56	U
1870	R	53	U
1872	R	55	U
1874	R	53	D-h
1876	R	49	D-h
1878	R	45	D

Year	President's Party	% of Seats Won by President's Party	Unified or Divided Government
1880	R	49	U
1882	R	43	D-h
1884	D	47	D-s
1886	D	44	D-s
1888	R	49	D-h
1890	R	45	D-h
1892	D	53	U
1894	D	45	D
1896	R	48	U
1898	R	46	U
1900	R	50	U
1902	R	48	U
1904	R	53	U
1906	R	49	U
1908	R	48	U
1910	R	46	D-h
1912	D	61	U
1914	D	57	U
1916	D	55	U
1918	D	54	D
1920	R	56	U
1922	R	47	U
1924	R	51	U
1926	R	51	U
1928	R	51	U
1930	R	46	D-h
1932	D	62	U
1934	D	64	U
1936	D	63	U
1938	D	60	U
1940	D	59	U
1942	D	57	U
1944	D	58	U
1946	D	54	D
1948	D	58	U
1950	D	57	U
1952	R	47	U

Year	President's Party	% of Seats Won by President's Party	Unified or Divided Government
1954	R	42	D
1956	R	44	D
1958	R	38	D
1960	D	59	U
1962	D	55	U
1964	D	59	U
1966	D	52	U
1968	R	48	D
1970	R	44	D
1972	R	48	D
1974	R	42	D
1976	D	57	U
1978	D	54	U
1980	R	48	D-h
1982	R	47	D-h
1984	R	48	D-h
1986	R	45	D
1988	R	46	D
1990	R	44	D
1992	D	51	U
1994	D	49	D
1996	D	49	D
1998	D	48	D
2000	D	48	D
2002	R	52	D-s
2004	R	53	U
2006	R	46	U

Sources: The American Presidency Project, http://www.presidency.ucsb.edu/data/ presparty.php, and U.S. House of Representatives, Office of the Clerk, http://clerk .house.gov (under "Member Information," then "Congressional Profile").

E. IDEA GENERATOR: PRESIDENTIAL POWER AND ROLES

The following chart provides some general guidelines for developing a research plan.

Specific Issue	Hypotheses	Hints
Power		
Presidential versus congressional power	If a president takes a firm stand on an appointment or legislative initiative, then Congress tends to accommodate him.	Look for clear confrontations between presidents and Congress. Determine the success rate of the president.
Presidential Role		
Agenda setting	If a president highlights an issue, then it becomes the focus of the media and Congress.	Follow the initiatives set out in the president's State of the Union address to determine the media attention the initiatives receive and the congressional response.

2. Participants

A. WHO ARE THE PRESIDENTIAL AND BUREAUCRATIC PARTICIPANTS AND WHY ARE THEY THERE?

Presidents

Viable presidential candidates represent a small slice of American citizens. The legal requirements of being at least thirty-five years of age and a native-born citizen of the United States have eliminated few who might be strong candidates. The constraints result more from cultural and political factors than legal ones. Until 2008, no female candidate or minority candidate had played a major role in a presidential general election, though several had competed for the party nomination. John F. Kennedy was the first (and so far the only) non-Protestant president. In the 2008 presidential race, Mitt Romney, a Mormon, found his religion to be a barrier among some voters, and Barack Obama (the first African American presidential candidate to win a major party nomination) was forced to denounce some of the statements of his longtime minister. Although we glorify the myth of "log cabin to White House," most viable candidates have had successful and remunerative careers. The rigors and time necessary for campaigning have tended to advantage governors (or former governors) in recent years.

Contemporary presidential candidates face two hurdles. First, they must win their party's nomination through a series of party caucuses and primaries that draw some of the more ideologically extreme members of their party. As figure

3.2 reveals, primaries have increasingly become the dominant source of convention delegates. Once they have won the nomination at their party's convention, the candidates must broaden their appeal to a larger general-election electorate that is more varied and moderate. Presidential candidates raise much of the money in the primaries on their own, having the option to get matching funds from the federal government for some private contributions. Once candidates have been nominated, the federal government gives candidates of the two major parties the funding to run their campaign as long as they agree not to raise other funds and to limit their spending. The increased cost of campaigns has enticed some presidential nominees such as George W. Bush to bypass federal funding and its limits. Third-party candidates who pass a minimum threshold of support receive some funding after the election.

The Bureaucracy

Until the 1880s, government employees were appointed largely on the basis of their political connections rather than their skill or expertise. The **spoils system** proved effective for building strong political parties but did not guarantee continuity or the appointment of the most qualified people. With the passage of the **Pendleton Civil Service Act** (1883), hiring became more competitive and was protected from political influence. Federal government positions are largely "white collar" jobs involving administrative tasks and professional duties (many government employees are scientists, lawyers, accountants, etc.). Today, most potential government employees compete for jobs by taking a civil-service examination, which tests their knowledge and skills. Only the top three thousand or so positions are reserved for political appointment by the president. Cabinet secretaries and other key officials are expected to be responsive to the president and assist him in carrying out the policies on which he ran for office.

B. COMPARATIVE PERSPECTIVE

Although American presidents arrive with considerable partisan experience, most often as governors of their states, they are not as tied to the national party and its Washington players as prime ministers are tied to their national parliaments. Prime ministers tend to be seen as "one of them" by parliamentarians, many of whom have served with the prime minister in the chamber for many years. Members of Congress, especially those not from the new president's party, recognize that presidents come and go, and they tend to see the new incumbent as a minor inconvenience. Prime ministers and their parliaments share political fortunes. If a prime minister calls an election by choice or loses a vote of no confidence, *all*

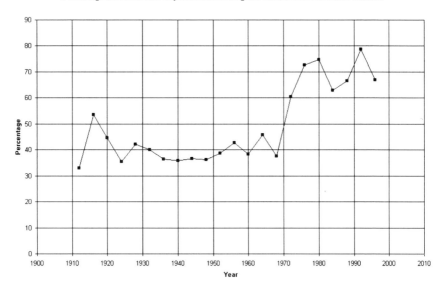

Percentage of Democratic Party Convention Delegates Selected In Democratic Primaries

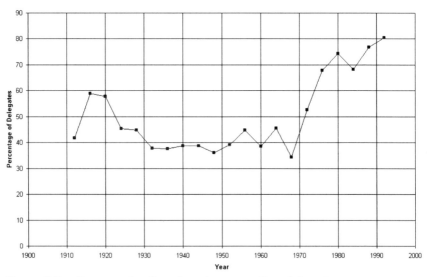

Percentage of Republican Presidential Convention Delegates Selected in Primary Elections

Figure 3.2.   Source of national party convention delegates.
Source: Reprinted from the American Presidency Project, http://www.presidency.ucsb.edu/
data/delegates_demo.php, and http://www.presidency.ucsb.edu/data/delegates_gop.php.
Note: The Democratic percentage is depressed by the party's addition of over 700 "super delegates," representing established political officeholders and activists, to the more than 4,500 total delegates.

members of the parliament, including the prime minister, must run for reelection. Presidents and members of their party in Congress are much less closely tied.

Bureaucracies vary even more across political systems. Developing countries are more likely to reward "ascriptive" characteristics (such as race, tribe, or gender), about which one can do nothing, in hiring. Individuals receive appointments to positions through "connections" such as family ties or ancestry rather than because of "achievement characteristics" associated with skills, credentials, and work ethic. It is important to note that the United States went through a stage where ascriptive characteristics dominated and that these characteristics can still be a factor, although ascriptive characteristics are generally considered illegitimate criteria for rewarding or punishing individuals.

American bureaucrats tend to be specialists, entering a specific bureaucracy early in their careers and sticking with that same agency until retirement. Lateral transfers between agencies tend to be relatively rare. Other political systems, such as that in Britain, take a different approach. They train bureaucrats for basic skills and encourage lateral transfers from one agency to another.

C. ENDURING QUESTIONS ABOUT THE PERSONNEL OF THE PRESIDENCY AND THE BUREAUCRACY

Is the Presidential Selection Process Designed to Result in the Election of Presidents with the Necessary Skills and Attributes?

Campaigning is not the same as governing. Successful candidates must raise funds, battle through a primary season to gain the support of a subset of the population, and then face the broader electorate, always with an eye toward the states

---

Sample Hypothesis

If a president is a strong campaigner, then he or she will have a difficult time governing.

Hints for Accomplishment

Outline the characteristics an ideal president would have. Consider such things as skills, behavior patterns, experience, and personal characteristics. Next outline the characteristics of an effective presidential candidate. Determine the specific areas of mismatch between the ideal candidate and the ideal president. Focus on the most detrimental characteristics encouraged by the selection process and suggest which aspects of the selection process should be changed.

most important to the Electoral College (i.e., swing states with the most electoral votes). Candidates must distinguish themselves from others, often emphasizing differences between themselves and fellow party members. On the other hand, the governing process requires organizational skills and the ability to find areas of agreement to forge compromise.

Is the Bureaucracy Representative, or Should It Be?

A bureaucracy that reflects the demographics of the population purportedly makes it more responsible to the public it serves and provides an example of fairness in hiring. On the other hand, particular bureaucracies serve unique subpopulations (the elderly, women, the disabled, etc.) and need specific insights and skills.

Sample Hypothesis

If government officials value diversity, then bureaucrats should reflect the diversity of the general public.

Hints for Accomplishment

Consider doing a demographic analysis of a sample of bureaucrats, comparing the breakdown of age, gender, race, education, or other relevant characteristics with that for the population as a whole (see section 5 below for sources).

Take one or more of the following sources and assess their arguments about representative democracy:

Naff, Katherine C. "Progress toward Achieving a Representative Federal Bureaucracy: The Impact of Supervisors and Their Beliefs." *Public Personnel Management* 27, no. 2 (1998): 135–150. Available at http://www.allbusiness.com/legal/laws-government-regulations-employment/690776-1.html.

Selden, Sally Coleman. *The Promise of Representative Bureaucracy: Diversity and Responsiveness in a Government Agency.* Armonk, N.Y.: M. E. Sharpe, 1998.

Meier, Kenneth J. "Representative Bureaucracy: A Theoretical and Empirical Exposition." *Research in Public Administration* 2 (1993): 1–35.

D. IDEA GENERATOR: WHO ARE THE PRESIDENTS AND BUREAUCRATS?

The following chart provides some general guidelines for developing a research plan.

Specific Issue	Hypotheses	Hints
Presidents		
Demographics	If you are a senator, then aspiring to the presidency is an unlikely goal.	Look at the demographics (especially previous political positions) of presidential candidates for the last twenty or thirty years. What kinds of candidates start out in the primaries? Which types get the nomination? Who wins?
Bureaucracy		
Demographics	If your agency represents a specific group in society, then your agency is likely to over-represent members from that sub-group.	Compare the demographics of bureaucrats in different agencies. You will need a clear set of demographic characteristics on which to compare the groups. Conclude with an evaluation as to whether the differences are positive or negative.
Presidential Nominations and Elections		
Convention delegates and electors	If you are a delegate or an elector, then you have a long record of party service.	Using newspaper accounts, identify convention delegates or electors. Interview them about how they became participants in the presidential selection process. Have them talk about their experiences and what it means for democracy.

3. Context and Performance of the Presidency and the Bureaucracy

A. HISTORICAL DEVELOPMENT

The Presidency

The office of the president has grown in size, prestige, and power. Public expectations for the government to solve domestic problems, international threats requiring quick and coordinated action, and activist presidents able to master modern communications technologies have all contributed to making this the "age of executive ascendancy." It is a mistake to focus on the president alone. Modern presidents have the ability to surround themselves with large professional staffs expected to support presidential initiatives.

The Bureaucracy

The growth of governmental programs required a dramatic expansion of government employees. The shift from political appointments to competitive hiring led to increased professionalism and careerism. Bureaucrats are evaluated both according to their ability to follow the laws passed by Congress and according to their ingenuity in judiciously using discretion to make the application of the law fit the "spirit of the law" in a way that slavish reliance on the "letter of the law" might not represent.

B. PUBLIC SUPPORT AND EXPECTATIONS

The Presidency

As the only nationally elected public official, the president is expected to gain and maintain public support. Gaining the office itself generally endows a new president with a reservoir of popular support. Presidential initiatives and world events can either boost or diminish that support. For most presidents, popularity declines over their time in office. Robust popularity is a potent resource for a president that translates into solid support from Congress and the bureaucracy. A president with low levels of popularity is often politically wounded.

The Bureaucracy

To many, the very word *bureaucrat* implies inefficiency and limited competence. Bureaucracies are seen as large, faceless entities that stand in the way of someone

Box 3.4.   Skill Box: Presidential Support

Take a look at the overall patterns of public support for recent presidents, shown in figure 3.3. What generalizations might you make? What is the lesson for both presidents and the public?

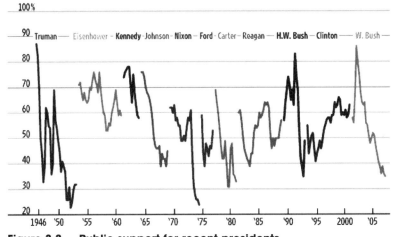

Figure 3.3.   Public support for recent presidents
Source: http://online.wsj.com/public/resources/documents/info-presapp0605-31.html

desiring a government-provided service. Even individuals that have positive encounters within the bureaucracy fail to translate that into a positive feeling about the bureaucracy as a whole. To some degree, public dissatisfaction emerges from the required tasks of the bureaucracy (see below).

C. THE PRESIDENT AND THE BUREAUCRACY AT WORK

The Presidency

Successful presidents must balance various constitutional and extraconstitutional demands (see section 1 above). Success in one realm (such as party leader) may have positive implications for the president's role as chief legislator. Failure as chief diplomat may place demands on the president's role as commander in chief. Above all, we expect the president to act on behalf of the nation.

There are a number of empirical measures of presidential success. Successful passage of one's legislative program by Congress is one measure. Presidents propose specific legislation, as well as take stands on legislation introduced by others. CQ

Table 3.1.   Presidential Vetoes, 1789-2006

President	Coincident Congresses	Regular Vetoes	Pocket Vetoes	Total Vetoes	Vetoes Overridden
Washington	1st–4th	2	—	2	—
Adams	5th–6th	—	—	—	—
Jefferson	7th–10th	—	—	—	—
Madison	11th–14th	5	2	7	—
Monroe	15th–18th	1	—	1	—
J. Q. Adams	19th–20th	—	—	—	—
Jackson	21st–24th	5	7	12	—
Van Buren	25th–26th	—	1	1	—
W. H. Harrison	27th	—	—	—	—
Tyler	27th–28th	6	4	10	1
Polk	29th–30th	2	1	3	—
Taylor	31st	—	—	—	—
Fillmore	31st–32nd	—	—	—	—
Pierce	33rd–34th	9	—	9	5
Buchanan	35th–36th	4	3	7	—
Lincoln	37th–39th	2	5	7	—
A. Johnson	39th–40th	21	8	29	15
Grant	41st–44th	45	48	93	4
Hayes	45th–46th	12	1	13	1
Garfield	47th	—	—	—	—
Arthur	47th–48th	4	8	12	1
Cleveland	49th–50th	304	110	414	2
B. Harrison	51st–52nd	19	25	44	1
Cleveland	53rd–54th	42	128	170	5
McKinley	55th–57th	6	36	42	—
T. Roosevelt	57th–60th	42	40	82	1
Taft	61st–62nd	30	9	39	1
Wilson	63rd–66th	33	11	44	6
Harding	67th	5	1	6	—
Coolidge	68th–70th	20	30	50	4
Hoover	71st–72nd	21	16	37	3
F. D. Roosevelt	73rd–79th	372	263	635	9
Truman	79th–82nd	180	70	250	12
Eisenhower	83rd–86th	73	108	181	2
Kennedy	87th–88th	12	9	21	—
L. B. Johnson	88th–90th	16	14	30	—
Nixon	91st–93rd	26	17	43	7
Ford	93rd–94th	48	18	66	12
Carter	95th–96th	13	18	31	2
Reagan	97th–109th	39	39	78	9
G. H. W. Bush	101st–102nd	29	15	44	1
Clinton	103rd–106th	36	1	37	2
G. W. Bush[a]	107th–110th	5	0	5	1

Source: The American Presidency Project, http://www.presidency.ucsb.edu/data/vetoes.php.
[a]Through 2007.

provides yearly "batting averages" for presidents in both the House and Senate (see section 5 below). If Congress takes an approach that the president opposes, the president can *threaten* a **veto** in hopes of changing the content, or exercise the veto power to block the legislation. Congress can override the president's veto by a two-thirds vote in both chambers. (See table 3.1 for statistics on presidential vetoes.)

The Bureaucracy

Bureaucracies are designed to increase efficiency and fairness by turning decisions into routine matters and by holding bureaucrats publicly responsible for their actions. Bureaucrats are expected to follow explicit rules no matter whom they are working with. Universal rules applied to everyone equally provide fairness and efficiency in general but may seem capricious in specific situations. While we might want police officers to ticket everyone going 70 in a 40-mile-per-hour zone, we also would like a police officer to ignore that rule for a husband trying to get his pregnant wife to the hospital. On the other hand, we would be offended if a procurement officer buying computers were to ignore the competitive-bidding rules and give the contract to a friend.

In a democracy, bureaucrats are employees of the citizens and are therefore expected to consider the interests of the public in general, rather than promote their personal interests or those of some small segment of the population. The standards of ethical conduct applicable to executive-branch employees (see box 3.5) provide the general standards. The key to ethical behavior lies in the ability to properly apply the standards to specific situations.

Box 3.5.   Executive Order 12731 of October 17, 1990

PRINCIPLES OF ETHICAL CONDUCT
FOR GOVERNMENT OFFICERS AND EMPLOYEES

Part 1—PRINCIPLES OF ETHICAL CONDUCT
Section 101. Principles of Ethical Conduct. To ensure that every citizen can have complete confidence in the integrity of the Federal Government, each Federal employee shall respect and adhere to the fundamental principles of ethical service as implemented in regulations promulgated under . . . this order:

(a) Public service is a public trust, requiring employees to place loyalty to the Constitution, the laws, and ethical principles above private gain.

(b) Employees shall not hold financial interests that conflict with the conscientious performance of duty.

(c) Employees shall not engage in financial transactions using non-public Government information or allow the improper use of such information to further any private interest.

(d) An employee shall not, except pursuant to such reasonable exceptions as are provided by regulation, solicit or accept any gift or other item of monetary value from any person or entity seeking official action

(e) Employees shall put forth honest effort in the performance of their duties.

(f) Employees shall make no unauthorized commitments or promises of any kind purporting to bind the Government.

(g) Employees shall not use public office for private gain.

(h) Employees shall act impartially and not give preferential treatment to any private organization or individual.

(i) Employees shall protect and conserve Federal property and shall not use it for other than authorized activities.

(j) Employees shall not engage in outside employment or activities, including seeking or negotiating for employment, that conflict with official Government duties and responsibilities.

(k) Employees shall disclose waste, fraud, abuse, and corruption to appropriate authorities.

(l) Employees shall satisfy in good faith their obligations as citizens, including all just financial obligations, especially those—such as Federal, State, or local taxes—that are imposed by law.

(m) Employees shall adhere to all laws and regulations that provide equal opportunity for all Americans regardless of race, color, religion, sex, national origin, age, or handicap.

(n) Employees shall endeavor to avoid any actions creating the appearance that they are violating the law or the ethical standards promulgated pursuant to this order.

The full text of the executive order is available at http://www.usoge.gov/pages/laws_regs_fedreg_stats/lrfs_files/exeorders/eo12731.html.

D. ENDURING QUESTIONS ON THE CONTEXT AND PERFORMANCE OF THE PRESIDENCY AND HOW TO RESEARCH THEM

What Does It Take to Be an Effective President?

According to the seminal work of Richard Neustadt (*Presidential Power*), presidential power is the power to persuade. Persuasion involves convincing others that what you want them to do is really what they want to do. Presidential persuasion techniques may be viewed from the perspective of the methods presidents have used to communicate with the public or by the arguments presidents have contributed to the political dialogue.

Sample Hypothesis

a. If a president has a high level of public support, then he or she will be more effective in getting a legislative program passed. (Also consider the possibility that effectiveness "causes" popularity.)

b. If a president uses many tools of public persuasion, then he or she will be more effective in getting a legislative program passed.

c. If a president is in the early years of his or her first term (the "honeymoon period"), then he or she will be more effective at getting a legislative program passed.

Hints for Accomplishment

Chose one of the hypotheses. Data on legislative success is available in each year's *CQ Almanac*. Data on presidential popularity is available from the American Presidency Project, at http://www.presidency.ucsb .edu/data/popularity.php, as well as from PollingReport.com, at http:// www.pollingreport.com/wh.htm. The American Presidency Project also provides historical data, which allows one to compare persuasion techniques of individual presidents (number of speeches, policy initiatives, press conferences, etc.). Categorize post–World War I presidents (the only presidents for whom relatively complete data are available) into two or more categories (such as "high" and "low") for your dependent variable (success rate) and independent variable (popularity, number of speeches, etc.). Enter your data in a contingency table (see box 2.4, in chapter 2) to test your hypothesis. Make sure you consider other factors that might be at work.

What Explains a President's Ability to Get a Particular Bill Passed?

No two legislative battles are identical. Each bill has its own historical and political environment. As political-coalition managers, effective presidents take the prevailing attitudes and political conditions and attempt to use them to their advantage.

Sample Hypothesis

If a president uses existing conditions creatively, then he or she can accomplish more in the legislative process.

Hints for Accomplishment

You will be doing a case study (see box 3.6) of a particular policy battle. Your first step is to choose a policy initiative on which there has been significant action. *CQ Almanac* provides a yearly summary of key legislation passed by Congress. Most legislation will reflect significant presidential involvement. The State of the Union address includes the president's policy goals for the upcoming year. An important step will be to determine what role(s) the president played in the legislative process. Potential roles include idea initiator; agenda setter (popularizer of the ideas of others); public spokesperson; coalition manager (who lines up support of decision makers); quality controller (who threatens a veto if legislation is not in accordance with the president's goals); and policy administrator. Next, you will want to determine what strategies the president employed and which power resources were brought to bear on the situation. Consider what would have happened if the president had not been involved. To what degree (if any) were the president's efforts crucial to the outcome? End with a discussion of the broader implications. What do we learn about the presidency in general from this particular case?

Box 3.6.   Skill Box: Conducting a Case Study

A case study is a detailed analysis of a particular event, trend, or person. Its strength lies in the richness of detail the researcher can provide through narrowly focused efforts. The weaknesses emerge from the fact that it may be impossible to generalize beyond the chosen case. Case studies are particularly helpful in the early stages of research, when the richness of detail has the potential for exposing variables one might have missed using a broader or more superficial method of gathering data.

Choosing the individual, trend, or event to study is crucial. Most often one chooses a "typical" case (e.g., a president's decision to sign or veto a bill) to increase the potential for generalization. In some cases, it makes sense to choose an extreme case to determine how things operate on the margins (e.g., a president's decision in a crisis). There are some tradeoffs involved in choosing a decision to analyze. More recent decisions might be more exciting, but there will have been less analysis of them. Historical decisions may well have academic articles or books written about them, but you may not have the sense of accomplishment in systematically analyzing a decision for yourself. You will have to decide whether you would gain the most from synthesizing the writings of others or doing more basic research.

The following is a summary of the steps involved in a good case study.

- Specify what is already known about this case or similar ones. Your literature review should indicate why others found such cases important.
- Clearly describe the case. Try to answer the five Ws: Who? What? Where? When? and Why?
- Outline your hypothesis. What do you expect to find? Most cases focus on *why* something happened. What were the legal constraints? What were the political opportunities and limitations? Your literature review should suggest possible hypotheses—for example, a president who lacks working majorities in the House and Senate is more (less?) likely to veto legislation.
- Use a wide variety of sources to flesh out your case and test your hypothesis. Beyond the academic literature, consider presidential and staff biographies.
- Outline your findings and compare them with previous conclusions. Answer the "so what" question: what have you found and why is it useful? Indicate any limitations in your research.

Is the Bureaucracy Effective in Carrying Out Its Task?

Bureaucrats serve many masters. Members of Congress provide the goals and guidelines for legislation and the debate that preceded such legislation. Those directly affected by legislation often have strong feelings about its wisdom and administration. Members of the public are often the ultimate beneficiaries of policies carried out by the bureaucracy. For example, the Occupational Safety and Health Act of 1970 was passed to protect workers from harm on the job. The Occupational Safety and Health Administration (OSHA) was created under the U.S. Department of Labor. Interest groups representing business and labor often took different positions on the cost and enforcement of the law. Individual businessmen and workers also differ on how effectively the law has been administered. A similar pattern of disagreement reinforces the general principle in politics that "where you stand often depends on where you sit."

Sample Hypothesis

If your job places you in a different political, economic, or personal risk, then you will see the effectiveness of the bureaucratic administration of policy differently.

Hints for Accomplishment

Think about policies that have an impact on a large number of individuals (taxes, health benefits, welfare, consumer safety, postal service, etc). The local telephone directory has a listing of state and federal agencies with local offices in your area. Many agencies have websites with policies they enforce. Look at the policy from the perspective of (1) legislative proponents, (2) bureaucratic administrators, (3) interest groups, and (4) individual citizens. The *Congressional Record*, available at http://www.thomas.loc .gov, will provide a clue to the legislative intent of the policy. Bureaucratic agencies spend considerable effort explaining the goals of the policies they administer and often collect statistics on their efforts. Interest groups often have strong views on the impact of the administration on their members. Relevant groups can often be found in the committee hearings for the legislation. The *Washington Information Directory*, published by CQ Press, provides cross-referenced citations to interest groups by policy area. Hearing about the direct impact of policy by talking to a random group of affected individuals is a meaningful measure of how the policy actually works. The previous three suggestions may require doing a series of telephone or face-to-face interviews (see box 3.7). In your research, look for varying definitions and measures of success and failure. To what degree do the players have the same goals and measures of success? Ultimately you will have to make a judgment call on success or failure.

Box 3.7.   Skill Box: What You Ask Is What You Get—Using Interviews to Acquire Information

For some projects it may be possible to interview experts or participants in the political process. Informant interviews are designed to acquire inside information and opinions of individuals.

Who Should I Talk To? Unlike polls where *respondents* are chosen randomly and everyone is asked the same questions so that their responses can be compared, *informants* are chosen because of their unique experience, position, or understanding. Look for:

- people in the media or academia who have written about your topic;
- individuals who have gone through relevant experiences; and
- those recommended by initial interview subjects.

Get in the habit of asking interview subjects, "Who else should I talk to about this topic?" and thus use the "snowball" technique of developing a list of interview subjects.

Some misconceptions to avoid:

- Don't assume you have to talk to the head of the organization (mid-level staff are often more accessible and insightful). The *Congressional Staff Directory*, *Federal Staff Directory*, and *Washington Information Directory* (all published by CQ) provide access to staff names.
- Don't avoid those no longer in office. Retired people have more time and are often eager to present their perspectives.

How Many People Should I Talk To? The number of interviews you conduct will be greatly constrained by the time you have available. It is important to talk to people on all sides of the issue you are dealing with. One signal that you have done enough is that the same names keep coming up when you ask your interview subjects who else to talk to.

Who Would Talk with Me? While there is a tendency to approach an interview subject as a lowly petitioner, hat in hand, the interview subject gets something out of being interviewed. There is the ego massaging of being asked. An interview is a chance to "set the record straight" and can be a stimulating opportunity to see a situation in new way. As a student, you are a rather benign threat and are going through an experience your interview subjects are likely to remember and want to help you with.

How Do I Get the Interview? The two keys are legitimacy and flexibility. Write, or call ahead, and explain in general terms what you are doing. If a previous interview subject has suggested the person, mention that fact. Offer to meet or call the interview subject *at his or her convenience*. Establish the ground rules. Will the interview be "on the record" (meaning that you can quote the person by name) or "off the record" (meaning that the person can only be identified by general descriptors)? Outline the amount of time you will need.

Do Your Homework. Find out as much as possible about the topic and the interview subject *before* the interview. Calling ahead for a résumé is an important first step.

What Should I Ask? Don't fritter away your opportunity with questions seeking information that you can get in other ways, questions that add nothing to your analysis, or questions that do nothing but aggravate the interview subject. In framing a question consider the following:

- Does the informant have the experience or knowledge to answer it?
- Is the question concrete enough to answer?
- Might the question be so embarrassing or sensitive as to threaten the rest of the interview? (If such a question is critical, save it until the end.)

Interviews are best for acquiring perceptions. One gains little by asking an elected official, "What was your electoral margin in the last election?" That fact is readily available. It may be legitimate to ask the perceptual question, "How politically secure do you feel after the last election?" That perspective comes from within. Carefully plan your questions, since you may well not get a second chance.

How Should I Ask It? It is useful to begin a question by signaling your level of knowledge with a brief preface. Open-ended questions that give the interview subject the opportunity to talk should dominate interviews. For example, you might preface your questions to an elected official by saying, "I realize that you spent ten years in the state legislature and were just reelected to your fourth term in Congress." Then you could ask, "Why did you originally run for office?" rather than "Did you run for office for money or power?" The latter, a close-ended question, may lead the informant toward an answer, but will not tap his or her true perspective. Avoid "loaded" questions. Rather than asking, "What do you see as the economic future of Communist China?" just ask, "What do you see as the economic future of China?"

Be a Good Listener. Master interviewer and C-SPAN founder Brian Lamb puts it as follows: "When you are talking, you are not learning." An interview is not the time to lobby or brag. You are there to tap the information of the interview subject.

Keeping the Interview Going. Always have ready a few questions to throw in quickly if an informant's answer ends abruptly. If an answer is not fully satisfying, be ready with follow-up questions that probe the subject more deeply.

Ending the Interview. As a researcher, you have a responsibility to maintain a positive research environment for subsequent students. Try to leave the interview subject pleased with the experience. A final "softball" question, with no right answer, allows the informant to speculate; for example, "How do you think people will look back on our efforts in this area a hundred years from now?" Make sure to thank the interview subject.

Creating an Interview Record. The goal of an interview is a written record providing raw material for insertion into a formal paper. Some interviewers like to record interviews, to allow for complete transcription, while others see recording as a distraction and as potentially intimidating to the interview subject. Even when an interview is recorded, taking handwritten notes provides a good backup and can send a positive signal to the interview subject. The body language of madly taking notes tells the subject that he or she is on track. Dropping a pen tells the subject that he or she is off track. However the interview is preserved, it is important to transcribe your notes or recording while everything is fresh in your mind.

Evaluating Interviews. Interviews do not guarantee finding the truth, only discovering the perception of the truth an interview subject is willing to share publicly with a stranger. We all tend to believe that the world revolves around us; so too, interview subjects often claim credit or eschew blame for things others would not necessarily attach to them. We all have rehearsed stories that reconstruct our own histories. Just think of your answer to the question, "Why did you go to this school?" Statements made to an interviewer may serve many purposes other than transmitting objective information. All that said, interviews are one of the premier methods of approaching the truth.

E. IDEA GENERATOR: EVALUATING PRESIDENTIAL AND BUREAUCRATIC PERFORMANCE

The following chart provides some general guidelines for developing a research plan.

Specific Issue	Hypotheses	Hints
Presidents		
Origins of popular support	a. If a president is a Republican (or Democrat) then his or her popularity is greater than if he or she is a Democrat	Look at one of the websites that provides data on presidential popularity. Isolate your proposed causal variable (party, portion of the president's

(continued)

Specific Issue	Hypotheses	Hints
	(Republican). b. If a president is in the later part of his or her term, then his or her popularity is less than it was in the first part of his or her term.	term). Using the *same* poll, compare presidential popularity under each of the conditions you identify.
	Bureaucracy	
Ethics	If you are a government bureaucrat, then you must work under different standards than people who don't work for the government.	Look at the standards of ethical behavior for federal bureaucrats. Which ones seem particularly applicable to government employees, and which would apply equally to any organizational employee? Why?

4. Original Research That Will Impress Your Professor

The Presidency

Barber, James D. *The Presidential Character: Predicting Performance in the White House.* Englewood Cliffs, N.J.: Prentice-Hall, 1985.

Jones, Charles O. *The Presidency in a Separated System.* 2nd ed. Washington, D.C.: Brookings Institution Press, 2005.

Lijphart, Arend, ed. *Parliamentary versus Presidential Government.* Oxford and New York: Oxford University Press, 1992.

Neustadt, Richard. *Presidential Power and the Modern Presidents: The Politics of Leadership.* New York: Free Press, 1990.

Pfiffner, James P. *The Strategic Presidency: Hitting the Ground Running.* 2nd ed. Lawrence: University Press of Kansas, 1996.

The Bureaucracy

Weber, Max. *Essays in Sociology.* Edited and translated by C. Wright Mills and Hans H. Gerth. New York: Oxford University Press, 1958. Weber's work provides the classic explication of the advantages of bureaucratic organization.

Weber, Max. *The Protestant Ethic and the Spirit of Capitalism.* Translated by Talcott Parsons. London: Harper Collins Academic, 1991.

5. In Their Own Words: Primary Sources

The *Weekly Compilation of Presidential Documents*, available online at http://www.gpoac-cess.gov/wcomp, provides transcripts of presidential speeches, press releases, and sum-maries of action.

The American Presidency Project, http://www.presidency.ucsb.edu, provides a treasure trove of data and digitized documents drawn from a wide variety of sources.

The Avalon Project at Yale Law School, http://www.yale.edu/lawweb/avalon, provides ac-cess to a wide variety of presidential documents and speeches, with an emphasis on law and diplomacy.

Richard Jensen's "Guide to Political Research Online," http://tigger.uic.edu/~rjensen/political.htm#News, provides a wide array of links to many political science topics, in-cluding the presidency. Links to more scholarly sources are at Jensen's "Scholars' Guide to WWW," http://tigger.uic.edu/~rjensen.

6. Where to Find It

How do I find out the president's agenda?
Presidential inaugural and State of the Union speeches (see below) are often the forum for presenting a president's policy agenda. CQ's presidential-support scores (available in the *CQ Almanac*) indicate key legislation on which the pres-ident took a public stand.

Where can I find a president's speech or statements about policy decisions?
Many presidential speeches are included in *Vital Speeches of the Day*, which is available in hard copy or online (by subscription).

The *Weekly Compilation of Presidential Documents*, available in most aca-demic libraries as well as online, at http://www.gpoaccess.gov/wcomp, provides access to the formal statements of presidents, as does the White House website, http://www.whitehouse.gov.

For statistics and searchable transcripts of all State of the Union addresses, go to the American Presidency Project, at http://www.presidency.ucsb.edu/sou.php, or the Avalon Project, at http://www.yale.edu/lawweb/avalon/21st.htm.

For audio and video of presidential speeches and statements, go to the Amer-ican Presidency Project, at http://www.presidency.ucsb.edu/media.php, or the Miller Center of Public Affairs, at http://millercenter.org (click on the "Scripps Library" tab).

Where can I find data on public support for a president?
Data on public support for the president is available at the American Presidency Project, at http://www.presidency.ucsb.edu/data/popularity.php, and PollingReport.com, at http://www.pollingreport.com/wh.htm.

Where can I find presidents' success rates in Congress?
Using presidential requests, CQ measures the percentage of times the president is successful in his dealings with Congress. Historical data are available in Lynn Ragsdale, *Vital Statistics on the Presidency* (Washington, D.C.: Congressional Quarterly Press, 1998). The data is also available online from the American Presidency Project, at http://www.presidency.ucsb.edu/data/concurrence.php. More recent data is available in the yearly *CQ Almanac*.

Where can I find data on presidential vetoes and presidents' ability to sustain them?
The American Presidency Project provides data on presidential vetoes, including the number of vetoes overridden by Congress, at http://www.presidency.ucsb .edu/data/vetoes.php.

How do I find out who is on the White House staff and more about the structure of the White House?
The *National Journal* website provides a list of White House staff members, including their salaries, at http://nationaljournal.com/about/njweekly/stories/ 2006/0711nj1.htm. The White House website provides descriptions of the various offices within the White House, at http://www.whitehouse.gov/government/ off-descrp.html. Information on the executive branch, including the White House, can also be found on the U.S. government's official website, at http:// www.firstgov.gov/Agencies/Federal/Executive.shtml.

Where can I find information about members of the president's cabinet?
The White House website contains information about the president's cabinet, at http://www.whitehouse.gov/government/cabinet.html.

Where can I find historical information on presidents and the presidency?
The Miller Center of Public Affairs provides a collection of materials on the presidents of the United States, as well as the history of the presidency, at http:// millercenter.org/academic/americanpresident.

Where can I find job descriptions and salaries of members of the bureaucracy, as well as the distribution of employment within the government?
Check out the website of the Bureau of Labor Statistics, at http://www.bls.gov/ oco/cg/cgs041.htm#emply.

Where can I find biographical information on members of the bureaucracy?
The following directories may be helpful:

Federal Staff Directory. Washington, D.C.: CQ Press.

Sobel, Robert. *Biographical Directory of the Executive Branch, 1774–1989.* Westport, Conn.: Greenwood Press, 1990.

Sobel, Robert, and David B. Sicilia, eds. *The United States Executive Branch: A Biographical Directory of Heads of State and Cabinet Officials.* Westport, Conn.: Greenwood Press, 2003.

Where can I find national demographic figures?

Basic information on the U.S. population from census figures and updated surveys are available in the *Statistical Abstract of the United States*, which is published annually and is available online, at http://www.census.gov/compendia/statab. Most libraries also carry the hard-copy version printed by the U.S. Government Printing Office.

7. Taking Action—Contacting and Influencing the President and the Bureaucracy

While the White House receives thousands of inquiries per week, there is little indication that such inquiries have much effect on the decision-making process. The White House receives public comments by e-mail, at comments@whitehouse.gov; by phone, at 202–456–1111; or by mail, at The White House, 1600 Pennsylvania Avenue NW, Washington, D.C. 20500.

The bureaucracy is better equipped to respond to specific inquiries on policies directly affecting individual citizens. The federal government's website provides a general access point for questions of government agencies at http://answers.firstgov.gov/cgi-bin/gsa_ict.cfg/php/enduser/ask.php. From the main page of the site (http://www.firstgov.gov), one can also navigate to each government agency and find contact information.

Agencies also reach out for public comments on impending rules designed to implement legislation. The *Federal Register* outlines proposed rules and asks for public comments. The Government Printing Office provides online access to the *Federal Register* at http://www.gpoaccess.gov/fr/index.html.

Notes

1. Two states use different methods. Maine and Nebraska have separate votes in each congressional district and award their final two electoral votes to the statewide winner.

Since the statewide winner has always won a majority in every district, the variation from the other states has made no difference.

2. For up-to-date figures on government employment, see the U.S. Department of Labor, Bureau of Labor Statistics website, at http://www.bls.gov/oco/cg/cgs041.htm#emply.

3. See comments on the American Political Science Association website, at http://www.apsanet.org/content_5221.cfm.

CHAPTER 4

The Federal Judiciary

Laws mean little if they are not evaluated and enforced. The federal (national) judiciary helps keep the actions of the policymakers, policy administrators, and the general public true to the Constitution and federal law. The federal judiciary resembles a pyramid, with each successive level reviewing the one below it. The Supreme Court, with its nine justices, reviews decisions by federal appeals courts (the next level in the pyramid) and provides definitive final judgments on the content of federal laws and their applications. The Supreme Court also has original jurisdiction in special cases.

1. The Structure and Function of the Federal Judiciary

A. CONSTITUTIONAL BASIS

Article III of the Constitution outlines the basic structure and function of the federal judiciary.

> Section 1.
> *The judicial Power of the United States, shall be vested in one supreme Court, and in such inferior Courts as the Congress may from time to time ordain and establish. The Judges, both of the supreme and inferior Courts, shall hold their Offices during good behavior, and shall, at stated Times, receive for their Services, a Compensation, which shall not be diminished during their Continuance in Office.*

Article III of the Constitution is the most vague of the institutional articles and the only article that required an act of one of the other branches (Congress) to

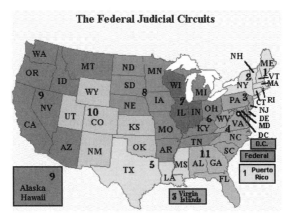

The Federal Judicial Circuits

Federal court of appeals circuits
Reprinted from the Mine Safety and Health Administration,
Office of the Solicitor, http://www.msha.gov/SOLICITOR/
KIDS/usa.gif.

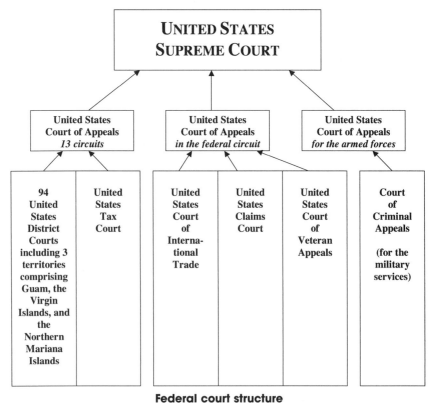

Federal court structure
http://www.usdoj.gov

Figure 4.1. Structure of the U.S. federal courts.

be enacted. Even the size of the Supreme Court, now set at nine justices, is determined by Congress.

B. GOALS AND INTENTIONS

Trial courts in the federal system gather evidence, assess wrongdoing in relation to federal laws, and mete out punishment when appropriate. The application of laws in the U.S. legal system is based on **precedent**, the traditional ways in which the law has been applied in the past. Precedent gives some predictability to the law and helps ensure fair treatment. Lower courts closely watch as the cases they have decided are appealed to upper-level courts, since being overruled by a higher court questions their skill and authority.

The federal court system is a three-tiered hierarchy, with the nine members of the Supreme Court at the top. Below the Supreme Court are thirteen U.S. courts of appeals (or circuit courts) organized geographically. The lowest-level federal courts are the ninety-four U.S. district courts (or trial courts). In addition, a number of special federal courts hear designated types of cases (bankruptcy, international trade, military courts martial, etc.). (See figure 4.1.)

Trial courts generally focus on questions of fact (e.g., in criminal law, whether a defendant is guilty or not guilty), whereas higher-level courts generally focus on questions of law, reviewing a lower-level court's interpretation and procedural application of the law. There was considerable debate early in the republic as to the proper role of the courts and the degree to which the Supreme Court should truly be supreme. While it is reasonable to argue that the framers intended that the courts exercise **judicial review**, in which courts could question both the law and

Box 4.1.   I Know Madison, but Who Was This Marbury Guy?

| William Marbury | John Adams | Justice John Marshall | Thomas Jefferson | James Madison |
| The contenders | | The chief referee | The defenders | |

Behind seemingly legalistic and philosophical issues often lie highly personal and political factors. After his Federalist Party was defeated by Thomas

Jefferson in the 1800 election, outgoing president John Adams appointed a number of Federalists to judicial positions. William Marbury had received an appointment, but the formal letter (commission) had not been delivered. He sued the new secretary of state, James Madison. Trying to maintain the Supreme Court's independence, Chief Justice John Marshall crafted a decision chastising Jefferson and Madison for not fulfilling the appointment, but also ruled that the law under which the appointment was made was unconstitutional. The decision in *Marbury v. Madison* was accepted by Jefferson, since it allowed him to help break the Federalist hold on the judiciary. In the process, he upheld the right of judicial review. Though it had the power, the Court held off using judicial review again for over fifty years.

Pictures of Marbury and Madison from Beyond Books, http://www.beyondbooks .com/gov91/9a.asp, of Marshall from http://www.army.mil/cmh-pg/books/RevWar/ ss/p257b.jpg, of Adams from www.priceofliberty.net/?m=200509, and of Jefferson: http://www.american-pictures.com/genealogy/descent/photos/Thomas.Jefferson.jpg.

its administration relative to the Constitution, that power was not explicitly outlined in the Constitution. It took a fortuitous situation and a clever political gambit to ensconce it in American legal tradition (see box 4.1).

There remains a continuing conflict over the rationale the courts should use in deciding a case. Supporters of **strict constructionism** argue that the courts should rely solely on the actual words and phrases in the Constitution. **Broad constructionism** involves taking into account legislative intent and social conditions. The conflict is often framed as one of "finding" the law versus "making" law.

C. COMPARATIVE PERSPECTIVE

Judicial review has become the norm for most democratic countries. Among the holdouts *not* allowing judicial review are Andorra, Barbados, Estonia, Lebanon, North Korea, and Tajikistan.

D. ENDURING STRUCTURAL QUESTIONS AND HOW TO RESEARCH THEM

Are Current Procedures Necessarily Consistent with Democracy?
Should We Reconsider the Power of Judicial Review?

On the surface, federal courts look very undemocratic. Judges are appointed rather than elected, they are almost impossible to remove from office, and much of their decision making occurs in secret. The power of judicial review gives them the final say in the application of a particular law. Opponents of such power fear authoritative "rogue" courts acting in ways contradictory to democracy.

Sample Hypothesis

a. If the courts have judicial review, then they will check the other branches of government making those branches more responsible.
b. If the courts have judicial review, then they will interpret the Constitutions differently than the other branches of government.
c. If the courts have judicial review, then they will overstep their bounds.

Hints for Accomplishment

Build a case either for or against judicial review. Consider which institutions of government could take on the task of reviewing laws if the Supreme Court were denied such power.

   Look at the *Federalist* No. 78, written by James Madison, to see what one of the framers had to say about the role of the courts. A number of authors have attempted to discuss the arguments for and against judicial review. For example, see "Rights-Based Judicial Review: A Democratic Justification," by Alon Harel, available at http://papers.ssrn.com/sol3/papers .cfm?abstract_id=364120. See also books such as John Ely, *Democracy and Distrust: A Theory of Judicial Review* (Cambridge, Mass.: Harvard University Press, 1980) and Christopher F. Zurn, *Deliberative Democracy and the Institutions of Judicial Review* (New York: Cambridge University Press, 2007).

Should the U.S. Supreme Court Cite Foreign Precedents?

While precedent-based rulings are well-established staples of American judicial procedures, an emerging conflict has arisen over what constitutes a legitimate precedent. Although Supreme Court justices swear to uphold the U.S. Constitution, some increasingly use precedents established in the courts of other countries to bolster their arguments.

Sample Hypothesis

Develop the arguments you would use to justify one of the two following hypotheses. To be effective, you must counter the opposing hypothesis.

a. If the Court uses foreign precedents, then it will improve decisions and bring its decisions more in line with widely accepted international principles.

b. If the Court uses foreign precedents, then the Court will produce unacceptable rulings not supported by the U.S. Constitution and the credibility of the judicial process will be diminished.

Hints for Accomplishment

Develop a "consensus of experts" approach. See what the justices and legal scholars have to say. Decide who makes the best case, both in terms of logic and in the context of examples of cases they provide. The justices themselves differ on the legitimacy and utility of using foreign precedents (see quotes on MSNBC available at http://www.msnbc.msn.com/id/6824149). The following sources may also be useful.

Yoo, John C. "Peeking Abroad? The Supreme Court's Use of Foreign Precedents in Constitutional Cases." *University of Hawaii Law Review*, 2004. Available online at http://papers.ssrn.com/sol3/papers.cfm?abstract_id=615962. (Mr. Yoo is controversial, given his role in the Bush administration. Look at his arguments on the basis of both their internal logic and how they might relate to his role in the policy process.)

Flaherty, Martin S. "Judicial Globalization in the Service of Self-Government." *Ethics & International Affairs* 20, no. 4 (2006): 477–503.

Flynn, William J. "Should the U.S. Supreme Court Cite Foreign Precedents?" Available online at http://hnn.us/articles/23499.html.

E. IDEA GENERATOR: HOW THE COURTS ARE STRUCTURED

The following chart provides some general guidelines for developing a research plan.

Specific Issue	Hypotheses	Hints
Court Decisions		
Partisanship	If a justice is Republican, then he or she is more likely to vote along with other Republicans than with Democrats on the Court.	Virtually all presidents appoint members of their own party to the Supreme Court. Take a series of cases and look at the continuing voting blocs by determining who votes with whom most often. Are these voting blocs related to the party of the president who appointed them?

Specific Issue	Hypotheses	Hints
Democratic Institutions		
The Supreme Court's role in our democracy	a. If the Supreme Court takes a stand, then the public will follow. b. If the public is not basically supportive of a position, then the Supreme Court is constrained in how far it can go in changing public policy.	Look at public opinion on key issues before and after Supreme Court decisions on those issues. To what degree does the Court lead public opinion, and to what degree does it follow? Does the Court tend to be split on issues when there is a deep split among the public? (Recent polls on issues can be found at PollingReport.com, http://www.pollingreport.com.) Earlier polls are reported in newspapers and books.

2. Participants in the Judicial Process

A. WHO ARE THE PARTICIPANTS AND WHY ARE THEY THERE?

While state and local judges are often elected to office and face the potential insecurity of being displaced from office by the voters, appointment to the federal judiciary means a lifetime job. Presidents nominate federal judges and must secure **confirmation** by the U.S. Senate. Presidents clear potential appointees with a committee of the American Bar Association for legal capabilities, and with key senators—particularly of their party—for political acceptability.

The Senate Judiciary Committee holds hearings on nominees. While the public emphasis is on qualifications, senators are also looking for potential justices who share their political philosophy and, often, who share their opinion on specific types of cases. Some confirmation processes end up as full-fledged pitched political battles, with interest groups weighing in both at the hearing and through mass-media advertising. Some nominees are either asked by the president or decide on their own to take their name out of consideration. At times vote margins in the Senate are razor thin, and at times there is little opposition (see figure 4.2).

Presidents generally prevail in the Senate-confirmation process when it comes down to an actual vote (see figure 4.3). In many cases, the primary tactic in the

Senate Votes On Supreme Court Nominees

YEAR	NOMINEE		VOTES FOR	VOTES AGAINST
2006	Samuel A. Alito Jr.		58	42
2005	John G. Roberts Jr., *chief justice*		78	22
1994	Stephen G. Breyer		87	9
1993	Ruth Bader Ginsburg		96	3
1991	Clarence Thomas		52	48
1990	David H. Souter		90	9
1988	Anthony M. Kennedy		97	0
1987	Robert H. Bork		42	58
1986	Antonin Scalia		98	0
1986	William H. Rehnquist, *chief justice*		65	33
1981	Sandra Day O'Connor		99	0
1975	John Paul Stevens		98	0
1971	William H. Rehnquist		68	26

Figure 4.2.   Recent Senate votes on Supreme Court nominations.
Source: http://www.senate.gov/pagelayout/reference/nominations/Nominations.htm

Senate is delay, as opponents hope to discourage the president, dishearten the nominee, or wait until a new president takes over. Presidents may be dissuaded from nominating individuals who they fear could not overcome the hurdle of senatorial confirmation. Table 4.1 contains unsuccessful nominations to the Supreme Court. Individuals on this list may have been appointed and confirmed at a later date.

While there is no requirement that a potential judge be a lawyer or have judicial experience (see table 4.2), these two criteria are usually considered to be the minimum qualifications. The Senate considers a mix of the potential nomi-

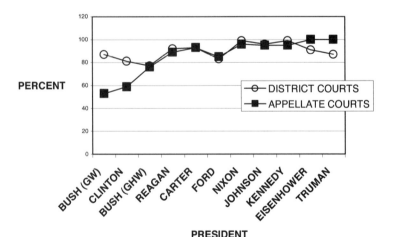

PRESIDENTIAL APPOINTMENT SUCCESS

Figure 4.3.   Presidential success in federal court appointments.
Source: http://www.senate.gov/reference/resources/pdf/RL31635.pdf

Table 4.1.   Failed Nominations to the Supreme Court

Nominee	Year	Nominating President	Outcome
William Paterson	1793	Washington	Withdrawn
John Rutledge	1795	Washington	Rejected
Alexander Wolcott	1811	Madison	Rejected
John J. Crittenden	1828	J. Q. Adams	Postponed
Roger B. Taney	1835	Jackson	Postponed
John C. Spencer	1844	Tyler	Rejected
Reuben H. Walworth	1844	Tyler	Withdrawn
Edward King	1844	Tyler	Postponed
Edward King	1845	Tyler	Withdrawn
John M. Read	1845	Tyler	No action
George W. Woodward	1845	Polk	Rejected
Edward A. Bradford	1852	Fillmore	No action
George E. Badger	1853	Fillmore	Postponed
William C. Micou	1853	Fillmore	No action
Jerimiah S. Black	1861	Buchanan	Rejected
Henry Stanberry	1866	A. Johnson	No action
Ebenezer R. Hoar	1869	Grant	Rejected
George Henry Williams	1873	Grant	Withdrawn
Caleb Cushing	1874	Grant	Withdrawn
Thomas Stanley Matthews	1881	Hayes	No action
William B. Hornblower	1893	Cleveland	Rejected
Wheeler Hazard Peckham	1894	Cleveland	Rejected
John J. Parker	1930	Hoover	Rejected
Abe Fortas	1968	L. B. Johnson	Withdrawn
Homer Thornberry	1968	L. B. Johnson	No action
Clement Haynsworth	1969	Nixon	Rejected
G. Harrold Carswell	1970	Nixon	Rejected
Robert H. Bork	1987	Reagan	Rejected
Douglas H. Ginsburg	1987	Reagan	Withdrawn
Harriet Miers	2005	G. W. Bush	Withdrawn

Summary: 8 withdrawn, 12 rejected, 4 postponed, 6 no action.

nee's credentials and previous legal decisions. The president and the Senate realize that they are "hiring" an individual with a particular way of reading the Constitution and whose influence on public policy may extend well beyond the president's or a senator's term of office. As table 4.3 indicates, successful Supreme Court nominees come from some of the most prestigious law schools.

B. COMPARATIVE PERSPECTIVE

There is no universally accepted method of selecting constitutional judges. While some countries emphasize academic credentials, others give more weight

Table 4.2.   The Exception That Proves the Rule: Supreme Court Justices without Judicial Experience Prior to Becoming Justices

Justice	Previous Occupations	Years on Court	Appointing President
William Rehnquist[a]	Assistant U.S. attorney general	1972–2005	Nixon
Lewis Powell	President of the American Bar Association; private practice	1972–1987	Nixon
Abe Fortas	Private practice	1965–1969	Johnson
Byron White	Deputy U.S. attorney general	1962–1993	Kennedy
Arthur Goldberg	U.S. secretary of labor	1962–1965	Kennedy
Earl Warren	Governor of California	1953–1969	Eisenhower
Tom Clark	U.S. attorney general	1949–1967	Truman
Harold Burton	U.S. senator	1945–1958	Truman

Note: Some justices, such as Clarence Thomas, served as judges for only a few months before appointment.
[a]William Rehnquist was appointed associate justice by President Nixon in 1972 and chief justice by President Reagan in 1986.

to judicial experience. (See table 4.4.) Particular problems occurred in the former Communist countries and Iraq as they experienced dramatic political changes. A number of the former Communist countries allowed judges appointed by the Communists to remain on the bench, arguing that they were repositories of great knowledge and experience who could operate under a new set of laws. In Iraq, on the other hand, the alleged complicity of the judiciary with Saddam Hussein's regime was judged so grievous that they were replaced. An important issue for the judiciary lies in public trust.

Table 4.3.   Educational Backgrounds of the Current Supreme Court Members

Justice	Appointing President	Undergraduate Degree	Law Degree
John Roberts (chief justice)	G. W. Bush	Harvard	Harvard
John Paul Stevens	Ford	Chicago	Northwestern
Antonin Scalia	Reagan	Georgetown	Harvard
Anthony Kennedy	Reagan	Stanford	Harvard
David Souter	G. H. W. Bush	Harvard	Harvard
Clarence Thomas	G. H. W. Bush	Holy Cross	Yale
Ruth Bader Ginsburg	Clinton	Cornell	Columbia
Stephen Breyer	Clinton	Stanford	Harvard
Samuel Alito	G. W. Bush	Princeton	Yale

Source: U.S. Supreme Court, "The Justices of the Supreme Court," http://www.supremecourtus.gov/about/biographiescurrent.pdf.

Table 4.4. Some Comparative Procedures for Appointing Constitutional Judges

Country	Qualifications	Nominating Body	Tenure
France	None (some political, legal, and parliamentary experience required)	President of the republic; presidents of both chambers of Parliament	9 years (nonrenewable)
Germany	Judges or professors qualified for judicial office; typically all were politically active in some way	8 nominated by each chamber of Parliament; list of possible candidates produced by ministry of justice and political parties and by the court itself	12 years (nonrenewable)
Spain	Judges or professors (mainly the latter)	Consejo General del Poder Judicial (Judicial System General Council) and both chambers of Parliament	9 years (nonrenewable)

Source: John Bell, "Judicial Appointments: Some European Experiences" (paper presented at a conference held by the Centre for Public Law, University of Cambridge, October 4, 2003). http://www.law.cam.ac.uk/docs/view.php?doc=865.

Table 4.5.   Demographics of the Federal Judiciary, 2006

	% of Judiciary	% of U.S. Population
Male	75	49
Female	25	51
White	81	75
African American	11	12
Hispanic	7	12

Source: Data on the federal judiciary is from Alliance for Justice, http://www
.judicialselectionproject.org/index.asp

Demographically, the federal judiciary does not look like the U.S. population as a whole (see table 4.5). With lifetime tenure and the concern over demographics a relatively recent issue, changing the overall composition of an institution like the judiciary will take many years.

C. ENDURING QUESTIONS ABOUT THE PARTICIPANTS AND HOW TO RESEARCH THEM

To What Degree Is the Imbalance in Demographic Representation Being Addressed?

Judges tend to move up within the judicial system. Appointment from outside is relatively rare. Unless one is on the "bench" awaiting appointment to a higher court, there is relatively little chance for success. Therefore, appointment to a lower federal court is crucial for determining the eventual composition of the higher courts.

Sample Hypothesis

If the lower-level federal courts are no more demographically diverse and than upper-level courts, then the potential for a more diverse upper-level judiciary is likely to be more limited.

Hints for Accomplishment

Using demographic data collected by the Alliance for Justice (see http://www.judicialselectionproject.org/demographics.asp), compare the demographics of district courts (the lowest level) with that of the circuit courts and ultimately that of the Supreme Court. You might also look at the degree to which the circuits vary demographically and look for factors that might help explain the variation.

To What Degree Does Partisanship Drive the Confirmation Process?

While it is clear that presidents usually choose members of their own party for top judicial positions, that does not necessarily translate into a partisan battle in the Senate.

Sample Hypothesis

If a conflict develops over a judicial appointment in the Senate, then the competing coalitions of Senators will be characterized by partisanship.

Hints for Accomplishment

Do case studies of two or three judicial-confirmation votes. (Nominations and overall votes can be found on Thomas, the congressional website, at http://www.thomas.gov/home/nomis.html, using "Supreme Court" or "circuit court" as search terms.) To find votes of individual senators, use CQ publications, newspaper accounts, or the *Washington Post*'s Votes Database, at http://projects.washingtonpost.com/congress/nomination-votes. Determine the degree to which the votes broke along partisan lines. For further information on the politics of confirmation, see Lee Epstein and Jeffrey A. Segal, *Advice and Consent: The Politics of Judicial Appointments* (New York: Oxford University Press, 2005).

D. IDEA GENERATOR: WHO SERVES ON THE COURTS AND HOW DO THEY GET THERE?

The following chart provides some general guidelines for developing a research plan.

Specific Issue	Hypotheses	Hints
Court Appointments		
Partisanship	If the president's party does not control the Senate, then there will be a greater split in the confirmation vote.	Compare confirmation votes where the Senate was controlled by the opposing party with those where the Senate was controlled by the president's party.
Court Appointments		
Demographics	If one looks over time, then one will find that	Using the biographical sources in section 5 below,

(continued)

Specific Issue	Hypotheses	Hints
	the same prestigious law schools have populated the court.	look at the educational backgrounds of justices from previous periods and compare them with the educational backgrounds of the justices today.

Court Appointments

Timing	If there is a possible change of party control of the presidency, then justices of the departing president's party are more likely to retire while the president is still in office, while justices of the opposing party will try to wait out the election and retire under a president of their party.	Look at the timing of retirements of justices and try to determine political motivations.

Court Appointments

Strategy, success, and failure	If a nominee faces a hostile Senate, then the nominee may not be approved despite being qualified.	Do a case study of a failed court-nomination battle. Look at the arguments used by the opponents and attempt to determine whether these arguments are legitimate or whether they are simply hiding partisan or ideological reasons. Look at the role of the media, interest groups, and public opinion.

3. Context and Performance of the Courts

A. HISTORICAL DEVELOPMENT

The Supreme Court has long been the least public of American national institutions. The Court does the majority of its business behind closed doors. The decision to hear a case (see the discussion below) occurs with virtually no public input or awareness. Once a case gets formal consideration, the door to the public is opened a crack, most often to the media acting on behalf of the general public. Although there is a public gallery that seats a few dozen people, the Supreme Court has refused to open its proceedings to cameras or simultaneous broadcasting of the audio recording. After the public hearing, the justices meet privately to discuss the case.

B. PUBLIC SUPPORT

Because the judiciary is a nonelected branch of government whose key players have lifetime tenure, one might conclude that public support means little except to stroke the ego of the judges. In reality, all political institutions require enough public support that their decisions are followed largely without question. Lacking its own enforcement arm, the Supreme Court is fortunate in having significant public regard. Unique among national institutions, the Supreme Court maintains a consistently high level of public support. About two-thirds of the American public approves of the "way the Court is handling its job."[1] This level of support far surpasses that of the other branches of the national government.

Figure 4.4.   Confidence in institutions, June 1–4, 2006.
Source: The Gallup Poll, national adult sample

The Court is not viewed as leaning consistently in one political direction. In a September 2006 Gallup Poll, 21 percent of the public saw the court as "too liberal," 31 percent saw it as "too conservative," and 43 percent viewed it as "about right." Such balance probably contributes to the Court's overall rating and to the perceived **legitimacy** of the Court and its decisions. (See figure 4.4.)

C. THE JUDICIARY AT WORK

The Supreme Court reviews cases decided by the lower federal courts, considering the constitutionality of the judicial procedures used or, in rarer cases, the constitutionality of the law under which a person or organization was charged, and in even rarer cases (such as suits between states), the Supreme Court exercises original jurisdiction and rules on innocence or guilt. Parties losing in the lower courts have the option of appealing their cases on constitutional grounds, while the Supreme Court can pick and choose which cases it feels worthy of review. The volume of cases is significant. In 2005, over 8,000 cases were appealed to the Supreme Court. The Court granted review of only 170 of those cases, by granting a **writ of certiorari**. The Court eventually issued full opinions for 85 of those cases, issuing brief memoranda for the remainder. The selectivity of the Court in choosing cases with serious questions about procedure or legislation is borne out by the fact that during the 2005 term, only 27 percent of the cases saw the rulings of the lower courts fully affirmed.[2]

The number of cases chosen for review from the thirteen circuit courts varies significantly, indicating the ideology of the judges, the kinds of cases they face, and differing views of the law. For example, in 2005, the Ninth Circuit (Alaska, Arizona, California, Hawaii, Idaho, Montana, Nevada, Oregon, Washington, Guam, and the Northern Mariana Islands) generated twenty-four cases and the Eleventh Circuit (Alabama, Florida, and Georgia) generated thirty-four, while the Second Circuit (Connecticut, New York, and Vermont) was responsible for only nine.

Justices interact in a number of ways on the Court. At least four justices must sign the writ of certiorari. During oral arguments, justices seek clarification and often attempt to present their own views of the legal aspects of the case to their colleagues. The two parties and other interested groups present **briefs** that outline their views of the case. During the public hearing of the case, lawyers for each side of the dispute are given a limited amount of time (often only a half hour) to present their arguments and field questions by the justices. After the public hearing, the justices meet in private to help frame a response. As the positions become clear, the chief justice assigns one justice the job of writing the opinion of the Court, which must be endorsed by at least four other justices who join the opinion or write a separate "concurring opinion" endorsing the general thrust of the decision. The justices who disagree have the option of writing an individual or group "dissenting opinion." While the assignment of written decisions on the Court are relatively equal, dissents vary greatly. During the 2005 term, the leaders in dissent were John Paul Stevens, with twenty-eight dissenting opinions; Stephen Breyer, with twenty-three; and Antonin Scalia, with twenty-one. On the other end of the scale, Sandra Day O'Connor wrote three dissenting opinions and Samuel Alito nine.[3] Agreement among the justices can tell us a great deal about the voting blocs on the Court. In the 2005 term, the highest percentage of agreement on nonunanimous cases was between Samuel Alito and John Roberts (90 percent) and Antonin Scalia and Clarence Thomas (84 percent).[4] The greatest percentage of disagreement was between Stevens and Thomas (81 percent) and Stevens and Alito (77 percent). Different justices join the majority at widely differing rates. In 2005, Justice Roberts voted with the majority in 86 percent of the cases, while Justice Stevens did so only 56 percent of the time.[5] (See table 4.6.)

D. ENDURING QUESTIONS ON THE CONTEXT AND PERFORMANCE OF THE COURTS AND HOW TO RESEARCH THEM

What Is the Nature of Voting Blocs on the Supreme Court?

Those who argue that justices should simply read the Constitution and "find" the law soon recognize that different groups of justices consistently find differing things in the law. Using all the cases in a particular Supreme Court term (the November issue of the *Harvard Law Review* presents statistics for the previous term and is available at http://www.harvardlawreview.org, under "Recent Issues") or select particular cases (perhaps dealing with specific subjects, such as criminal procedure, constitutional guarantees, business law), look at the degree to which each justice agrees with the others. For a more in-depth look (1994–2003), see "Nine Justices, Ten Years: A Statistical Retrospective," *Harvard Law Review* 118 (2004): 510–523, available at http://www.harvardlawreview.org/issues/118/ Nov04/Nine_Justices_Ten_YearsFTX.pdf. After completing your statistical analysis, look at the factors that might explain varying levels of agreement.

How Have Constitutional Interpretations Changed over Time?

One of the strengths of our living Constitution is its ability to be applied in different ways as social and technological conditions have changed. Take one of the

Table 4.6. Voting Agreement among U.S. Supreme Court Justices, 2005 Term (percent)

	Thomas	Scalia	Roberts	Alito	Kennedy	Breyer	Souter	Ginsburg	Stevens
Thomas		84	74	68	68	27	24	19	19
Scalia			85	68	62	38	41	35	30
Roberts				90	65	44	44	44	32
Alito					77	32	41	32	23
Kennedy						46	51	46	41
Breyer							78	70	62
Souter								70	73
Ginsburg									76

Source: "The Statistics," Harvard Law Review 120 (2006): 372–384, available online at http://www.harvardlawreview.org/issues/120/nov06/statistics06.pdf.

hot issues such as free speech or the right to bear arms or abortion and follow it through the major court cases refining its application. For a section-by-section analysis of cases related to the Constitution, see Sue Davis, *Corwin & Peltason's Understanding the Constitution*, 17th ed. (Belmont, Calif.: Thompson/ Wadsworth, 2008) (earlier editions listed Peltason as the lead author).

What Happened in the XYZ Case?

A significant learning tool in law school involves "briefing" a case. As box 4.2 in-dicates, briefing is a process of summarizing the key aspects of a case in such a way as to efficiently communicate its basic characteristics to others.

Box 4.2.   Briefing a Case

A Guide to Legal Case Briefs

I. Citation

From what specific source is the case taken? For example, was the case reported in the *United States Reports*?

II. The Facts

A. **Material:** What materially happened?

B. **Legal:** From what legal circumstances did the case originate?

III. Legal Issues

A. **Specific:** What specific legal questions does this case raise?

B. **General:** What more general legal questions does this case raise?

IV. The Holding

What decision was made? That is, in support of which side did the court hold?

V. Legal Rationale

• What legal reasoning informed the court's decision?

• What rules of law did it apply?

• How did it interpret legal principles, documents?

• How did it construe the facts?

VI. Questions

• What existing legal questions, if any, are unresolved by this case?

• What new questions, if any, does it raise?

Source: Adapted from the University of Virginia School of Law, http://www.people .virginia.edu/~rjb3v/briefhow.html.

Why Are Some Circuit Court Rulings So Often Reversed?

The U.S. Court of Appeals for the Ninth Circuit is composed of nine states and two territories. It includes Alaska, Arizona, California, Hawaii, Idaho, Montana, Nevada, Oregon, Washington, Guam, and the Northern Mariana Islands. This court has become the example of a circuit whose decisions are often overruled by the Supreme Court. The Supreme Court, as final arbiter of constitutionality, is designed to send signals to lower courts and thus bring the entire federal court system into line.

Sample Hypothesis

If a lower federal court is regularly overruled, then it is (not) functioning properly.

Hints for Accomplishment

First make the case for your evaluation as to whether being overruled is positive or negative. What are the implications for the residents of the circuit, the circuit court, and the Supreme Court? Determine whether the Ninth Circuit has had an inordinate number of cases overruled. To expand your analysis, look at the arguments about why the Ninth Circuit has been overruled and determine which are most important. Decide which factors might be amenable to change through reform. You may want to read the House Committee on the Judiciary, *Federal Judgeship and Administrative Act of 2005*, 109th Cong., 2d sess., 2006, H.R. Rep. 109-373, at 15–19 ("The Ninth Circuit: Structure and Concerns"), available on Thomas, the congressional website, at http://www.thomas.gov (under "Committee Reports"), or GPO Access, the Government Printing Office's website, at http://www.gpoaccess.gov/legislative.html (under "Congressional Reports"). The Center for Individual Freedom provides statistics regarding Supreme Court reversals of circuit court opinions at http://www.centerforindividualfreedom.org/legal/supreme_supervision.htm.

E. IDEA GENERATOR:
JUDGING THE PERFORMANCE OF THE JUDGES

The following chart provides some general guidelines for developing a research plan.

Specific Issue	Hypotheses	Hints
Public Support		
Variation over time	If you compare public support of the Supreme	Create a graph showing public support for the

Specific Issue	Hypotheses	Hints
	Court with that of other national political institutions, then you will find less variation in the Court's evaluation than in that of other institutions.	Supreme Court and for other institutions. Some data is available at PollingReport.com, http://www.pollingreport.com.
	Workload	
Explaining sources of cases	If you look at the Supreme Court docket, then you will find great variation in the type and origin of cases.	Look at the Supreme Court docket and determine whether certain subjects or originating circuits dominate.

4. Original Research That Will Impress Your Professor

Abraham, Henry J. *An Introductory Analysis of the Courts of the United States, England, and France.* 7th ed. Norman: University of Oklahoma Press, 1998.
Hall, Kermit L., James W. Ely, and Joel B. Grossman. *The Oxford Companion to the Supreme Court of the United States.* New York: Oxford University Press, 2005.
Irons, Peter H., and Howard Zinn. *A People's History of the Supreme Court: The Men and Women Whose Cases and Decisions Have Shaped Our Constitution.* New York: Penguin Books, 2006.
McCloskey, Robert G., *The American Supreme Court.* 4th ed., revised by Sanford Levinson. Chicago: University of Chicago Press, 2005.
Neubauer, David W., and Stephen S. Meinhold. *Judicial Process: Law, Courts, and Politics in the United States.* Elmont, Calif.: Wadsworth Publishers, 2006.
O'Brien, David M. *Storm Center: The Supreme Court in American Politics.* New York: W. W. Norton, 2005.

5. Where to Find It

Where can I find out what is on the Supreme Court docket (schedule)?
The Supreme Court docket is available on the Court's website, at http://www.supremecourtus.gov/docket/docket.html, and is searchable by keyword. Brief summaries of current and past dockets are available from Northwestern University, at http://docket.medill.northwestern.edu, or from FindLaw, at http://supreme.lp.findlaw.com/supreme_court/docket/index.html.

Where can I find biographies of judges?
Try the Federal Judicial Center, at http://www.fjc.gov/public/home.nsf/hisj, or for Supreme Court justices, Oyez, at http://www.oyez.org, FindLaw, at http://supreme.lp.findlaw.com/supreme_court/justices/index.html, or the Supreme Court, at http://www.supremecourtus.gov/about/about.html.

Where can I find statistics on the caseload of the Supreme Court?
The *Harvard Law Review* is available either in hard copy or online. Each court term (year), the November issue presents statistics on case dispositions and voting patterns of the justices for the previous term. The online version can be found at http://www.harvardlawreview.org (under "Recent Issues"). A ten-year summary analysis (ending in 2003) is available at http://www.harvardlawreview.org/issues/118/Nov04/Nine_Justices_Ten_YearsFTX.pdf.

How do I find voting patterns of members of the Supreme Court?
See A Vacancy on the Court, at http://partners.is.asu.edu/~george/vacancy/justices.html#table2, or the statistics published by *Harvard Law Review* (see the question above).

Where can I find summaries of cases?
Both FindLaw, at http://caselaw.lp.findlaw.com/casesummary/index.html, and Oyez, at http://www.oyez.org/oyez/portlet/justices, provide case summaries.

How can I take a virtual tour of the Supreme Court building?
The Oyez website provides a virtual Supreme Court tour at http://www.oyez.org/tour. Think of yourself as an anthropologist studying a strange "tribe." What does the setting of the Supreme Court tell you about how we respect the justices and the power relationships of those with business before the court?

Where can I find analyses of landmark Supreme Court cases?
The Supreme Court Historical Society provides a gateway to sources about key Supreme Court cases at http://www.landmarkcases.org.

How do I find significant cases that split the Court?
Check out the Oyez website, at http://www.oyez.org/?justice_id=88.

Where can I find a list of past nominees to the Supreme Court and the Senate vote on their nomination?
The U.S. Senate website provides a table summarizing all nominations at http://www.senate.gov/pagelayout/reference/nominations/Nominations.htm. For a more detailed analysis of the nomination process, see Denis Steven Rutkus,

Supreme Court Appointment Process: Roles of the President, Judiciary Committee, and Senate, CRS Rep. No. RL31989 (Washington, D.C.: Congressional Research Service, 2005), available online at http://fpc.state.gov/documents/organization/50146.pdf.

How do I determine which states are in which judicial circuits?
The U.S. Courts website provides a circuit court map at http://www.uscourts.gov/courtlinks.

To what degree do presidents limit Supreme Court nominations to members of their party?
The chart from Professor George Watson lists the parties of all nominees and the party of the president who nominated them, at "A Vacancy on the Court," http://partners.is.asu.edu/~george/vacancy/justices.html.

How do I determine the public's view of the court?
PollingReport.com provides evaluations of the major institutions. Supreme Court polls are available at http://www.pollingreport.com/Court.htm.

6. Taking Action—Contacting and Influencing the Courts

While the federal courts are not immune to public opinion, there is no formal or effective way for an individual to affect judicial outcomes, aside from becoming part of a court case or joining an interest group with a judicial agenda. Becoming part of a court case requires, aside from financial backing, the existence of legal **standing**. The courts will not handle hypothetical cases, only those brought by an individual who was actually harmed by the law or its application. Interest groups often financially back courts cases or submit **amicus curiae** ("friend of the court") **briefs**, which explain the groups' perspective on a case.

Notes

1. The Gallup Poll regularly asks national samples of adults this question. The alternative question as to "how much confidence" respondents have in the Supreme Court results in over 40 percent choosing the top category of "a great deal."

2. Statistics are from "The Statistics," *Harvard Law Review* 120 (2006): 372–384, available online at http://www.harvardlawreview.org/issues/120/nov06/statistics06.pdf (hereafter referred to as *Harvard Law Review* 2005 Statistics). *Harvard Law Review* provides

statistics on the Supreme Court each year, generally in the November issue. Recent issues are available at http://www.harvardlawreview.org/recentissues.shtml.

3. *Harvard Law Review* 2005 Statistics.

4. Statistics on concurrence are from "A Vacancy on the Court," http://partners.is.asu .edu/~george/vacancy/justices.html#table2.

5. *Harvard Law Review* 2005 Statistics.

CHAPTER 5

State and Local Government

The framers of the U.S. Constitution faced a dilemma regarding **federalism** (the relationship between the federal government and state governments). They did not desire to reestablish the type of relationship they had experienced under British rule, namely, **unitary federalism**, a system in which the state governments derive their power from the federal government. Nor did they desire to continue the system of **confederated federalism**—a system in which the federal government derives its authority from the state governments—that they had established under the Articles of Confederation. Instead, the founders attempted to create a unique system of federalism commonly referred to as **American federalism**, a division of power between the federal government and state governments in which each derives power directly from the people and both remain sovereign in their separate spheres.

1. The Structure of American Federalism

A. THE CONSTITUTIONAL RELATIONSHIP BETWEEN STATE AND FEDERAL GOVERNMENTS

The U.S. Constitution did not firmly establish the balance of power between the federal government and the state government, but instead set the stage for a power struggle. The "**supremacy clause**" (Article VI), the "**necessary and proper clause**" (Article I, Section 8), and the "**commerce clause**" (Article I, Section 8, Clause 3) appear to give the upper hand to the federal government, while the **Tenth Amendment** sets the boundaries on federal power in favor of states' rights. The Constitution grants the federal government certain **express powers**, that is, specific powers enumerated in the Constitution, and **implied powers**, that is, powers not specifically described but implied from the enumerated powers. **Reserved powers** are those powers specifically resting with the states (e.g., the power to charter local governments and to conduct elections). The Constitution also establishes certain **concurrent powers**, which are governmental powers granted to both the federal and state governments (e.g., the power to make laws, impose taxes, and establish courts).

- *Supremacy clause:* Article VI of the U.S. Constitution states that the Constitution, federal laws, and treaties are "the supreme Law of the Land; and the Judges in every State shall be bound thereby."
- *Necessary and proper clause:* Article I, Section 8 of the U.S. Constitution states that Congress shall have the power to enact all laws that are "necessary and proper" for performing its enumerated powers. This clause gives Congress implied powers beyond those specifically stated in the Constitution.
- *Commerce clause:* Article I, Section 8, Clause 3 of the U.S. Constitution grants Congress the power to regulate commerce among the states. This power has been broadly interpreted over the years and used as a powerful mechanism for the federal government to regulate a wide range of activities at the state level.
- *Tenth Amendment:* This part of the Bill of Rights states that "the powers not delegated to the United States by the Constitution, nor prohibited by it to the States, are reserved to the States respectively, or to the people."

B. THE RELATIONSHIP BETWEEN STATE AND LOCAL GOVERNMENTS

In 1868, federal judge John F. Dillon made a famous ruling, known as **Dillon's Rule**, which clearly articulates the relationship between state and local governments. Judge Dillon ruled that municipal corporations derive their power and rights entirely from state legislatures. As Dillon's Rule makes clear, there is no power-sharing arrangement between the local and state government; the state government creates local governments to serve the state's interests. While all local governments are created by charters, granted by the state legislature, there remains a great deal of variation in the nature of charters.

- *General charter:* A **general charter** is a standard charter provided by the state that is granted to all jurisdictions and lists the specific areas in which a local government may legislate.
- *Classified charter:* A **classified charter** is a standard charter provided by a state that is granted to jurisdictions on the basis of their population and lists

the specific areas in which a local government may legislate. Local governments with larger populations are typically given more authority than those with smaller populations.

- *Optional charter:* An **optional charter** is a standard charter provided by the state that is selected by the jurisdiction by a direct vote of the citizens and lists the specific areas in which a local government may legislate.
- *Home-rule charters:* The concept of **home rule** allows an individual community to draft its own charter, though the charter must meet the general requirements determined by the state. Unlike other charters, home-rule charters do not list the specific areas in which a local government may legislate. Local governments are free to rule in all areas that do not conflict with state and federal laws.

C. TYPES OF STATE GOVERNMENTS

No two state governments are created exactly the same. Structural, as well as substantive, differences in their constitutions lead to substantial differences in the operation of state governments. Listed below are a few major structural differences that exist within state governments.

Unicameral versus Bicameral Legislative Bodies

While **unicameral legislatures**, or legislative bodies that are not divided into upper and lower chambers but instead contain a single chamber, are common in legislative bodies around the world, they have been the exception in the United States. Three states (Georgia, Pennsylvania, and Vermont) were established with unicameral legislatures but switched to **bicameral legislatures**, or legislative bodies that are divided into upper and lower chambers, by the mid-nineteenth century. Nebraska switched from a bicameral system to a unicameral system in 1934 and remains the only state with a unicameral legislature. Among the states there are major differences in the ratio of members in the House and Senate. Several states maintain a ratio of 2 to 1 (two members in the House for each state senator), though New Hampshire has a ratio of 16 to 1.

Professional Legislatures versus Amateur Legislatures

While it is now the norm for states to conduct annual legislative sessions, this has not always been the case. As recently as 1960, less than half the state legislatures met annually. Today, the legislatures in six states (Arkansas, Montana, Nevada, North Dakota, Oregon, and Texas) hold **biennial legislative sessions**, that is, sessions that meet every other year. The length of legislative sessions also varies substantially from state to state. The legislatures in some states meet for only a few months out of the year, while other states have full-time legislatures. Moreover the compensation for state lawmakers also varies from state to state, helping to make legislative positions in some states full-time careers, while it remains a part-time occupation in other states. Another institutional factor that influences the operations of a legislature is the size of the respective chambers. In New Hampshire, a relatively small state, the state legislature has 400 members in its House of Representatives, about 1 representative for every 3,300 people. In contrast, Colorado has only 65 members in its lower chamber, roughly 1 representative for every 73,000 people.

Term Limits versus No Term Limits

Term limits place legal limits on the number of consecutive terms an elected official can serve in office. The fifteen states with legislative term limits are Arizona, Arkansas, California, Colorado, Florida, Louisiana, Maine, Michigan, Missouri, Montana, Nebraska, Nevada, Ohio, Oklahoma, and South Dakota. A majority of states (thirty-five) limit the number of terms a governor can serve. The states with gubernatorial term limits are Alabama, Alaska, Arizona, Arkansas, California, Colorado, Delaware, Florida, Georgia, Hawaii, Indiana, Kansas, Louisiana, Maine, Maryland, Michigan, Mississippi, Missouri, Montana, Nebraska, Nevada, New Jersey, New Mexico, North Carolina, Ohio, Oklahoma, Pennsylvania, Rhode Island, South Carolina, South Dakota, Tennessee, Utah, Virginia, West Virginia, and Wyoming.

Strong Governors versus Weak Governors

The power of state governors varies dramatically from state to state. In some states governors not only have general **veto power**, the power of the chief executive to void a bill that has been passed by the legislature, but they also have the power of the **line-item veto**, the power of the chief executive to void part of a bill that has been passed by the legislature. In Maryland, which grants its governor vast budgetary powers, the governor introduces the state budget. In that state, the legislature can remove spending items from the governor's budget, but they can add no new spending items of their own. Some states permit the governor to select heads of executive agencies, while other states hold separate statewide elections for the offices of attorney general, secretary of education, secretary of agriculture, and other executive offices. In some states (e.g., New York and Ohio) the governor and lieutenant governor run as a ticket, but in other states (e.g., Virginia and California) the candidates for governor and lieutenant governor run separately and the offices can be held by members of competing political parties. There are also important differences among governors regarding their judicial powers: the power to **pardon**, or cancel a criminal's conviction; to **commute a sentence,** that is, cancel part or all of a criminal's sentence (but keep the conviction); and to grant **parole**, or release a criminal prior to the full completion of a sentence.

Direct Democracy versus No Direct Democracy

The **initiative** process is a mechanism that enables citizens, by collecting a sufficient number of signatures on a petition, to place a statute or constitutional amendment on the ballot for the voters to adopt or reject. Twenty-four states permit some version of the statewide initiative process. The **popular-referendum** process is the mechanism that enables citizens, by collecting a sufficient number of signatures on a petition, to force a popular vote on a measure that was preciously enacted by the state legislature. The **legislative-referendum** process is the mechanism that enables voters to accept or reject a measure (constitutional amendment, statute, bond issues, etc.) that was referred to them by the state legislature or other governmental body. All states permit some form of the legislative referendum.

State Courts: Fifty Separate Legal Systems

Each state has a unique legal system. While most states organize their state judicial system around a similar structure (municipal/special courts, circuit/county courts, courts of appeals, and a state supreme court), the structure and complexity of judicial systems vary by state. See the National Center for State Courts website, at http://www.ncsconline.org/D_Research/Ct_Struct/Index.html, for an analysis of the judicial systems in individual states. The selection process for judges also varies from state to state, with some states electing their judges in partisan elections, some electing judges in nonpartisan contests, others appointing judges either through legislative appointments or gubernatorial appointments, and still others making use of a hybrid selection process known as the **Missouri Plan**. States that use the Missouri Plan nominate judges through a nominating committee composed of legal experts. The committee names several nominees and then the governor selects one of them. In the first election following the governor's judicial selection, the voters are asked to approve or reject the judicial nominee. If the nominee is approved by the voters, he or she serves a full term as judge. If rejected, the selection process is repeated.

D. TYPES OF LOCAL GOVERNMENTS

Since each state determines its own laws regarding local governments, the laws and even the words used to describe local governments vary from state to state.

Municipal Government

Municipal governments come in all sizes, from the largest cities to the smallest villages. What they have in common is that they are incorporated by the state through a charter. The charter serves as the municipality's governing constitution and outlines the powers and responsibilities of the municipality. Municipal governments are typically run by a **mayor**, who is the chief executive authority of a municipality, and a **city council**, which is the legislative authority of a municipality. While the mayor-council arrangement remains the most common in municipal government, a substantial number of municipalities (more than two thousand) have replaced the job of mayor with an appointed **city manager**, a nonpartisan executive authority created to run the operations of a municipal government.

County Government

Most states have a level of local government referred to as a **county** government (Alaska uses the word *borough* and Louisiana uses the word *parish* to describe what other states generally call counties). Counties divide states into small political subunits. Some states divide counties into smaller **towns** and make use of town governments as the primary local form of government. In some states, municipalities (i.e., incorporated cities) operate as part of the county in which they belong, while in other states, municipalities function as independent government units outside of counties. Counties typically contain law enforcement agencies, courts, public utilities, libraries, and land records. County governments record marriages, deaths, and births that occur in the county. The legislative arm of the county is typically represented by an elected **county commission**, and the executive functions are carried out by an elected **county executive**.

Town Governments

In New England, **towns** serve the same political functions that are served by county governments in other states. New England towns have a tradition of highly participatory local government in which citizens have a direct impact on local governance. Pennsylvania and New Jersey subdivide their counties into townships, which provide some of the functions often associated with county governments. Southern states generally do not subdivide counties into towns. In southern states, the word *town* generally refers to a small municipality rather than a subsection of a county.

Special Districts

There are a greater number of special districts in the United States than all other forms of government combined. **Special districts** are created by state governments or local governments (county, town, or municipal) to meet a specific need of the community. The most common type of special district is the school district, though they exist for numerous other purposes, including flood control, water conservation, fire protection, hospitals, harbors and ports, libraries, police protection, recreation and parks, and sanitation. Special districts are often granted funding and administrative authority for their specific purpose. Typically, special districts are funded through property taxes, though their funding can come from any number of sources, including revenue from city, county, and state sources. Special districts are popular at the local level because they relieve a great deal of the administrative burden of local governments and often provide an independent source of revenue for programs that would otherwise be funded by counties, towns, or municipalities.

Common-Interest Communities

More than thirty million Americans live in what are known as **common-interest communities**. (a form of private government that includes homeowners

---

Box 5.1.   Skill Box: Applying Information

In the United States, government does not exist as a single entity but instead, as shown in table 5.1, as multiple layers of individual governments. A single person could fall under the jurisdiction of dozens of governmental bodies (e.g., the national government, state government, county government, municipal government, and numerous special districts). Ideally, the layering of governments provides a unique set of services that meet the individual interests and needs of specific communities, but it could also be argued that it results in the duplication of services and bureaucratic inefficiencies. Can you identify the various governmental entities that have jurisdiction over you?

Table 5.1.   Number of Governments in the United States

	No. of Governments
Federal	1
State	50
Local:	
Counties	3,034
Towns	16,504
Municipalities	19,429
Special Districts	48,558
Total	87,576

Source: U.S. Census Bureau, "Federal, State, and Local Governments" (from the 2002 census), http://www.census.gov/govs/www/gid2002.html.

associations, condominium associations, and housing cooperatives). Common-interest communities contain property held in common by all members (e.g., buildings, open spaces, playgrounds, clubhouses, pools) and require all members of the community to join the community's governing association (e.g., a homeowners' association, a condominium association) and abide by the association's rules. The association manages common property and sets rules for the community (e.g., rules regarding pets, house color, antennas, yard care).

E. AMERICAN FEDERALISM: GOALS AND INTENTIONS OF THE FOUNDERS

As is often the case, scholars look to the *Federalist Papers* to understand the goals and intentions of the nation's founders. The *Federalist* Nos. 45 and 46, both written by James Madison, specifically address the relationship between the federal government and the states. The primary purpose of these essays was to calm fears that the new government would dominate the states and that by ratifying the Constitution the states were signing away their sovereignty. As you review the major points of Madison's argument (outlined below), consider the extent to which they still hold true.

1. The federal government could not function without the cooperation of the states (e.g., could not select senators and a president), but the states could function without the involvement of the federal government.
2. The number of people employed by the state governments would be larger than the number of people employed by the federal government.

3. The powers delegated to the federal government are few and defined, while those held by the states are not limited under the U.S. Constitution.

4. The power of the federal government would be greatest during times of war, and war would be the exception rather than the rule.

5. The people's first and natural attachment would be to their states, not the federal government.

6. Those who rose to national office would hold a bias toward their states, but those who rose to state office would not hold a bias toward the federal government.

7. Encroachments of the federal government on the rights of a specific state would incite opposition from all states.

8. The national military would not pose a threat to the states because the state militias and citizens would collectively represent a superior force.

F. COMPARATIVE PERSPECTIVE

To this date, the American system of federalism remains the exception to the rule rather than the norm in national politics around the globe. Most modern political states implement a unitary system of federalism in which the national government controls the political process and dictates policies for state and local officials. The state and local officials are not seen as policymakers, but instead serve the role of policy implementers. In a unitary system a country is likely to have a single court system, a single set of executive agencies, and a national police department. In a unitary system, a nation might have a national curriculum for public education or a single set of laws related to environmental protection. France and Great Britain are two examples of countries with unitary systems. The advantages of this system include government accountability, less duplication in the bureaucratic structure, equitable allocation of resources, and ease in decision making. Examples of nations with American-style federalism include Brazil, Germany, Russia, and Canada. The advantages of this type of system include the protection of local identities and the policy experimentation that comes at the state level.

G. ENDURING STRUCTURAL AND INSTITUTIONAL QUESTIONS AND HOW TO RESEARCH THEM

Ballot Initiatives and Term Limits

The relative value of ballot initiatives at the state level can be debated in many respects (e.g., what the founders thought of direct democracy, whether citizens have sufficient information to make informed decisions, whether minority rights are trampled by majority rule). One interesting way to assess the value of ballot initiatives is to address the policy implications of the process—in other words, have the twenty-four states that offer ballot initiatives adopted different types of policies as a consequence of the mechanism? One interesting policy area to explore is term limits. Since politicians are likely to resist adopting electoral policies that force them from office, it is possible that states with ballot initiatives are more likely to have term limits than states without term limits. Using the same logic, you could also explore the relationship between ballot initiatives and strict campaign-finance rules and access to public financing for campaigns.

Sample Hypothesis

If a state permits ballot initiatives, then the state is likely to limit the number of terms that a state lawmaker can serve in office.

Hints for Accomplishment

This analysis can be conducted relatively easily by making use of information that is widely available and applying straightforward analytical procedures. A comprehensive list of states with term limits is available from U.S. Term Limits, a nonprofit group that tracks term limits in the United States, at http://termlimits.org/state-information. A list of ballot-initiative states is available from the University of Southern California's Initiative & Referendum Institute, at http://www.iandrinstitute.org. With information from these two organizations you can construct a simple contingency table showing the percentage of ballot-initiative states that have legislative term limits and the percentage of non-ballot-initiative states that have legislative term limits. Depending on your level of interest and available time, you could also compare initiative states and noninitiative states in other categories (e.g., public funding for campaigns, legislative salaries, women elected officials). Keep in mind the potential influence of third variables, and resist the desire to make causal claims from the relationships that you uncover.

Annual versus Biennial State Legislatures

While only six state legislatures currently meet biennially (Arkansas, Montana, Nevada, North Dakota, Oregon, and Texas), most states have considered this option for various reasons. One interesting way to compare the relative benefits of these systems is to compare governance in the six states with biennial sessions to states that meet annually.

Sample Hypothesis

a. If a state legislature meets biennially, then per capita taxes (i.e., taxes per person) in the state will be relatively low.
b. If a state legislature meets biennially, then the state's per capita operating budget will be relatively low.

Hints for Accomplishment

This type of analysis can be meaningfully explored through a straightforward comparative analysis or by implementing a more sophisticated statistical analysis. If you are interested in the comparative approach, you could choose two states that are demographically similar but that differ in that one state makes use of biennial legislative sessions and the other state makes use of annual sessions (e.g., North Dakota and South Dakota). You could then compare how the two states addressed a single legislative imperative (like homeland-security issues following the September 11 attacks) or more general issues (like state tax policies). Students with more time and more advanced statistical skills could create a simple database for all fifty states from data available from the Council of State Governments' annual publication *The Book of States* and could then make aggregate-level comparisons of policies in the six states with biennial sessions with those in states with annual sessions.

H. IDEA GENERATOR: STRUCTURAL AND INSTITUTIONAL QUESTIONS RELATED TO FEDERALISM

The following chart provides some general guidelines for developing a research plan.

Specific Issue	Hypotheses	Hints
Unitary Federalism versus American Federalism		
Is the British system of unitary federalism more efficient than the American system of federalism?	a. If unitary federalism is more efficient than American federalism, then British citizens should pay lower per capita taxes than Americans. b. If unitary federalism is more efficient than American federalism, then the percentage	For this type of comparative analysis, you would ideally select two countries that are identical in every important way other than the issue of concern (i.e., federalism). While the United Kingdom and the United States share much in common (history, language, values,

(continued)

Specific Issue	Hypotheses	Hints
	of British citizens who work for the government should be less than the percentage of American citizens who work for the government.	economic systems), they are certainly not identical. Be careful not to overstate federalism's importance when analyzing government efficiency. Also make sure to include state, local, and federal taxes when comparing tax rates in the United States with those in Britain.

Governors

Specific Issue	Hypotheses	Hints
What are the policy implications of strong versus weak governors?	a. If a state has a governor with substantial constitutional powers (i.e., a strong governor), then the state will have relatively low taxes. b. If a state has a governor with substantial constitutional powers (i.e., a strong governor), then the state will spend less on state programs.	While state legislators represent the interests of their respective districts, only governors represent the interests of the entire state. It could be argued that giving more authority to governors could limit pork-barrel projects championed by local lawmakers and could help control state spending. See Council of State Governments, *The Book of States* for a comparison of the relative power of governors.

Common-Interest Communities

Specific Issue	Hypotheses	Hints
What are the advantages and disadvantages of living in common-interest communities?	a. If a person places a high degree of value on individual autonomy, then that person is unlikely to choose to live in a common-interest community. b. If a person places a high degree of value on convenience, then that person is likely to choose to live in a common-interest community.	If you are reading this book, the odds are that you are living in one version of a common-interest community (campus housing), or at least had the option to live in a common-interest community. Many college campuses are well suited for exploring the factors that influence residential housing decisions. Assuming that students are provided a choice

Specific Issue	Hypotheses	Hints
		between on-campus housing and off-campus housing, a simple survey of students living in different housing types could help shed light on the issue.

2. Participants

A. GOVERNORS

In all fifty states, executive authority rests with the governor. The power of the governor varies from state to state, as do the rules concerning gubernatorial selection and the number of terms a governor may serve. Following the 2006 elections, there were twenty-two Republican governors and twenty-eight Democratic governors. The 2006 elections marked a significant change in the partisan composition of governorships, with Republicans controlling less than 50 percent of gubernatorial offices for the first time in over a decade. See table 5.2 for a list of governors and their party identifications in 2007.

B. LEGISLATURES

Democrats currently control a majority of state senate seats and state house seats, though there are significant regional variations across the country. Republicans currently find strong support in much of the South, while Democrats dominate the state legislatures in many northeastern states. In several states legislatures, one party controls the senate and a different party controls the house. See table 5.3 for a list of the partisan composition in the state legislatures.

C. JUDGES

There are over eleven thousand state judgeships in the United States. Most states select their judges in a nonpartisan manner (e.g., nonpartisan elections) or in an indirectly partisan manner (e.g., appointment by legislatures or governors), while fourteen states conduct partisan elections for the selection of state judges. The nonpartisan and indirectly partisan nature of judicial selection in most states makes it difficult to assess the aggregate partisan composition of state judges in

Table 5.2. State Governors, 2008

State or Jurisdiction	Governor (Party)	Present Term Began	Present Term Ends	No. of Previous Terms	Maximum Consecutive Terms
Alabama	Bob Riley (R)	1-07	1-11	1	2
Alaska	Sarah Palin (R)	12-06	12-10	0	2
Arizona	Janet Napolitano (D)	1-07	1-11	1	2
Arkansas	Mike Beebe (D)	1-07	1-11	0	2
California	Arnold Schwarzenegger (R)	1-07	1-11	1	2
Colorado	Bill Ritter (D)	1-07	1-11	0	2
Connecticut	M. Jodi Rell (R)	1-07	1-11	1	No limit
Delaware	Ruth Ann Minner (D)	1-05	1-09	1	2
Florida	Charlie Crist (R)	1-07	1-11	0	2
Georgia	Sonny Perdue (R)	1-07	1-11	1	2
Hawaii	Linda Lingle (R)	12-06	12-10	1	2
Idaho	C. L. "Butch" Otter (R)	1-07	1-11	0	No limit
Illinois	Rod Blagojevich (D)	1-07	1-11	1	No limit
Indiana	Mitch Daniels (R)	1-05	1-09	0	2
Iowa	Chet Culver (D)	1-07	1-11	0	No limit
Kansas	Kathleen Sebelius (D)	1-07	1-11	1	2
Kentucky	Ernie Fletcher (R)	12-03	1-07	0	2
Louisiana	Bobby Jindal (D)	1-08	1-12	0	2
Maine	John Baldacci (D)	1-07	1-11	1	2
Maryland	Martin O'Malley (D)	1-07	1-11	0	2
Massachusetts	Deval Patrick (D)	1-07	1-11	0	No limit
Michigan	Jennifer Granholm (D)	1-07	1-11	1	2
Minnesota	Tim Pawlenty (R)	1-07	1-11	1	No limit
Mississippi	Haley Barbour (R)	1-08	1-12	1	2

State	Governor				
Missouri	Matt Blunt (R)	1-05	1-09	0	2
Montana	Brian Schweitzer (D)	1-05	1-09	0	2
Nebraska	Dave Heineman (R)	1-07	1-11	1	2
Nevada	Jim Gibbons (R)	1-07	1-11	0	2
New Hampshire	John Lynch (D)	1-07	1-09	1	No limit
New Jersey	Jon Corzine (D)	1-06	1-10	0	2
New Mexico	Bill Richardson (D)	1-07	1-11	1	2
New York	Eliot Spitzer (D)	1-07	1-11	0	No limit
North Carolina	Mike Easley (D)	1-05	1-09	1	2
North Dakota	John Hoeven (R)	12-04	12-08	1	No limit
Ohio	Ted Strickland (D)	1-07	1-11	0	2
Oklahoma	Brad Henry (D)	1-07	1-11	1	2
Oregon	Ted Kulongoski (D)	1-07	1-11	1	2
Pennsylvania	Edward G. Rendell (D)	1-07	1-11	1	2
Rhode Island	Don Carcieri (R)	1-07	1-11	1	2
South Carolina	Mark Sanford (R)	1-07	1-11	1	2
South Dakota	Mike Rounds (R)	1-07	1-11	1	2
Tennessee	Phil Bredesen (D)	1-07	1-11	1	2
Texas	Rick Perry (R)	1-07	1-11	2	No limit
Utah	Jon Huntsman Jr. (R)	1-05	1-09	0	2
Vermont	Jim Douglas (R)	1-07	1-09	2	No limit
Virginia	Tim Kaine (D)	1-06	1-10	0	1
Washington	Chris Gregoire (D)	1-05	1-09	0	No limit
West Virginia	Joe Manchin III (D)	1-05	1-09	0	2
Wisconsin	Jim Doyle (D)	1-07	1-11	1	No limit
Wyoming	Dave Freudenthal (D)	1-07	1-11	1	2

Source: National Governors Association, "Governors' Political Affiliations & Terms of Office, 2008," http://www.nga.org/Files/pdf/GOVLIST2008.PDF.

Table 5.3. State Legislatures, 2007

State	Senate Total Seats	Dem.	Rep.	Ind./ Other	House Total Seats	Dem.	Rep.	Ind./ Other
Alabama	35	23	12	0	105	62	43	0
Alaska	20	9	11	0	40	17	23	0
Arizona	30	13	17	0	60	27	33	0
Arkansas	35	27	8	0	100	75	25	0
California	40	25	15	0	80	48	32	0
Colorado	35	20	15	0	65	39	26	0
Connecticut	36	24	12	0	151	107	44	0
Delaware	21	13	8	0	41	18	23	0
Florida	40	14	26	0	120	41	79	0
Georgia	56	22	34	0	180	74	106	0
Hawaii	25	20	5	0	51	43	8	0
Idaho	35	7	28	0	70	19	51	0
Illinois	59	37	22	0	118	66	52	0
Indiana	50	17	33	0	100	51	49	0
Iowa	50	30	20	0	100	54	46	0
Kansas	40	10	30	0	125	48	77	0
Kentucky	38	16	21	1	100	61	39	0
Louisiana	39	24	15	0	105	63	41	1
Maine	35	18	17	0	151	89	60	2
Maryland	47	33	14	0	141	106	35	0
Massachusetts	40	35	5	0	160	141	19	0
Michigan	38	17	21	0	110	58	52	0
Minnesota	67	44	23	0	134	85	49	0
Mississippi	52	26	26	0	122	74	47	0
Missouri	34	13	21	0	163	71	92	0
Montana	50	26	24	0	100	49	50	1
Nebraska	49	*	*	49	*	*	*	*
Nevada	21	10	11	0	42	27	15	0
New Hampshire	24	14	10	0	400	239	161	0
New Jersey	40	22	18	0	80	49	31	0
New Mexico	42	24	18	0	70	42	28	0
New York	62	29	33	0	150	108	42	0
North Carolina	50	31	19	0	120	67	52	0
North Dakota	47	21	26	0	94	33	61	0
Ohio	33	12	21	0	99	46	53	0
Oklahoma	48	24	24	0	101	44	57	0
Oregon	30	17	11	2	60	31	29	0
Pennsylvania	50	21	29	0	203	102	101	0
Rhode Island	38	33	5	0	75	60	15	0
South Carolina	46	20	26	0	124	51	73	0
South Dakota	35	15	20	0	70	20	50	0
Tennessee	33	16	17	0	99	53	46	0
Texas	31	11	20	0	150	69	81	0

State	Senate				House			
	Total Seats	Dem.	Rep.	Ind./ Other	Total Seats	Dem.	Rep.	Ind./ Other
Utah	29	8	21	0	75	20	55	0
Vermont	30	23	7	0	150	93	49	8
Virginia	40	17	23	0	100	40	57	3
Washington	49	32	17	0	98	63	35	0
West Virginia	34	23	11	0	100	72	28	0
Wisconsin	33	18	15	0	99	47	52	0
Wyoming	30	7	23	0	60	17	43	0
Total	1,971	1,011	908	52	5,411	2,979	2,415	15

Source: National Conference of State Legislatures, "2006 Post-Election/2007 Pre-Election Partisan Composition of State Legislatures," http://www.ncsl.org/statevote/partycomptable2007.htm

the United States. The racial composition of judges, however, can be compared. The nonpartisan group the Lawyers' Committee for Civil Rights under Law tracks the racial composition of judges at the state level and has found that judgeships are disproportionately filled by white males.

D. ENDURING QUESTIONS ABOUT THE PARTICIPANTS

The Partisan Divide in State Government

In recent years, partisanship in state politics has proved to be unpredictable. States that tend to be dominated by one party in the legislature are increasingly

Table 5.4.   Judges, Lawyers, and General Population by Race, 2005

Race	Judges		Lawyers		U.S. Population %
	Number	%	Number	%	
Nonminority:					
White	10,200	89.9	786,730	90.3	75.1
Minority:					
African American	665	5.9	33,865	3.9	12.3
Hispanic	320	2.8	28,630	3.3	13.0
Asian	122	1.1	20,160	2.3	3.6
Native American	13	0.1	1,730	0.2	0.9
Other	24	0.2	—	—	5.5
Minority total	1,144	10.1	84,385	9.7	35.3

Source: Lawyers' Committee for Civil Rights Under Law, "Answering the Call for a More Diverse Judiciary" (Washington, D.C., 2005), available online at http://www.lawyerscommittee.org/2005website/publications/images/judicialdiversity.report.pdf.

Box 5.2.   Skill Box:
Analyzing Cross-Tabulations

Table 5.4 presents several interesting findings and raises many questions. The most obvious finding is that racial minorities (African Americans, Hispanics, Asians, and Native Americans) are underrepresented on the bench. It is also interesting to note that the percentage of lawyers who are African American (3.9 percent) is less than the percentage of judges who are African American (5.9 percent), a trend that is not consistent for other minority groups. Why might there be a larger percentage of African American judges than African American lawyers, and why might this trend not hold for other minority groups? When considering the question, think about the differences in the selection process for law school and the selection processes that exist for judges. Would you expect states that appoint judges to have more or fewer minority judges than states that elect their judges?

electing governors from a different party. For example, states with strong Democratic majorities in their state legislatures (e.g., California, Connecticut, and Hawaii) have recently elected Republican governors. The same is true for states with strong Republican majorities in their state legislatures (e.g., Arizona, Kansas, and Wyoming), which recently elected Democratic governors. A few possible explanations for this phenomenon include (1) the fact that voters might prefer that no one party dominates state politics, (2) the fact that gubernatorial

Sample Hypothesis

If political corruption is prevalent in a state dominated by one party, then the state is likely to elect a governor from the minority party.

Hints for Accomplishment

With a broad research topic like this one, it is often wise to focus your attention on either (1) several cases but few hypotheses or (2) a single case and several hypotheses. If you choose the first option, you might want to analyze the complete list of states that currently have a governor from the state's minority party and look for the prevalence of a single factor (e.g., scandal). If you choose the second option, you may decide to take an in-depth look at a single gubernatorial election, considering all the factors that might have led to the unlikely outcome.

races might be more competitive than races in legislative districts that have been drawn for partisan advantage, or (3) the fact that voters might punish corruption within the dominant party by electing governors from the minority party.

Judicial Selection Procedures and Judicial Composition

In the previous section we saw that there are numerous ways that state judges are selected. Some states elect judges in partisan elections, some elect them in non-partisan elections, others rely on governors to appoint judges, and still others rely on the legislature to make appointments, while some states make use of a hybrid approach known as the Missouri Plan. One interesting question is to explore whether the judicial selection process influences judicial composition—that is, whether one selection process increases the chance of minority or female representation on the bench.

Sample Hypothesis

a. If a state makes use of gubernatorial appointments, then the state is likely to have greater minority and female representation on the bench.
b. If a state makes use of partisan elections, then the state is likely to have a low level of minority and female representation on the bench.

Hints for Accomplishment

While studying this issue in the aggregate would most likely be beyond the scope of an undergraduate research project, making use of a simple comparative approach and case studies is possible. Select a small number of states that make use of different selection procedures and investigate the racial and gender composition of judges in those states. See the Lawyers' Committee for Civil Rights under Law report "Answering the Call for a More Diverse Judiciary," available online at http://www.lawyerscommittee.org/2005website/publications/images/judicialdiversity.report.pdf, for an example of this type of analysis.

E. IDEA GENERATOR: ADDITIONAL QUESTIONS RELATED TO STATE-LEVEL PARTICIPANTS

The following chart provides some general guidelines for developing a research plan.

Specific Issue	Hypotheses	Hints

Gender and State Politics

Do state and local elections afford women a meaningful entry point into electoral politics?	a. If a state legislature has term limits, then the likelihood of women serving in the legislature increases. b. If a state has small legislative districts, then the likelihood of women serving in the legislature increases.	Many politicians gain their initial political experience at the state or local level. Logic suggests that as women continue to become more active in the political arena, their presence will first be felt at the state and local level. Logic also suggests that women will be most successful in states that have few obstacles for entry into the political process. The hypotheses listed here are just a sample of questions related to this important issue.

Race and Gubernatorial Politics

Why have there been so few African American governors in American history?	a. If attitudes about race have changed substantially in the United States, then race should have been less of a campaign issue in the election of Deval Patrick of Massachusetts in 2006 than it was for Douglas Wilder of Virginia in 1990. b. If attitudes about race have changed substantially in the United States, then Deval Patrick should have won a greater percentage of the white vote in 2006 than Douglas Wilder of Virginia won in 1990.	While African Americans have made substantial inroads into state legislative politics and congressional politics, only two African Americans have been elected governor in the United States: Deval Patrick of Massachusetts (2006) and L. Douglas Wilder of Virginia (1990). Comparing the issue of race in these two elections provides a meaningful opportunity to explore changes in racial attitudes that have occurred in the last fifteen years and to assess the prospects for additional African American governors in the near future.

Specific Issue	Hypotheses	Hints
Term Limits and Gubernatorial Ambition		
Do gubernatorial term limits increase the chance that a governor will run for president?	a. If a governor is from a non-term-limit state, then the governor is unlikely to run for president. b. If term limits create an incentive for governors to run for president, then presidential candidates who were former governors, or are sitting governors, should disproportionately come from term-limit states.	The majority of states limit the number of consecutive terms a governor may serve. This limitation could influence the way that governors behave as they position themselves to run for another office. This issue could be explored by looking at governors who recently ran for president or by analyzing the career paths of two governors, one from a term-limit state and one from a state without term limits.

3. Context and Performance

A. HISTORICAL DEVELOPMENT OF AMERICAN FEDERALISM

State-Centered Federalism (1787–1834)

The initial period of American federalism was one in which the states retained a great deal of autonomy and the balance of power rested with the states. Paradoxically, it was the period in which the states enjoyed the greatest influence, but it was also a period in which federal authority was rapidly increasing. A series of court decisions issued by the **Marshall Court** (i.e., the Supreme Court under the leadership of Chief Justice John Marshall) increased the influence of the federal government at the expense of the states. Two of the most important cases that had this effect were *McCulloch v. Maryland* (1819), which denied states the right to tax a federal bank, and *Gibbons v. Ogden* (1824), which granted Congress broad powers over interstate commerce. The Landmark Supreme Court Cases website provides a thorough discussion of these cases at http://www.landmarkcases.org.

Dual Federalism: Layer-Cake Federalism (1834–1932)

Chief Justice Roger B. Taney and subsequent chief justices attempted to rein in the powers of the federal government and to establish a balance between federal and state rights. It was a period in which the courts generally took a conservative posture, while the legislative and executive branches worked to expand federal influence through a series of constitutional amendments. Political scientists sometimes use the "layer cake" metaphor to describe this period of federalism, also referred to as **dual federalism**, because the federal government and state governments were separate and relatively equal players during this period. Important factors that influenced the state-federal relationship during this period include the following:

- *Dred Scott v. Sandford (1857):* The Supreme Court ruled that Congress lacked the authority to bar slavery in new territories.
- *Civil War Amendments:* The **Civil War Amendments** are a series of constitutional amendments adopted after the Civil War: the **Thirteenth Amendment** (1865) barred slavery, the **Fourteenth Amendment** (1868) extended legal rights to all citizens, and the **Fifteenth Amendment** (1870) barred states from denying voting rights because of race, color, or previous condition of servitude.
- *Plessey v. Ferguson (1896):* The Supreme Court held that state laws that provided separate but equal accommodations for blacks and whites did not violate the equal protection clause of the Fourteenth Amendment.
- *Sixteenth Amendment (1913):* The **Sixteenth Amendment** granted the federal government the power to impose an income tax.
- *Seventeenth Amendment (1913):* The **Seventeenth Amendment** took the Senate selection process away from the states and granted it to the citizens.
- *Eighteenth Amendment (1919):* The **Eighteenth Amendment** prohibited the manufacturing, sale, and importation of intoxicating liquors in all states.
- *Nineteenth Amendment (1920):* The **Nineteenth Amendment** granted women the right to vote in all states.

Cooperative Federalism: Marble-Cake Federalism (1933–1964)

The period of **cooperative federalism** was one in which the federal government began to dominate the federal-state relationship. Political scientists sometimes refer to this period as "marble cake" federalism because the lines between the federal government and the states became blurred. The period began with the presidency of Franklin D. Roosevelt and his **New Deal** programs (a series of federal government programs enacted between 1933 and 1939 that were designed to create jobs and alleviate economic hardships felt during the Great Depression). During this period the federal government and state governments entered into a cooperative arrangement in which the federal government exerted influence over the states through financial assistance.

Creative Federalism (1965–1980)

President Lyndon B. Johnson's **Great Society programs**, which were designed to confront racial discrimination and end poverty in the United States, further concentrated power at the federal level. During this period of **creative federalism**, the federal government's role in funding state projects increased, federal regulations increased, and the use of **categorical grants**, that is, federal grants to the states that require states to spend resources for specific purposes, increased, as did the use of **matching grants**, that is, federal grants that are awarded to states only if they agree to match the federal funds with additional state resources. By end of this period, the Tenth Amendment had lost much of its power to limit federal influence.

New Federalism (1981–2001)

Ronald Reagan's presidency marked a significant shift away from the previous period of federalism. Reagan embarked on process often referred to as **devolution** (public policies that attempt to return power back to the states and local governments). Toward this end, Reagan promoted policies that reduced federal regulations; eliminated **unfunded mandates**, that is, federal requirements that impose additional costs on states but that provide no federal funding; and replaced categorical grants and matching grants with **block grants**, which are broad federal grants awarded to states without the restrictions often associated with categorical grants and matching grants.

Federalism in the Post–September 11 Context (2001–)

Following the terrorist attacks of September 11, 2001, President George W. Bush pursued a course of action that significantly altered the federal-state relationship. Under the Bush administration, the size of the federal government grew substantially (most noticeably in the area of defense spending); the Department of Homeland Security was created and became the nation's largest federal agency; Congress passed the Patriot Act, which increased the powers granted to federal law enforcement agencies; and the states increased their reliance on the federal government to fund state programs. While the influence of the federal government increased during the Bush presidency, it is too early to determine if power will continue to flow toward the federal government in the modern context.

B. THE HISTORICAL DEVELOPMENT OF HOME RULE

Throughout much of American history, local governments were part-time operations. Only the largest cities had full-time elected officials. As cities grew and the services that local governments provided expanded (e.g., education, public health, safety, transportation, zoning), the need for full-time local officials also increased. States addressed the growing need for local services by allowing urban areas to apply for special charters granting them powers once reserved for the state. As more local governments were requested, states began to issue general charters, charters that standardized the functions of local governments in a state. In more recent years, states have given local governments more options when applying for charters. One way states currently do this is by allowing local governments to select among various standard charters (known as optional charters), which enables local governments to select a charter that suits their preference while still allowing the states to achieve a degree of standardization. Another recent trend has been to give local governments more control over their charters by establishing the main criteria of a charter and allowing local leaders to draft their own charter and charter amendments, so long as they stay within the state's guidelines and seek approval from the state (i.e., home rule).

C. THE DECLINE OF POLITICAL MACHINES
AND PARTY BOSSES

The urban politics of large metropolitan areas has traditionally been dominated by a single party, typically the Democratic Party. In the absence of meaningful partisan competition, the dominant party was often able to make use of government contracts, patronage, social programs, and outright corruption to consolidate power in the hands of party leaders. Collectively, the party leaders who dominated urban politics, and sometimes the politics of an entire state, through the mid-twentieth century were referred to as **party machines. Tammany Hall**, the name for New York's political machine, was one of the most notorious machines, though most major metropolitan areas had their own political machines (Chicago, Boston, Philadelphia, Cincinnati, Baltimore, and others). The person who leads a party machine is known as the **party boss**. Party bosses were either elected officials, like Mayor Richard J. Daley in Chicago, or nonelected party leaders, like William Tweed ("Boss Tweed") in New York City. Progressive reforms in the early twentieth century (including competitive bids for government contracts and the replacement of patronage with professional civil-service positions) weakened the urban party machines. Federal social-welfare programs, as well as major shifts in urban demographics, also played major roles in loosening the grip of party machines.

Box 5.3.   Skill Box:
Data-Driven Research Questions

Note that annual federal grants to both state governments and local governments have more than doubled since 1991. Federal grants to state governments have increased by more than $25 billion per year in recent years, and federal grants to local governments have increased by more $2 billion per year in recent years. Table 5.5 raises several interesting research questions: (1) What factors might help explain the upswing in federal spending at the state and local levels? (2) Why do federal contributions to local governments remain relatively low compared with federal contributions to state governments? (3) How does the increase in federal funding change the nature of American federalism? (4) If you were to look at the federal contributions to individual states, rather than the aggregate data for all fifty states, would you expect to see certain states receiving disproportionate funding? (5) Would you expect federal funding to state and local governments to increase or decrease when a single party controls the presidency and Congress? (6) Would you expect differences in funding depending on which party controls federal spending?

Table 5.5.   Federal Government Grants to State and Local Governments (billions of dollars)

Year	State	Local	State and Local
1991–1992	159	20	179
1992–1993	177	21	198
1993–1994	191	23	215
1994–1995	202	26	228
1995–1996	207	26	234
1996–1997	215	28	244
1997–1998	224	30	255
1998–1999	238	31	270
1999–2000	259	32	291
2000–2001	288	35	324
2001–2002	317	42	360
2002–2003	343	45	389
2003–2004	374	50	425
2004–2005	386	52	438

Source: U.S. Census Bureau, http://www.census.gov/govs/www/estimate.html.

Table 5.6. Number of Employees and Gross Payrolls by Governmental Function for Local and State Governments, 2006

	Local		State	
	Employees	Monthly Payroll ($ millions)	Employees	Monthly Payroll ($ millions)
Financial Admin.	223,320	839	169,312	657
Government Admin.	231,747	893	54,556	219
Judicial and Legal	249,553	1,030	170,416	783
Police: Officers	620,411	3,037	65,201	342
Police: Other	194,342	670	39,323	139
Firefighters	301,550	1,537	—	—
Fire: Other	26,162	110	—	—
Correction	249,551	931	238,185	922
Highways	306,904	1,066	3,359	15
Air Transportation	42,575	180	3,359	15
Water Transport	7,280	36	4,838	22
Public Welfare	278,870	942	231,971	774
Health	250,163	911	182,694	687
Hospitals	530,045	2,056	396,728	1,458
Insurance Admin.	—	—	3,297	311
Waste Management	107,506	367	1,886	9
Sewerage	125,795	499	1,730	9
Parks and Rec.	233,213	695	33,913	100
Housing	114,100	435	—	—
Natural Resources	41,715	146	146,593	541
Water Supply	165,221	650	694	3
Electric Power	73,580	393	4,030	24
Gas Supply	12,632	45	—	—
Transit	195,656	867	32,357	167
Elem & Sec: Instr.	4,580,028	18,081	35,644	174
Elem & Sec: Other	2,016,355	4,893	13,296	36
Higher Ed: Inst.	135,048	721	518,385	2,929
Higher Ed: Other	185,565	599	1,049,821	3,467
Other Ed	—	—	91,118	353
Libraries	128,080	376	573	1
Liquor Stores	—	—	7,493	20
Other	258,178	954	205,645	900
Total	11,885,145	43,971	4,250,554	16,769

Source: Compiled by the author from U.S. Census Bureau data, available online at http://ftp2.census.gov/govs/apes/06locus.txt and http://ftp2.census.gov/govs/apes/06stus.txt.

D. STATE AND LOCAL GOVERNMENTS AT WORK

Over 15 million people work for state and local governments, with local government employees accounting for more than 11 million of the total. More than half of public employees at the local level (6.5 million) work in elementary and secondary education. In fact, more people work in elementary- and secondary-education positions than in all other state jobs combined. At the state level, higher education is the largest provider of public jobs, providing more than 1.5 million jobs. Corrections facilities and hospitals are also large sources of public jobs at both the local and state levels. (See table 5.6.)

E. ENDURING CONTEXTUAL QUESTIONS AND HOW TO RESEARCH THEM

Factors That Influence Differences in State Spending Priorities

Table 5.6 suggests that significant services are provided by state and local governments. What this aggregate-level data does not reveal, however, are the substantial differences in the operation of state governments. For example, why do some states invest heavily in higher education while others invest less? Why do

---

Sample Hypothesis

a. If a state government is dominated by a Democratic legislature, then the state will spend a relatively large percentage of its budget on education and social-welfare programs.
b. If a state government is dominated by a Republican legislature, then the state will spend a relatively large percentage of its budget on police protection and corrections facilities.
c. If a state government is dominated by a Republican legislature, then the state will have relatively low per capita state spending.

Hints for Accomplishment

The U.S. Census Bureau maintains an excellent website for investigating spending priorities at the state level (http://www.census.gov/govs/www/state.html). From this site you can obtain state government spending data by year for each state. This data allows you to explore how spending has changed in a specific state over time (i.e., time-series analysis) or to compare spending across states (comparative analysis). The spending information from this site can be combined with other political information to test the sample hypotheses above.

some states spend a relatively high percentage of their budget on highway construction, natural resources, healthcare, or police protection?

American Federalism and the War on Terror

One way the federal government responded to the September 11, 2001, terrorist attacks was to create the Department of Homeland Security. The department's annual budget exceeds $40 billion (the budget is larger than the annual budget of most American states), and the department has a professional staff of more than 180,000 people. Many of the functions of the new department are designed to assist local and state personnel or to provide services previously led by state and local officials, including disaster relief and the protection of critical infrastructure. The Department of Homeland Security also provides more than $1 billion in grants to state and local governments.

Sample Hypothesis

a. If a state spent little on security-related issues prior to 2001, then Homeland Security grants should have a large impact on state and local practices.

b. If Homeland Security grants are being used to increase state and local security capacity, rather than to pay for existing state programs, then the total spent on security issues at the state level should have increased substantially following 2001.

Hints for Accomplishment

The Department of Homeland Security lists the grants given to each state on its website, at http://www.dhs.gov/xgovt/grants/index.shtm. This information can be coupled with state spending information available from the Census Bureau, at http://www.census.gov/govs/www/state.html. Combining these two pieces of information, you can explore the hypotheses above and gain a meaningful understanding of how the Department of Homeland Security is influencing state funding priorities.

F. IDEA GENERATOR: A SAMPLE OF
ADDITIONAL CONTEXTUAL QUESTIONS RELATED
TO STATE AND LOCAL POLITICS

The following chart provides some general guidelines for developing a research plan.

Specific Issue	Hypotheses	Hints

Party Bosses

Specific Issue	Hypotheses	Hints
Searching for evidence of a modern party boss: the case of Chicago	a. If Mayor Richard M. Daley, Richard J. Daley's son, is a modern party boss, then there should be strong evidence that he has made use of patronage in hiring city employees. b. If Mayor Richard M. Daley, Richard J. Daley's son, is a modern party boss, then there should be strong evidence that he has used city contracts to consolidate political power.	Mayor Richard J. Daley dominated Chicago politics from the mid-1950s through the early 1970s, representing one of the last urban bosses. His son, Richard M. Daley, has served as the mayor of Chicago since 1989. Conducting a comparative analysis of the two Daleys could help explain the changing nature of machine politics in the United States. For historical analysis of the Richard J. Daley machine, see Roger Biles, *Richard J. Daley: Politics, Race, and the Governing of Chicago* (Dekalb: Northern Illinois University Press, 1995) and Milton J. Rakove, *Don't Make No Waves—Don't Back No Losers: An Insider's Analysis of the Daley Machine* (Bloomington: Indiana University Press, 1976).

Federalism and Public Education

Specific Issue	Hypotheses	Hints
Do decentralized education policies in the United States lead to funding inequalities in public education?	If schools in a particular state rely primarily on local funds for public education, then the state will have a sizeable gap between funding for schools in wealthy areas and poor areas.	In the United States, public education remains funded primarily at the local level, with local property taxes accounting for the bulk of primary- and secondary-education revenue in most states. One negative consequence of the reliance on local revenue for school funding is that it can lead to a situation in which students from poor

(*continued*)

Specific Issue	Hypotheses	Hints
		areas receive fewer resources than students from affluent areas. A few states, however, fund their schools primarily at the state level, making for interesting comparative analysis. For an excellent source of data on this topic, see Kevin Carey, *The Funding Gap 2004: Many States Still Shortchange Low-Income and Minority Students* (Washington, D.C.: Education Trust, 2004), available online from the Education Trust, at http://www2.edtrust.org (under "Reports and Publications").

The State of American Federalism

Specific Issue	Hypotheses	Hints
In the modern context, do the states truly seek independence from the federal government?	a. If modern states prefer independence from the federal government, then the organization that represents state governors (the National Governors Association) should express concerns regarding the rise in federal influence. b. If modern states prefer independence from the federal government, then the organization that represents state legislatures (the National Conference of State Legislatures) should express concerns regarding the rise in federal influence.	The federal government now freely engages in issues that were once thought of as the domain of state governments (homeland security, public education, highway construction, and others). Some argue that the states actively seek federal influence by sending lobbyists to the nation's capital to obtain additional federal funds and accepting the strings that inevitably come with federal funding. This analysis allows you to consider whether the push for increased federal influence is being actively resisted or welcomed at the state level. A content analysis of the policy positions identified on the websites of the National

Specific Issue	Hypotheses	Hints
		Governors Association (http://www.nga.org) and the National Conference of State Legislatures (http://www.ncsl.org) should help you gauge the level of concern that currently exists among state elected officials regarding federal influence.

4. Secondary Sources That Will Help You Get Started

Bowman, Ann O'M., and Richard C. Kearney. *State and Local Government.* 6th ed. Boston: Houghton Mifflin, 2005.

Beyle, Thad L., ed. *State and Local Government.* Washington, D.C.: CQ Press, 2007.

Council of State Governments. *The Book of States.* Lexington, Ky.: Council of State Governments, 2007.

Dye, Thomas R., and Susan MacManus. *Politics in States and Communities.* 12th ed. Englewood Cliffs, N.J.: Prentice Hall, 2006.

Kincaid, John. *The Encyclopedia of American Federalism.* Washington, D.C.: CQ Press, 2005.

Magleby, David, David O'Brien, Paul Light, James MacGregor Burns, and J. W. Peltason. *State and Local Politics: Government by the People.* 12th ed. Englewood Cliffs, N.J.: Prentice Hall, 2006.

Saffell, David C., and Harry Basehart. *State and Local Government.* 8th ed. New York: McGraw-Hill, 2004.

Stinebrickner, Bruce, ed. *Annual Editions: State and Local Government.* 13th ed. New York: McGraw-Hill, 2006.

5. Original Research That Will Impress Your Professor

Barton, Stephen E., and Carol J. Silverman, eds. *Private Governments and Public Interest.* Berkeley, Calif.: Institute of Government Studies Press, 1994.

Beer, Samuel H. *To Make a Nation: The Rediscovery of American Federalism.* Cambridge, Mass.: Harvard University Press, 1993.

Biles, Roger. *Richard J. Daley: Politics, Race, and the Governing of Chicago.* DeKalb: Northern Illinois University Press, 1995.

Carey, Kevin. *The Funding Gap 2004: Many States Still Shortchange Low-Income and Minority Students.* Washington, D.C.: Education Trust, 2004. Available online from the Education Trust, at http://www2.edtrust.org (under "Reports and Publications").

Clucas, Richard A., ed. *Readings & Cases in State and Local Politics.* Boston: Houghton Mifflin, 2006.

Dahl, Robert A. *Who Governs? Democracy and Power in an American City.* New Haven, Conn.: Yale University Press, 1961.

Dye, Thomas R. *American Federalism: Competition among Governments.* Lexington, Mass.: Lexington Books, 1990.

Elazar, Daniel J. *The American Partnership.* Chicago: University of Chicago Press, 1962.

Erikson, Robert, Gerald C. Wright, and John P. McIver. *Statehouse Democracy: Public Opinion and Policy in the American States.* Cambridge, U.K.: Cambridge University Press, 1993.

Gray, Virginia, and Russell L. Hanson, eds. *Politics in the American States: A Comparative Analysis.* 8th ed. Washington, D.C.: CQ Press, 2003.

Horn, Carl E. Van, ed. *The State of the States.* 4th ed. Washington, D.C.: CQ Press, 2006.

Light, Paul C. *The New True Size of Government: Organizational Performance Initiative.* Organizational Performance Initiative Research Brief no. 2. New York: Robert F. Wagner Graduate School of New York University, 2006. Available online at http://wagner.nyu.edu/performance/files/True_Size.pdf.

Nagel, Robert F. *The Implosion of Federalism.* New York: Oxford University Press, 2001.

Rakove, Milton J. *Don't Make No Waves—Don't Back No Losers: An Insider's Analysis of the Daley Machine.* Bloomington: Indiana University Press, 1976.

Renzulli, Diane. *Capitol Offenders: How Private Interests Govern Our States.* Washington, D.C.: Public Integrity Books, 2000.

Rosenthal, Alan. *Drawing the Line: Legislative Ethics in the States.* Lincoln: University of Nebraska Press, 1996.

Sabato, Larry J., Bruce A. Larson, and Howard R. Ernst, eds. *Dangerous Democracy? The Battle over Ballot Initiatives in America.* Lanham, Md.: Rowman & Littlefield, 2001.

Tarr, G. Alan. *Understanding State Constitutions.* Princeton, N.J.: Princeton University Press, 1998.

Walker, David B. *The Rebirth of Federalism.* 2nd ed. Chatham, N.J.: Chatham House, 2000.

6. Where to Find It

Where can I find the complete text of the *Federalist Papers*?

Yale Law School's Avalon Project has a complete set of the *Federalist Papers*, at http://www.yale.edu/lawweb/avalon/federal/fed.htm.

Where can I find links to state governments and information on trends in state politics?
The Council of State Governments maintains a website, at http://www.csg.org, with links to state governments, as well as information on state trends and policies. You can also find helpful links at State and Local Government on the Net, http://www.statelocalgov.net.

Where can I find data about disparities in education funding at the state level?
The Education Trust, an education advocacy group, supports research on this topic, and you can find helpful data and publications on their website, at http://www2.edtrust.org.

Where can I find information about the diversity of state judges?
The Lawyers' Committee for Civil Rights under Law, http://www.lawyers committee.org, conducts studies on this topic and has published a report, "Answering the Call for a More Diverse Judiciary," available online at http://www .lawyerscommittee.org/2005website/publications/images/judicialdiversity.report .pdf.

Where can I find information about recent ballot measures and data about the initiative and referendum processes?
The Initiative & Referendum Institute at the University of Southern California maintains a great website on this topic, at http://www.iandrinstitute.org.

Where can I find information about state and local governments?
For information on state courts, see the National Center for State Courts website, at http://www.ncsconline.org/D_Research/Ct_Struct/Index.html. For information on state legislatures, see the National Conference of State Legislatures website, at http://www.ncsl.org. For information on governors, see the National Governors Association website, at http://www.nga.org. And for information on mayors, see the United States Conference of Mayors website, at http://www .usmayors.org/USCM/home.asp.

Where can I find a brief history of Nebraska's unicameral legislature?
Go to the Nebraska legislature's website, at http://nebraskalegislature.gov/web/ public/history.

Where can I find more information about landmark Supreme Court cases related to federalism?

The Landmark Supreme Court Cases website, http://www.landmarkcases.org, developed by Street Law and the Supreme Court Historical Society, provides summaries (as well as links to the full opinions) of landmark Supreme Court cases, including *Marbury v. Madison* (1803), *McCulloch v. Maryland* (1819), *Gibbons v. Ogden* (1824), and *Dred Scott v. Sandford* (1857).

How can I compare state tax policies?

You can find information on state tax policies on the Tax Foundation website, at http://www.taxfoundation.org/research/topic/9.html.

Where can I find aggregate data for state and local spending and revenue sources?

Go to the U.S. Census Bureau website, at http://www.census.gov/govs/www/index .html.

Where can I find information about term limits in all fifty states?

U.S. Term Limits, a nonprofit group, tracks state term limits, and has compiled a summary, available at http://termlimits.org/state-information.

CHAPTER 6

The Media

The media play a critical role informing the public. The term *media* is both grammatically and conceptually plural, indicating a wide variety of communications technologies (newspapers, radio, television, the Internet, etc.) that serve as intermediaries between real-world events and interested audiences. None of us wants to know everything about everything. Such information overload would overwhelm and debilitate us. On the other hand, there are certain important facts and ideas we need to know about our world in order to effectively engage in it. As "mediators," the media must pick and choose among events to cover and decide what story will be told. As media consumers, we audience members ideally pick and choose among the individual mediums that best serve our information needs.

1. The Structure and Function of the Media

A. CONSTITUTIONAL AND LEGAL BASIS

The First Amendment to the Constitution gives the media special protection: "The *Congress shall make no law* respecting an establishment of religion, or prohibiting the free exercise thereof; or *abridging the freedom* of speech, or *of the press*; or the right of the people peaceably to assemble, and to petition the Government for a redress of grievances."

The framers were, of course, limited by their understanding of the technology of the day. While the printing press is now only one communication tool, the courts have struggled to fit new technologies into the general goal of the framers to provide wide and unfettered access to information. James Madison set

187

the tone in arguing that "*a popular Government, without popular information, or the means of acquiring it, is but a Prologue to a Farce or a Tragedy; or, perhaps both. Knowledge will forever govern ignorance: And a people who mean to be their own Governors, must arm themselves with the power knowledge gives.*"[1]

Working from the context of these constitutional guarantees, the courts have attempted to preserve the free "press," while recognizing particular dangers and limitations. The courts have, as a general rule, disallowed **prior restraint**, which refers to blocking the publication or broadcast of information before it is disseminated, but have allowed punishment in some cases after the fact. The media, like all individuals, can be punished for libel (written untruths) and slander (spoken untruths).

As new technologies developed, each medium was eventually placed into one of two tracks. Newspapers, other print media, and eventually the Internet became classified as *publications* over which the government had little responsibility or control. The number of newspapers, magazines, newsletters, and Internet sites are expandable without harming the initial practitioners. Television and radio, on the other hand, use limited electronic frequencies, which if overused, would lead to the babble of multiple signals fading in and out. These media became classified as **common carriers** using inherently public resources, the frequencies. This opened the door for licensing, with approval based on a politically defined set of criteria for the public good. As the physical limitations declined with technologies such as cable television, the impetus for governmental regulation declined. Countries vary significantly as to the freedom they provide their media (see table 6.1).

Table 6.1.   Just How Free Is the Free Press? The Lower the Score, the Freer the Media

Rank	Country	Score
1	Finland	0.50
—	Iceland	0.50
—	Ireland	0.50
—	Netherlands	0.50
5	Czech Republic	0.75
6	Estonia	2.00
—	Norway	2.00
8	Slovakia	2.50
—	Switzerland	2.50
10	Hungary	3.00
—	Latvia	3.00
—	Portugal	3.00
—	Slovenia	3.00
14	Belgium	4.00
—	Sweden	4.00

Rank	Country	Score
16	Austria	4.50
—	Bolivia	4.50
—	Canada	4.50
19	Bosnia and Herzegovina	5.00
—	Denmark	5.00
—	New Zealand	5.00
—	Trinidad and Tobago	5.00
23	Benin	5.50
—	Germany	5.50
—	Jamaica	5.50
26	Namibia	6.00
27	Lithuania	6.50
—	United Kingdom	6.50
29	Costa Rica	6.67
30	Cyprus	7.50
31	South Korea	7.75
32	Greece	8.00
—	Mauritius	8.00
34	Ghana	8.50
35	Australia	9.00
—	Bulgaria	9.00
—	France	9.00
—	Mali	9.00
39	Panama	9.50
40	Italy	9.90
41	El Salvador	10.00
—	Spain	10.00
43	Taiwan	10.50
44	South Africa	11.25
45	Cape Verde	11.50
—	Macedonia	11.50
—	Mozambique	11.50
—	Serbia and Montenegro	11.50
49	Chile	11.63
50	Israel	12.00
51	Japan	12.50
52	Dominican Republic	12.75
53	Botswana	13.00
—	Croatia	13.00
—	Tonga	13.00
—	United States	13.00
57	Uruguay	13.75
58	Fiji	14.00
—	Hong Kong	14.00
—	Poland	14.00

(continued)

Table 6.1. *(continued)*

Rank	Country	Score
—	Romania	14.00
62	Central African Republic	14.50
—	Cyprus (North)	14.50
—	Guinea-Bissau	14.50
—	Honduras	14.50
66	Madagascar	15.00
—	Togo	15.00
68	Ecuador	15.25
69	Nicaragua	15.50
70	Burkina Faso	16.00
—	Kosovo	16.00
—	Lesotho	16.00
73	Congo	17.00
—	Kuwait	17.00
75	Brazil	17.17
76	Argentina	17.30
77	Mauritania	17.50
—	Senegal	17.50
—	United Arab Emirates	17.50
80	Albania	18.00
—	Qatar	18.00
82	Paraguay	18.25
83	Timor-Leste	18.50
84	Liberia	19.00
85	Moldova	19.17
86	Mongolia	19.25
87	Haiti	19.50
88	Tanzania	19.82
89	Georgia	21.00
90	Guatemala	21.25
91	Angola	21.50
92	Malaysia	22.25
93	Comoros	22.50
—	Zambia	22.50
95	Niger	24.50
—	Seychelles	24.50
97	Morocco	24.83
98	Bhutan	25.00
—	Ivory Coast	25.00
—	Turkey	25.00
101	Armenia	25.50
—	Malawi	25.50

Source: Country rankings based on the Reporters without Borders press freedom index, available at http://www.rsf.org/rubrique.php3?id_rubrique=639. Low index values indicate more freedom.

B. GOALS AND INTENTIONS OF THE MEDIA

Understanding the goals and intentions of the media requires recognizing the three participants in the process of transmitting a story. *Newsmakers* may be intentional (a politician holding a news conference) or accidental (the store owner shot in a robbery). They may want to promote the story, attempt to control how it is told, or try to keep it from the public. The *media* (which include the reporters who cover a story and the editors who run the newsroom) serve as transmission vehicles, identifying stories of greatest interest or importance and passing them on to the larger public. They may be attempting to promote a certain outlook, but more often are attempting to maintain their economic viability by garnering an adequate audience to satisfy whoever is underwriting their costs. Both the newsmakers and media are interested in the impact of the story (or nonstory) on the *audience.* Increasingly that audience has a choice of what they will tune in to, to get the information they deem necessary.

There is no clear definition of what *news* is. News is essentially something out of the ordinary, something new and different. It is often something different happening to someone of extraordinary importance. Automobile accidents happen every moment of every day, but if one involves a public official or an entertainment figure, it is more likely to be news, especially if it involves alcohol or drugs. In writing a story, journalists are trained to answer the five Ws: Who? What? Where? When? and Why?

No concept related to the media is more controversial than **bias**. The media's attention to the unique interjects a bias in and of itself, but the criticism is more associated with perceptions that the media picks and chooses from among unique events in an unfair manner. News consumers ask, "Why can't the media just tell it like it is?" Bias is a misleading representation of reality. It is more than reporting something good or bad about a news subject. It is focusing on the bad or good to the exclusion of legitimate stories on the other side. If a president loses a crucial vote in Congress, that is legitimate news. If, on the other hand, he also won three crucial votes that day, it would be biased to present a story with the headline "President Loses Crucial Vote" without mentioning that his legislative record for that day was really three out of four. Focusing on things that are out of the ordinary makes news interesting but creates the impression that crime, conflict, and other rare occurrences are the norm. News would be pretty boring if it covered the routine. The unbiased journalist has the responsibility to provide the context as to why a particular news item was out of the ordinary and important enough to be included.

Some bias is both intentional and legitimate. The *Wall Street Journal* focuses on business news, often to the exclusion of other topics. It is appealing to the substantive interests of its readers, who have some expectation of its intentional focus. Bias is more problematic when a medium presents only one political viewpoint, especially if its consumers are expecting a balanced story that gives them all relevant perspectives.

The expectations and operations of the media have changed over the course of U.S. history. Many of the earliest newspapers in America were closely tied to one of the political parties. Consumers chose the newspaper that best fit their own political perspectives. The newspaper was used more to gather ammunition than for objective edification. The goal of providing objective reporting took a backseat to promoting a political perspective in the partisan era. Once in office, the party would reward printers from their party with government printing contracts.

During the second half of the nineteenth century, newspapers began to depend on wider circulation and advertising for revenue. To secure new readers, they cut their prices (the so-called **penny presses**) and became less partisan. Journalism became more of a profession, with formal training and accepted norms. The goal of objectivity became more established.

Throughout much of the twentieth century, the concept of "**mass media**" legitimately described the media environment. Local independent newspapers declined as newspaper chains brought about more uniformity in news coverage. The locally controlled newspapers that remained depended on national news services for other than local coverage. Radio and television began with a plethora of locally owned stations, but soon the news, especially on the national level, was dominated by a small number of networks. Increasingly there was a great deal of overlap in the national news one received, no matter where one lived. News became more homogeneous and instantaneous.

By the end of the twentieth century, new waves of technological change emerged. Cable television, from its infancy in the 1970s, had grown into a major medium by the end of the century, stealing viewers from the major networks by providing niche programming that appealed to relatively narrow segments of the public. Closely on the heels of cable, the Internet provided a vast array of information and a vehicle through which interested individuals could seek out only the information they desired. Newspapers and television news found their audiences dropping in size and lacking many of the younger generations. Websites and cable programming could take more of a political perspective and still appeal to a large enough niche of consumers to survive economically. Blogs have created a new variety of self-publishing that political candidates and causes have capitalized on. The modern era is one of fragmented audiences in which only the most momentous stories are spread widely in a uniform manner. The 24-hour news cycle gives both political leaders and the public little time to consider their reaction to stories that are often reported in real time.

There is no complete consensus on the role of the media. The media as a *proponent of narrow partisan or ideological perspectives* (the **partisan press**) has largely been discredited. A more neutral version of an activist media is promoted by the advocates of **civic journalism**. They encourage journalistic initiatives supporting democracy by actively encouraging civic engagement. Civic journalistic efforts include media-supported issues forums, polling, and get-out-the-vote drives. Serving as *objective observers of reality* or as *watchdogs* over government and society are journalistic roles that receive almost universal support among journalists and the public.

C. COMPARATIVE PERSPECTIVE

Probably the most unique characteristic of American media is its almost universal grounding in private enterprise. Unlike most countries, the U.S. government does not control or directly subsidize major media outlets, but the government certainly attempts to influence the media by creating media events and catering to the information needs of journalists. The U.S. government does establish the business and civil-liberties environment in which media outlets have the opportunity to succeed or fail according to the same criterion, the ability to make a profit.

The U.S. guarantees freedom of expression in almost all cases. Prepublication censorship is virtually unheard of. The test of acceptable taste and utility provided to the customer determines one's ability to sell a media product.

The United States leads the world in access to electronic media, with more than 2,000 television broadcast stations, 13,000 radio stations, and more than 200 million Internet users. India, on the other hand, a nation with more than one billion people, has only 562 television stations and 60 million Internet users, though it produces far more newspapers per person than the United States does.[2] Access to media is generally correlated to a country's income.

D. ENDURING STRUCTURAL QUESTIONS ABOUT THE MEDIA AND HOW TO RESEARCH THEM

To What Degree Has the Media Become Concentrated?

Variety and choice have long been seen as positive hallmarks of a vibrant media environment. Changing consumer habits and economies of scale have led to the concentration of media ownership, since chain operations allow a number of media outlets to share news-collection and production costs. However, concentrated ownership and production reduces variety. Despite population growth,

Number of U.S. Daily News Papers (1940-2005)

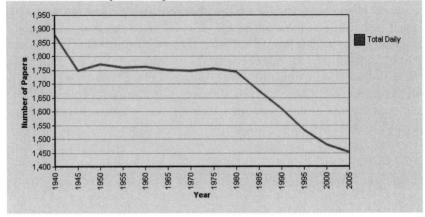

Circulation of U.S. Daily News Papers (1940-2005)

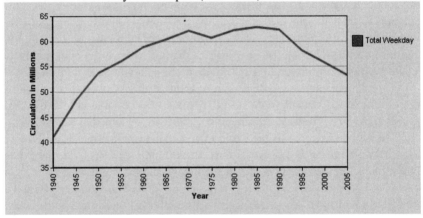

Figure 6.1.   Number of U.S. newspapers.
Source: Project for Excellence in Journalism "The State of the News Media 2007" (http://www.state
ofthenewsmedia.org/2007/narrative_newspapers_charts_and_tables.asp?cat=9&media=3)

the number of newspapers published, and the number of copies printed, has declined (see figure 6.1). Not all types of newspapers have been equally affected.

How Has the Constitutional Definition of "the Press" Been Expanded?

While the framer's physical image of "the press" involved a rather crude process
of inking trays of letters and transferring them under pressure to paper, their
philosophical commitment was to grant broad freedom to those who spread information throughout society.

Sample Hypothesis

If you wanted access to a newspaper in the 1970s (or some other previous date), then you would have had more options than if you wanted access in the 2000s.

Hints for Accomplishment

Harold Stanley and Richard Niemi, *Vital Statistics on American Politics* (Washington, D.C.: CQ Press), provides additional data. If you are interested in who owns a particular media outlet (print or electronic), or the media outlets in a particular city, the *Columbia Journalism Review* offers a keyword-searchable database at http://www.cjr.org/tools/owners.

Sample Hypothesis

If the courts view the framers' intentions as a philosophical commitment to free expression by the media, then they will apply the constitutional principle broadly and permit only the most pressing limitations on the media.

Hints for Accomplishment

The courts are tasked with applying general constitutional principles to specific cases. At times, two or more constitutional principles seem to be in conflict. By tracking Supreme Court cases over time, you can see how the Court's thinking has changed, especially as it has been challenged by new technologies or new uses of old technologies. A number of sources will help you. Linda Monk, *The Bill of Rights: A User's Guide* (Alexandria, Va.: Close Up Publishing, 1991) provides a concise discussion of freedom of the press and the key court cases associated with it. J. Sue Davis, *Corwin & Peltason's Understanding the Constitution*, 17th ed. (Belmont, Calif.: Thomson/Wadsworth, 2008) provides similar coverage. The FindLaw website provides a searchable catalog of free-press cases at http://caselaw.lp.findlaw.com/data/constitution/amendment01.

E. IDEA GENERATOR:
THE ROLE OF THE MEDIA IN SOCIETY

The following chart provides some general guidelines for developing a research plan.

Specific Issue	Hypotheses	Hints
Free Press		
Advantages and disadvantages	If press rights were more limited, then society would be more stable.	While most Americans take a free press as an absolute given, many countries see a free press as a luxury having costs. Look at statements by leaders of countries with more constrained media to see how they justify the limitations. (See the Freedom House classification of countries, at http://www .freedomhouse.org/ template.cfm?page=16.)
Role of the Media		
Civic journalism	a. If a media outlet joins the civic-journalism initiative, then it has lost its objectivity. b. If a media outlet joins the civic-journalism initiative, then it becomes a productive partner in its political community.	Join the debate over civic journalism by exploring both sides of the issue and taking a stand yourself. The Pew Center for Civic Journalism provides a broad range of arguments supporting civic journalism, at http://www .pewcenter.org. Arguments in opposition to civic journalism can be found in various journalism journals.
Press Freedom		
Correlates	a. If a country's political system is less democratic, then it will grant its press less freedom. b. If a country has high illiteracy, then it will grant its media less freedom.	Divide countries into three or four press-freedom categories (see table 6.1). Then categorize them into three or four other categories according to other criteria you think might be relevant and see if there is a pattern. Democracy rankings are provided by World Audit, at http://www.worldaudit .org.democracy.htm, and

Specific Issue	Hypotheses	Hints
		by Freedom House, at http://www.freedomhouse .org/template .cfm?page=15. Country economic and educational data are available from UNESCO, at http://www.uis.unesco .org/profiles.

2. Participants

A. THE MEDIA PLAYERS

Politics in representative democracies is a conversation between citizens and public officials facilitated by the media. The nature of the conversation is affected by the *newsmakers* who do newsworthy things, the *media professionals* who report it, and the *audience*, which has the choice of what captures its attention and how that is interpreted. News does not exist in a vacuum but is animated by choices the participants make.

The Journalists

As journalism has become a profession, educational requirements and career paths have become more structured. As in most professions, journalists are not a random sample of the U.S. population. Journalists tend to be educated in the humanities and social sciences. Research indicates that individuals with liberal outlooks are drawn to those majors. While considerably more women graduate from college in journalism,[3] men have a greater, but declining, percentage of key positions in the media.

Demographics mean relatively little if they fail to translate into the nature of the news reported. The critical unanswered question is the degree to which personal political preferences affect political reporting. If men collect and report news differently from women, or if ethnic minorities cover stories differently from nonminorities, then demographics are key variables. It is also important to ask if editors share the political preferences of their journalists, as it is the editors who ultimately decide which stories make the paper. Another important factor to consider is the preferences of advertisers, as they fund the papers and contribute to the salaries of editors and reporters.

The Newsmakers

Only a small portion of the population acts in such a way as to make news. Public officials (and those battling to become officials) dominate stories about politics and government and seek to guide the conversation. The U.S. media tends to be particularly personality oriented. Journalists develop stories around **news hooks**, well-known individuals whose activities and experiences are easy to describe, which reduces the time needed to introduce the main character.

By adjusting the rules of access, officials gain some control over what stories the media tell. In the 2000 presidential campaign, John McCain (R-Ariz.) gained good coverage by widely opening all aspects of his campaign to the media and in the process forced his opponents to be more open. After experimentation with widely varying sets of rules in previous conflicts, the Pentagon changed its policy during the early stages of the Iraq war and allowed journalists to **embed** themselves with military units. Presidents getting good news coverage tend to provide more access to the media than presidents who are struggling and thus prefer to limit contact.

Most public officials and interest groups have press secretaries, if not an entire office, charged with managing their news coverage. Press secretaries not only arrange positive settings in which the official faces the media but also serve as spokespersons when the official is not available. Both officials and their spokespersons attempt to **spin** stories, focusing on the positive and downplaying the negative.

Given the fragmented media audience, strategic officials have expanded the types of media through which they attempt to communicate. While the national news programs once had almost exclusive access to key public officials, cable networks such as CNN, Fox, and C-SPAN can now draw public officials. These officials have recognized the value of appearing on networks that appeal to news and public-affairs "junkies."

The Audience

With increasing choices between media, it has become clear that it is not enough to know what the media broadcasts; one must also know who is tuning in to which media. It is no surprise that the media themselves, as commercial enterprises competing for the same advertising dollars, help underwrite detailed analyses of viewers and readers. Public-opinion polling and direct monitoring are used to determine who tunes in to which media and at what time so that advertisers can select the audiences they want to hear their advertisements. Individual demographics (age, gender, education, race, etc.) differ across various media. Readership of hard-copy newspapers has declined as consumers, led by younger age groups, first moved to television and now show considerable interest in using the Internet to gather information. Political news is not the first choice of most news consumers, which presents a challenge to those desiring to inform and change political views through the media.

B. ENDURING QUESTIONS ABOUT THE PARTICIPANTS AND HOW TO RESEARCH THEM

Who Are the Journalists, How Do They View Politics, and What Difference Does It Make?

Some observers argue that professional journalists are able to serve as objective observers despite their own views, or that other constraints, such as differing views of editors and owners, dampen bias. Others believe that it is virtually impossible to "check one's political preferences at the door." The potential for bias is clear to many observers when considering the heavy liberal and Democratic Party preferences of the major media players. Other observers argue that journalists can rise above their personal preferences and cover events objectively. Rather than testing a particular hypothesis, you might begin a research paper with a description of the political preferences of journalists, proceed to an analysis of competing assertions about journalists' political preferences, and then come to a conclusion yourself.

Sample Hypothesis

a. If you are a member of the media, then you have different ideological views than the general public.
b. If you are a member of the media, then you have different partisan preferences than the general public.
c. If you are a member of the media, then your political views will lead to bias in your reporting.

Hints for Accomplishment

In 2001, the Media Research Center (a conservative watchdog group) conducted an extensive survey of media professionals on their ideological and partisan views. The results are available at http://secure.mediaresearch.org (check out "Special Reports," "Profiles in Bias," and "Media Reality Check"). Results from a 2005 survey by the University of Connecticut can be found at http://importance.corante.com/archives/UCONN_DPP_Press_Release.pdf. Arguments both for and against the bias of journalists can be found in books such as Bernard Goldberg, *Bias* (Washington, D.C.: Regency Press, 2002) and Eric Altman, *What Liberal Media?* (New York: Basic Books, 2003). After outlining the demographics and political views of media professionals, speculate on the "worst-case scenario." What if they reported only on the basis of their personal views and self-interest? To what degree do you see the media rising above its personal biases and reporting objectively?

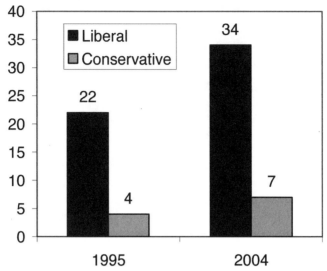

Figure 6.2.   Percent of journalists and media executives identifying themselves as liberal or conservative.
Source: Pew Research Center for the People and the Press, May 2004. Further information and data available at http://www.mediaresearch.org/SpecialReports/2004/report063004_p3.asp, and http://people-press.org/reports/pdf/214topline.pdf.

Who Gets Covered by the Media?

News stories need a "**news hook**," the character of the story from which the eventual news report proceeds. Many political news stories focus on events surrounding a limited number of individuals or institutions. Journalists ask, "Who did what?" or "Who had what happen to them?" Being seen as a legitimate news hook invites careful scrutiny but also grants the potential for getting one's views heard. Whatever the president does is almost by definition news, while similar actions (speeches, news conferences, etc.) by junior members of Congress are seldom covered. Some variations in being a news subject are obviously based on the importance of the position, while others may reflect the skills of the news subject or bias by the media.

Good news hooks are well-known individuals who hold important positions. A well-known individual does not have to be introduced to the audience, something that eats up significant space or broadcast time. Having access to the news allows one to make his or her case. It is possible that spokespersons and commentators are chosen for convenience or out of habit rather than according to news criteria. In the following project, you are interested in the degree to which the "usual suspects" dominate the news.

Sample Hypothesis

Someone from the president's party (not from the president's party, from a large state, etc.) is more likely to be a guest on a Sunday news program.

Hints for Accomplishment

A number of sources allow you to determine who has access to the American public through the media. Your task is to determine whether particular types of people are quoted or serve as talk-show guests. Variations in the frequency of access to the media is not necessarily inappropriate, since some people are simply much more in the middle of important news. Your goal is to determine whether the distribution of opportunities seems reasonable. For example, if 52 percent of the Senators are Democrats, should they make up 65 percent of the guests on the Sunday news programs? If only 26 percent of the governors are from the eastern portion of the United States,[4] should they get 50 percent of the opportunities to make their case? You will need to establish a "baseline" against which you can compare media access. Each of the Sunday programs has a website that lists guests. For *Meet the Press*, go to http://www.msnbc.msn.com/id/8987534. For *Face the Nation*, try http://www.cbsnews.com/stories/2005/07/25/podcast_nation/main711465.shtml. For a liberal analysis of talk-show guests, see Media Matters for America, *If It's Sunday, It's Conservative* (Washington, D.C., 2006), http://mediamatters.org/static/pdf/MMFA_Sunday_Show_Report.pdf. The Vanderbilt Television News Archive, http://tvnews.vanderbilt.edu/, and Google provide search engines that allow you to determine who is mentioned in the media. A search by title ("governor," "senator," etc.) would generate data for evaluation and analysis. In doing database searches, watch for inappropriate hits. There may be more than one "Senator Smith," so you could pick up a mention of a state senator when you are monitoring a national one.

To What Degree Can Newsmakers Control the Stories about Themselves?

The press conference and formal speech remain the key vehicles for setting or changing the political agenda. They are the rare times when a public official has direct access to the media and the public. Public officials attempt to use such events to transmit visual, oral, and symbolic messages.

Who Tunes in to Which Media?

While the dictionary does not include the word "municate," it represents "communication" without the "co." If no one is tuning in to the media, it is irrelevant. The mix of media audiences is critical as media search out advertisers and news subjects to cover. Over time, the fortunes of different media have changed dramatically, forcing them to shut down (the fate of most afternoon newspapers),

---

Sample Hypothesis

If a public official makes a public statement, then his or her key points will make it to the public via the media.

Hints for Accomplishment

Find the full recording or transcript of a speech or news conference (see section 5 below for sources). Think about how the event was "staged" for maximum positive coverage. What was the setting, and what were the hoped-for implications? Which words were chosen, and which words were rejected? How did the newsmaker accommodate the needs of the different kinds of media? Look at media coverage for a few days prior to the event and follow it for a few days after the event. Did the media pick up on the key issues? Did they fairly represent the views of the speaker? For a current speech, you might want to use blogpulse.com to measure the immediate amount of discussion generated among bloggers. By going into the "trends" section and placing the speaker and the topic in the search line with an "and" between them, you can see the relevant discussion over time and see if changes correlate with a speech or press conference. Remember that bloggers are not a large or representative sample of the public.

---

change their role (radio moving from hot news to more "background noise" that one pays little attention to), or expand its services (newspapers with websites and network television moving into cable). Media executives spend a great deal of time looking at audience and readership surveys in an attempt to determine the future. A major question mark is the degree to which current usage patterns will carry over into the future.

Sample Hypothesis

The media habits of (members of a specific demographic) differ from those of other groups.

Hints for Accomplishment

The most extensive current polling on media usage is done by the Pew Research Center for the People and the Press, whose data can be found at http://people-press.org. Use the search box and enter "media consumption" to find a wide variety of national poll results.

First, put yourself in the place of a media executive. What do these figures tell you about the future of each medium? What advice would you be most comfortable in giving about change? Second, think of yourself as a politician (you select the position and constituency). Think about which medium you would like to use. Justify your answer by indicating your goal and audience preference.

C. IDEA GENERATOR: WHO ARE THE MEDIA PLAYERS?

The following chart provides some general guidelines for developing a research plan.

Specific Issue	Hypotheses	Hints
Journalists		
Demographics and bias	If you "make it" in the media, then you are different from the public as a whole.	Compare the demographics of different types of media players (anchors, morning news personalities, foreign correspondents, etc.). Compare their demographics with those of the U.S. population as a whole. Most outlets list biographies of their key players on their websites. You will need to determine which demographic characteristics are important (age, gender, race, education, etc.). Speculate on the causes and consequences of the variations you find.
Newsmakers as News Hooks		
Individuals versus organizations	If a story is written, then the news hook is more likely to be the individual than the organization of which that individual is a part.	Calculate the number of references in a story, or set of stories, to an individual as opposed to the individual's position or organization.
Audience		
Changing preferences	If younger citizens use certain types of news media today, then they are likely to continue that pattern of usage in the future.	Different usage patterns could be generational or associated with life stage. Generational arguments assume that once established, usage patterns are unlikely to change. Life-stage

(continued)

Specific Issue	Hypotheses	Hints
		arguments rest on the idea that at different times in one's life, different media are of more interest and use. Speculate on which of these arguments seems most valid to you.
	Public Relations	
Strategies	If you do it "right," then you will get good news coverage.	Set up an interview with one of the professionals in your college or university public-relations office or with a public-relations person (often called press secretary) in a political or governmental office. Ask him or her to outline strategies for getting good coverage.

3. Context and Performance of the Media

A. HISTORICAL DEVELOPMENT

The media has had to adapt to technological developments, societal change, and public preferences. There is often a delicate balance between what *can* be done and what *should* be done. Contemporary media attempt to appeal to an audience that increasingly wants summarized, relevant, and instant information delivered according to the audience's schedule.

The age of the local newspaper editor or electronic media producer attempting to please a relatively homogeneous local readership or audience gave way to large chain newspapers and network television. Just as the mass media industry reached its stride, it was refragmented. This time audiences and readerships were based not on geography but along the lines of preferences. Cable television and then websites attracted people with narrow interests by providing them with information tailored to their preferences. Some stories percolated through the entire media spectrum, while many bypassed the bulk of the population as they were picked up by people tuned in to only a small segment of the media.

Table 6.2.   What Kind of Media Coverage Does the Public Want?

Better if coverage of the war on terror is . . .	March 1991 (%)	April 2003 (%)	June 2005 (%)
Neutral	71	69	68
Pro American	22	23	24

Source: The Pew Research Center for the People and the Press, http://people-press.org/reports/display.php3?ReportID=248.

B. PUBLIC SUPPORT AND EXPECTATIONS

In one sense, audiences "vote" with their remotes, keyboards, and checkbooks. Shifting audiences tell a great deal about what people want and what they willingly ignore. Specific television programs are evaluated by ratings, the percentage of households with televisions tuned in to a program at a particular time. Extensive surveys by the Nielsen Company outline the audience size and demographics. Hit counters on some websites provide another measure of the appeal some sites have. (See section 5 below.) Survey data indicate that the public prefers media coverage that is neutral, even on a sensitive issue such as terrorism (see table 6.2).

Views on the performance of the media tend to be filtered through one's political views. More Republicans than Democrats see the media as too critical of America (see tables 6.3 and 6.4).

C. THE MEDIA AT WORK

The media often find themselves in a bind. The dominance of privately owned media in America means that media must find an audience in order to have a product to sell to advertisers. In appealing to an audience, the media often find that the potential audience says one thing and does another. They say they want in-depth coverage of policy yet gravitate toward **tabloid stories** of murder, rape, and mayhem; the cliché "if it bleeds, it leads" reflects a great deal of coverage.

Table 6.3.   Is the Media Too Critical of America?

	July 2002 (% yes)	June 2005 (% yes)
Republicans	42	67
Democrats	26	24
Independents	39	33
Total	35	40

Source: The Pew Research Center for the People and the Press, http://people-press.org/reports/display.php3?ReportID=248.

Table 6.4 Does the Media Hurt Democracy?

	July 2002 (% yes)	June 2005 (% yes)
Republicans	36	43
Democrats	28	27
Independents	22	33
Total	29	33

Source: The Pew Research Center for the People and the Press, http://people-press
.org/reports/display.php3?ReportID=248.

Political journalists gather news in a variety of ways. Some are on a **beat** (the White House, Congress, the Supreme Court), where they cover the same people and issues over a period of time. This offers them a great deal of detailed information and personal contacts but can bias them toward the people whose help they need for good stories. Other journalists cover a wide range of newsmakers and institutions, making them less knowledgeable but potentially able to have a broader perspective.

D. ENDURING QUESTIONS ON THE CONTEXT AND PERFORMANCE OF THE MEDIA AND HOW TO RESEARCH THEM

What Is Bias and How Can We Discover It?

For the media analyst, bias is a distorted presentation of reality. Biased coverage may result from either the *amount* of coverage or its *political slant*.

Bias as an Unjustified Amount of Coverage. Remaining uncovered in politics means being invisible. Most newsmakers want as much coverage as, if not more coverage than, their opponents. In a political campaign, for example, we would expect that all legitimate candidates have equal access to the public through the media. If one candidate receives more coverage than another, the public is receiving less information on which to base their voting choice. Journalists might justify different amounts of coverage by arguing that some candidates (e.g., third-party candidates) are less legitimate newsmakers since they have little chance of winning. Or they might argue that some candidates are better at generating coverage. One could compare the amount of coverage of various candidates, elected officials, institutions, or policy realms by measuring the number of column inches in a set of newspapers or the number of mentions on television news. This would serve as the basis for testing hypotheses about bias toward different news subjects and comparing bias in different media outlets. See box 6.1, on content analysis, before creating your hypothesis and planning your research.

In creating your hypothesis, you might want to determine whether different media outlets provide different amounts of coverage for the same events (the events of the previous few days). Alternatively, you might want to see if different newsmakers receive different amounts of coverage across a number of media outlets.

Box 6.1. Skill Box: Content Analysis

Content analysis is a systematic and replicable technique for gathering comparable empirical data on witten or spoken content. In studying the media, the unit of analysis might be an entire newscast, the home page of a website, a paragraph in a newspaper story, or the adjectives used to describe a political figure. In other contexts, content analysis is used to evaluate speeches, political campaign advertisements, or any other phenomena with differing content. The **unit of analysis** is *that entity on which the researcher gathers data.* The next step is to determine what data to gather. The process might be simple. For example, you might look at the websites of the two major political parties and two third parties to determine effectiveness, recording characteristics such as number of hits, timeliness, quality of graphics, and so on. This would allow you to test a hypothesis such as "The websites of the major political parties tend to be more effective than those of minor parties." Since we cannot measure effectiveness directly, it is important to create a set of criteria others will accept as relevant. The best way to assure you are coding your data objectively is to have others recode the data. If they code the data the same way you did, this suggests inter-code reliability and provides strong evidence that your data collection method is reliable.

Since the media have the same reality to report, one way to measure bias is to compare how different media outlets cover reality. Starting from the presumption that various media differ in their evaluation of the president, you might choose the same dates and compare the lead presidential stories of two or more newspapers. Your hypothesis would be, "Readers of [names of newspaper] are more likely to get a positive slant on stories about the president than arc readers of [different newspapers]. Using the paragraph as the unit of analysis, you could code (categorize) each paragraph as positive (the kind of information the president and his supporters would want published), neutral, or negative. By comparing the percentage of positive, neutral, and negative paragraphs in each paper, you can test your hypothesis. A more detailed analysis might count the positive, neutral, and negative adjectives describing the president. This would require creating a justifiable set of adjectives that fall into each category.

Sample Hypothesis

a. If you read (names of newspapers), then you are likely to get differing information than if you read (names of other newspapers).
b. If you are a Republican official, then you are quoted more often than if you are a Democratic official. (You will probably want to eliminate coverage of the president.)

Hints for Accomplishment

Compare the front pages of four or more different newspapers for the same day (or two newspapers over a number of days). Most college libraries subscribe to several newspapers. For a large selection of today's front pages, go to the Newseum website, at http://www.newseum.org (see section 5 below for details on how to get readable images), or PressDisplay, at http://www.pressdisplay.com. Alternatively, you could evaluate the network news programs. Abstracts by date are available from the Vanderbilt Television News Archive, at http://tvnews.vanderbilt.edu.

Indicate some characteristics on which you expect the sources to vary. You might think in terms of characteristics such as number of pictures, size of headlines, number (or length) of stories, subject matter of stories, number of wire-service stories (indicated by initial references to AP, UPI, Reuters, etc.) versus original stories. For example, you might expect a local newspaper to differ from a national newspaper in the number of national stories, their placement, and their enhancement with pictures or graphics. Each of these differences implies a hypothesis both predicting differences and ideally helping us understand the reasons behind the differences. Create a set of "coding" categories for the relevant characteristics (e.g., for story content you might use "local versus national," "entertainment or human interest versus hard news," etc.). Record your findings in such a way that you can create a graphical representation (such as a bar graph) of the data. Provide a conclusion about the differences you found and their possible causes and potential consequences.

Bias as a Political Slant.   What the media cover may be less important than how they cover it. Newsmakers can be made to look impressive or ridiculous. Content analysis can be used to measure the quality of coverage as well as the quantity. It is possible to test hypotheses asserting that different media outlets cover the same news subjects in different ways. Alternatively, you might want to compare two or more newsmakers across a number of media outlets. Such an approach is particularly useful in analyzing the coverage of candidates during campaigns.

Sample Hypothesis

a. If you read the *Washington Times*, then you will get a more positive image of (Republican politician) than if you read the *Washington Post*.
b. If the media covers (a specific politician, political organization, or subject), then the media will be more negative than if they cover (another specific politician, political organization, or subject).

Hints for Accomplishment

If you are comparing different media outlets or using a set of media outlets to represent the full spectrum, it is important to justify your choices. You will probably want to collect separate data on each outlet and initially report it in that way. The key to a valid content analysis lies in creating a justifiable set of evaluation criteria. Measuring quality of coverage can be tricky. At a minimum, some standards must be applied upfront and applied consistently. For example, if you categorize the adjective "stubborn" as a negative characterization when applied to one news subject, it should be seen as negative when applied to others. You will need to decide on your **unit of analysis**. Are you going to summarize large blocks of material (whole articles or paragraphs) or are you going to adopt a narrower focus, such as on adjectives? Record your findings in such a way that you can create a graphical representation of the data (such as a bar graph). Provide a conclusion about the differences you found and their potential causes and consequences.

Sample Hypothesis

a. If you cover a political event, then what you choose as important will be different from what the media chooses.
b. If one compares coverage of an event presented by one media source, then it is likely to be different in predicable ways from the coverage in another media source.

Hints for Accomplishment

If you cannot actually go to an event, C-SPAN (http://www.c-span.org) provides video of recent events. Newspapers and other websites (e.g., the White House website, at http://www.whitehouse.gov) provide transcripts of speeches. Remember that typical news stories cover the who, what, where, when, and why of a specific event. Think about the type of constraints you have in covering a story and the type of constraints faced by members of the media. Look at the differences between your ideal story and those actually showing up in the media (see sources listed below). Recent print stories are available on newspaper websites. The national networks are beginning to provide online access to recent news broadcasts as well.

Why Can't the Media Just Tell It Like It Is?

Watch an actual news event in its entirety on television (a presidential press conference, a debate, a congressional committee meeting on C-SPAN, etc.). Develop an outline of the news story you would write about this event if you were a journalist, and then compare your story with what actually showed up in a variety of media.

E. IDEA GENERATOR: HOW WELL DOES THE MEDIA MEDIATE?

The following chart provides some general guidelines for developing a research plan.

Specific Issue	Hypotheses	Hints
Bias		
Bias in the eye of the beholder	If a conservative (liberal) observer evaluates the media, then he or she will evaluate it differently from a liberal (conservative) observer.	Go to one of the media watch groups and scan its evaluations of the media. Which site seems to make the most sense? What biases do you see *in the group's* evaluations
Media Proliferation		
Fragmentation	If you get your news from a particular medium, then the picture of the world you receive will be very different from the one you receive if you get your news from a different medium.	Compare publications, websites, and television news to see if they pay the same attention to the same issues and personalities.
Media Evaluation		
Trust in media	If your party is in power, then you will be less trusting of the media.	Look at audience polls over time. Are Republicans always more distrusting of the media, or does it go along with the natural media criticism of those in power?

Specific Issue	Hypotheses	Hints
Use of Media		
Strategy	If you want to communicate with particular kinds of voters, then you need to choose specific media.	Develop a detailed media plan for television or the Internet. Identify the kinds of voters you want to reach. Using hard data, choose the specific television programs or websites on which you would advertise.

4. Secondary Sources That Will Help You Get Started

Murray, Michael D., ed. *Encyclopedia of Television News.* Phoenix, Ariz.: Oryx Press, 1999.
Newcomb, Horace, ed. *Encyclopedia of Television.* 2nd ed. New York: Fitzroy Dearborn, 2004. Contains over a thousand articles on the personalities and components of television.

5. Original Research That Will Impress Your Professor

Graber, Doris A. *Mass Media & American Politics.* Washington, D.C.: CQ Press, 2006.
Jones, Steve, ed. *Encyclopedia of New Media: An Essential Reference to Communication and Technology.* Thousand Oaks, Calif.: Sage, 2003.
McLuhan, Marshall. *Understanding Media: The Extensions of Man.* New York: McGraw Hill, 1964. Reissued by Gingko Press, 2003. Although his many books are difficult to read, McLuhan's pithy summaries ("the medium is the message," "instant information creates involvement," "the global village," etc.) provide key insights into the contemporary and developing media environment.

6. Where to Find It

Where can I find the biographies of journalists?
Yahoo (http://dir.yahoo.com/News_and_Media/Journalism) and Google (http://www.google.org/alpha/Top/News/Media/Journalism) provide extensive listings of links to both contemporary and historical journalists.

Who evaluates the media?
Among the conservative groups are the Media Research Center, http://www
.mediaresearch.org; Accuracy in Media, http://www.aim.org; and the Center for
Media and Public Affairs, http://www.cmpa.com. Among the liberal groups are
Media Matters for America, http://mediamatters.org, and Fairness & Accuracy
in Reporting (FAIR), http://www.fair.org.

What do the various media audiences look like?
The Pew Center does regular polling on the demographics of media usage and
trust, and the results can be found at http://people-press.org/reports/index
.php?TopicID=1.

How can I find out what is happening on the blogs?
Blogging is an activity carried on by a small, and probably atypical, segment of
the population. Nonetheless, conversations on blogs do measure hot topics per-
meating the rest of society. Blogpulse, at http://www.blogpulse.com provides the
ability to track blogs over time using keywords (use "Trend Search").

Where can I find copies of political cartoons?
Cartoonist Daryl Cagle operates an extensive website of political cartoons organized by subject at http://www.cagle.com/.

Where can I find pictures to enhance my presentation?
Google's image search provides a wide array of pictures and graphics. Corbis, a
commercial photography broker, allows free searching and use of their photos for
noncommercial, educational purposes, at http://pro.corbis.com.

Where can I find the full text of press conferences or speeches?
For the president, go to the website of the American Presidency Project, http://
www.presidency.ucsb.edu/index.php (see also chapter 3, section 5 for additional
resources).

For speeches on the floor of Congress, go to Thomas, at http://www.thomas
.gov, and search the *Congressional Record*.

Many agencies post the speeches and press conferences of their key personnel. Begin at USA.gov, the federal government's website, at http://www.first-
gov.gov. Go to the agency in which you are interested and find the individual on
whose speeches or public statements you want to focus. Key individuals will usually have a section containing their speeches and media comments.

CommonDreams is a liberal website that gives direct access to many
unedited transcripts of news events, at http://www.commondreams.org.

How free is the press?
Two organizations rank countries using both hard and soft data: Freedom
House, http://www.freedomhouse.org/template.cfm?page=251&year=2006,

and Reporters without Borders, http://www.rsf.org/rubrique.php3?id_rubrique
=639.

How much does the public trust the media?
Several organizations have conducted studies to determine the level of confidence
in the media, among them, the American Society of Newspaper Editors (http://
www.asne.org/kiosk/news/98jcp.htm) and the Pew Research Center for the People
and the Press (http://people-press.org/reports/display.php3?ReportID=248). (The
Pew surveys are updated regularly; from the "Survey Reports" tab, narrow the
search to "News Media.") For a compilation of various surveys, go to the Media
InfoCenter, at http://www.mediainfocenter.org/journalism/press_confidence.

Where can I find television ratings?
The Nielsen Company makes money by selling ratings data to the media and advertisers. It only makes a portion of its data available to the public. Basic demographics such as race are available on the Nielsen website, at http://www.nielsen-
media.com/nc/portal/site/Public (go to "Top Ten TV Programs" and "Ratings").
The *Los Angeles Times* presents ratings data regularly at http://www.calendarlive
.com/tv/ratings/more.

How can I determine the popularity of websites?
Alexa (http://www.alexa.com) allows you to see the popularity of a website (you
can search for a particular site). It also shows changes in the popularity of the
most popular sites.

How can I get access to the content of various media?
A large number of newspapers have their own websites. Usually today's issue is free.
There may be a charge for previous issues. The Newseum website (http://www
.newseum.com) provides screen captures of over five hundred of today's newspaper
front pages from around the world. They archive the front pages for certain days
that had coverage of significant events. To get a readable page, click on the thumb-
nail and then download a pdf file from the "take a closer look" link. You can also
use this site to go to the website of each newspaper. Some newspaper articles show
up in Google. Most college libraries have access to one or more electronic databases
to replace the microform access of the past. PressDisplay is a fee-based database
that your library might have. Individuals can get limited access to the full text of
hundreds of newspapers at http://www.pressdisplay.com.

The Vanderbilt Television News Archive provides a searchable index of the
major network news programs, at http://tvnews.vanderbilt.edu. The abstracts
can be searched by date, word, or phrase. Registration to use the database is free.
C-SPAN provides live coverage of full events and digitized versions of selected
events, at http://www.c-span.org.

**Box 6.2.   Skill Box:
Reading in the Internet Age**

For many, "reading" a newspaper means going to its website. It is important to recognize that the online versions of major newspapers are not the
same as the hard-copy versions. In some cases, the articles are written by
different people. At a minimum, the website is selective in what it covers
and often includes only summaries. Web "reading" is different from reading the hard copy in other ways. Hard-copy readers receive a great deal of
inadvertent information as they scan headlines for articles they choose to
read. They are limited to one newspaper, or at best a few newspapers, available in their area. Internet "reading" is more intentional, as users choose
from a vast array of sites, which makes it easier for users to avoid those that
challenge their currently held views. Within the articles, which they click
through, they are likely to get ever-narrower information. From a research
perspective, the Web leads to another problem. Websites, by design,
change regularly, making a basic principle of scientific research—the ability to replicate findings—impossible. There is no way for an interested
reader or future researcher to go back to what you found and verify it. Using a publication's archive of its printed version in electronic form often
involves a subscription fee. If you plan to use a website as your raw material for analysis, you should save printouts of the pages you used, for bibliographic and rechecking purposes.

7. Taking Action— Contacting and Influencing the Media

Writing a letter to the editor:

- Make one point (or at most two) in your letter, e-mail, or fax. State the point
  clearly, ideally in the first sentence.
- Make your letter timely. If you are not addressing a specific article, editorial,
  or letter that recently appeared in the paper to which you are writing, then try
  to tie the issue you want to write about to a recent event.
- Familiarize yourself with the coverage and editorial position of the paper to
  which you are writing. Refute or support specific statements and address relevant facts that are ignored, but avoid blanket attacks on the media in general
  or the newspaper in particular.

- Check the letter specifications of the newspaper to which you are writing. Length and format requirements vary from paper to paper. (Generally, roughly two short paragraphs are ideal.) You also must include your name, signature, address, and phone number. Look at the letters that appear in your paper.
- Monitor the paper for your letter. If your letter has not appeared within a week or two, follow up with a call to the editorial department of the newspaper.
- Direct your letter to the appropriate section of the newspaper. Sometimes the issue you want to address is relevant to the lifestyle, book review, or other section of the paper.
- Always sign your letters as an individual or representative of a community group.[5]

Box 6.3. Avoiding Death by PowerPoint

PowerPoint is an effective tool to present the results of your paper, but it can easily be overused and misused. PowerPoint is effective for *visual* representations of material. It is deadly for presentations of long or detailed lists. Think of PowerPoint as a way to engage listeners, create visual memory hooks, and highlight what you are saying verbally.

Some tricks of the trade:

- *KISS (keep it simple, stupid):* No slide should have more than six lines or more than six words to a line. This allows the listener to see the words and forces you to present ideas with clarity.
- *Avoid being the child with a hammer who sees the whole world as a nail:* Limit the number of slides. Not everything should be on a slide; otherwise, you, as the presenter, are nothing but a button pusher.
- *A picture is worth a thousand words:* Pictures become visual memory hooks, helping your listeners understand your message. Don't be afraid to use a *little* humor.
- *Active learning is better than passive learning:* PowerPoint has the potential for letting your message unfold, encouraging your listeners to try to anticipate the next point you are going to make.

- ***Bigger is better:*** Don't ever get caught saying, "If you could see this picture (chart, quote, etc.) you would know that. . . ." If a person in the back of the room can't read your slide, you have cheated the audience and demeaned your presentation.
- ***Duh:*** Never get caught simply reading your slides. The message to your listeners is that you don't think they are smart enough to read.

8. Presenting Your Findings

The media teach us some lessons about getting and maintaining an audience. Throughout history, features such as photographs and cartoon strips drew in readers. The launch of *USA Today* in the 1980s, with short stories, lots of visuals, and front-page color challenged the more traditional newspapers, which were forced to come along to survive. Even the *New York Times*, called the "grey lady" for its dense, text-filled front page, began adding pictures and eventually color. There are certainly times to add pictures, graphs, and charts to your paper. They should not simply be "fluff," but rather should add something of substance to your presentation. A graphic in your paper should be "a self-contained whole." It should mean something in and of itself. That means it should include a brief title and a full bibliographic citation if it is not entirely your work. Charts and graphs should have their axes clearly labeled. In addition, a graphic should not simply float around in your paper. You should refer to the graphic in the text and expand on it. A good graphic will enhance your written work. At times you will be expected to present your paper orally. This may be the time to harness a tool such as PowerPoint (see box 6.3).

Notes

1. James Madison to W. T. Barry, August 4, 1822, in *The Writings of James Madison*, ed. Gaillard Hunt, vol. 2, *1819–1836* (G. P. Putnam's Sons, 1910), 103. The letter is also available online at The Founder's Constitution, http://press-pubs.uchicago.edu/founders/documents/v1ch18s35.html.

2. *World Factbook, 2008* (Washington, D.C.: Central Intelligence Agency, 2008), http://www.bartleby.com/151/ (calculated from country outlines).

3. Lee B. Becker, Tudor Vlad, and Amy Jo Coffey, *2004 Annual Survey of Journalism and Mass Communication Graduates* (Athens, Ga.: Grady College of Journalism and Mass Communication, 2004), http://www.grady.uga.edu/annualsurveys/grd04/GraduateReport.pdf.

4. Official regions of the country can be found on the U.S. Department of Labor's website, at http://www.dol.gov/esa/programs/dbra/regions.htm.

5. From Fairness & Accuracy in Reporting (FAIR), "How to Communicate with Journalists," http://www.fair.org/index.php?page=122.

CHAPTER 7

Political Parties and Interest Groups

Political parties in the United States are loosely bound coalitions that work to gain and maintain positions of authority through the electoral process. **Interest groups** are voluntary associations, typically outside of government, that are composed of individuals who share policy objectives and who work collectively in pursuit of their shared objectives. Both political parties and interest groups represent individuals working collectively in pursuit of a common end. For parties, the primary objective is typically winning elections. For interest groups, elections are more often a tool that members use to achieve their policy preferences. The differences between interest groups and political parties are often a matter of degree and in the modern context the lines are often blurred.

1. The Structure and Intention of Political Parties and Interest Groups

A. CONSTITUTIONAL AND LEGAL BASIS

Political parties and interest groups are not part of the formal political structure outlined in the U.S. Constitution. Rather than sanction political parties and interest groups, the **Bill of Rights** (the first ten amendments to the U.S. Constitution) left the door open for the formation of organized political groups. The First Amendment guarantees, among other rights, freedom of speech, the right to peaceably assemble, and the right to petition the government for a redress of grievances, rights that protect the actions of interest groups and political parties.

In the *Federalist* No. 10, James Madison explains the founders' general philosophy for handling the mischief of "**factions**"—the founders' word for organized interest groups and political parties. Madison and others hoped to create a system in which numerous groups would compete for power, counterbalancing the influence of each other and making it highly unlikely that any single group would come to dominate the political process. Others, like George Washington, were less ambivalent about factions and hoped that the nation's leaders could rise above the spirit of faction (see Washington's Farewell Address[1]).

Structure (Parties)

The U.S. political system is considered a **two-party system**, as two major political parties dominate the political environment. In the United States there is no legal prohibition against the formation of **third parties** (i.e., parties other than the two dominant parties in a two-party system). However, several structural elements are believed to contribute to the two-party system. One of these elements is the **winner-take-all system**, also known as "first past the post," in which a candidate wins an election by receiving at least one more vote than all the other candidates. Another of these structural elements is the reliance on **single-member districts**, in which a single official represents a given geographic district. Outside the United States, parliamentary systems tend to make use of **proportional representation**, under which legislative seats are allocated to political parties in proportion to the percentage of the vote the parties receive in a national election. Since minor parties receive representation in proportional systems, proportional systems generally lead to a **multiparty system**, in which several parties are presented in government. The tendency of political systems that make use of winner-take-all or single-member districts to produce two-party systems is known as **Duverger's Law**, named for Maurice Duverger, the French sociologist who first observed the trend in the late 1950s.

In the United States, the major political parties are divided into local, state, and national components. At the local level, party activists fill numerous leadership posts (e.g., precinct committees, city committees, and county committees). These local party branches, which are somewhat independent from the state and national parties, provide much of the manpower that drives the major parties. At the state level are the state central committees, state conventions, and congressional district committees. Since the state parties enjoy a degree of autonomy from the national parties and the laws that govern state political parties are mostly determined by the individual states, there is a great deal of variation in the operation of the state parties.

At the national level are the parties' national campaign committees: the Democratic National Committee (DNC) and the Republican National Committee (RNC). These committees tend to focus on party activities that relate to presidential elections. Focusing on congressional elections are the parties' House and Senate congressional committees: the Democratic Congressional Campaign Committee (DCCC); the National Republican Congressional Committee (NRCC); the Democratic Senatorial Campaign Committee (DSCC); and the National Republican Senatorial Committee (NRSC).

Power is also distributed within Congress according to party affiliation. The party leaders within the House and Senate are known as **floor leaders**. The highest leadership positions are controlled by the **majority party** (the party that controls a majority of the seats in a legislative body). In the House, the highest leadership position is Speaker of the House, followed by majority leader, and a host of lesser positions called whips. The **minority party**, a party that controls some seats in a legislative body, but less than a majority, elects a minority leader and has its own whips, but has no position comparable to the Speaker of the House. The highest leadership positions in the Senate are the Senate majority leader (controlled by the majority party), followed by the Senate minority leader (controlled by the minority party).

Structure (Interest Groups)

The interest-group system in the United States is often considered a **pluralist system**, that is, a system in which numerous groups compete for influence within the political system. Groups are often classified by the issues they represent (see section 2 below) and by their tax status (specified by the Internal Revenue Service)[2] as well as their status under the Federal Election Commission.

- **501(c)(3) groups** (not-for-profit and charitable organizations) operate exclusively for one of the following purposes: charitable, religious, educational, scientific, literary, or public safety. Examples of this type of group include the American Red Cross, the Chesapeake Bay Foundation, the Salvation Army, churches, and Books for International Goodwill. Contributions to these groups are tax exempt to the donor, and the group is exempt from paying income tax. The amount of lobbying that these types of groups can undertake is limited, and they are prohibited from participating in the electoral process.
- **501(c)(4) groups** (civic leagues and social-welfare organizations) are not organized for profit, but instead promote social welfare. Examples of this type of group include homeowners' associations, AARP, the Sierra Club, and the National Rifle Association. Contributions to these organizations are not tax exempt, but the organizations themselves are not required to pay income tax. Groups in this category are subject to some limits on participation in electoral politics but face fewer restrictions than the 501(c)(3) groups.
- **501(c)(5) groups** (labor unions) consist of workers organized to promote the interests of their members through collective bargaining. Examples of this type

of group include the United Mine Workers of America, the National Education Association, and the United Auto Workers. Contributions to these organizations are not tax exempt, but the organizations themselves are not required to pay income tax. Groups in this category can actively lobby congress, but can only contribute to political campaigns through political action committees.

- **501(c)(6) groups** (trade or professional associations) are not-for-profit groups that represent business leagues, chambers of commerce, and real estate boards. Examples of this type of group include the National Bankers Association, the U.S. Chamber of Commerce, and the American Association for Justice (formerly the Association of Trial Lawyers of America)). Contributions to these organizations are not tax exempt, but the organizations themselves are not required to pay income tax. Groups in this category can actively lobby congress, but can only contribute to political campaigns through political action committees.
- **527 groups** (political groups) are those that directly or indirectly accept contributions or make expenditures for political purposes. In recent elections, this type of group has become increasingly active in national, state, and local elections. These groups typically make use of **issue advertisements** that indirectly benefit or harm a candidate, rather than giving money directly to a candidate's campaign.
- **Political action committees (PACs)** accept contributions and make expenditures for the purpose of electing or defeating candidates for public office. Federal law prohibits PACs from contributing more than $5,000 per candidate per election cycle (primary and general elections are considered separately) and from contributing more than $15,000 to the national political parties per year. Examples of this type of group include the Committee on Political Education (COPE) and the American Medical Association Political Action Committee (AMPAC). The Federal Election Commission distinguishes between two distinct types of PACs:
- 1. **Separate segregated funds (SSFs)** are PACs that are established and administered by corporations, labor unions, membership organizations, or trade associations. These committees can solicit contributions only from individuals associated with the sponsoring organization.
- 2. **Nonconnected committees** are PACs that are not connected to corporations, labor unions, membership organizations, or trade associations and are permitted to solicit contributions from the general public.[3]

B. GOALS AND INTENTIONS

Political Parties

Political parties in the United States are loosely bound coalitions that work to gain and maintain positions of authority through the electoral process. They exist within government and outside government. The primary goal of political parties is to support candidates running for office under the party label.

- *Influence elections:* The basic goal of political parties is to elect fellow partisans to public office. Toward this end parties recruit candidates, hold nomination contests, register voters, help get out the vote on Election Day, raise campaign funds, and provide resources and expertise to candidates.
- *Provide political unity:* After elections, parties help provide unity within the political system. A party provides useful links within specific branches of government (Congress is internally organized by political party), between the different branches of government (the executive, the legislative, and to a lesser extent the judicial branches), and between the different levels of government (national, state, and local).
- *Provide accountability:* Since party members often support a common set of political goals, parties have the ability to enhance political accountability. The presence of a party label enables voters to reward or punish a group of elected officials, depending on how well the voters feel the party in power has governed.
- *Provide voting cues:* The electorate is often called on to make decisions with limited information. A party label provides voters with a useful information shortcut, also known as a **voting cue**, that can help them make informed decisions with limited information. Knowing that a candidate is a Democrat or a Republican is often sufficient information for voters to recognize the candidate as someone they are likely to support or oppose.
- *Determine policy objectives:* Political parties debate and adopt national **party platforms**, which are formal policy statements adopted at the parties' quadrennial conventions that discuss the parties' policy objectives in general terms.

Interest Groups

Interest groups in the United States are voluntary associations, typically outside government, that are composed of individuals who share policy objectives and who work collectively in pursuit of their shared objectives. They differ from political parties in the extent to which they focus on electoral politics. While interest groups may participate in electoral politics, they generally do so in pursuit of specific policy objectives.

Lobbying.   **Lobbying** is the process by which interest groups attempt to influence key policymakers and promote their policy objectives. Traditional lobbying is conducted by a group's **lobbyists**, paid representatives of an interest group who are responsible for promoting the group's policy objectives to key policymakers.

Lobbyists attempt to influence the policy process through various activities including conducting private meetings with policymakers, having constituents contact policymakers, drafting legislation, testifying at hearings, providing research to policymakers, identifying coalitions of supporters, running advertisements in the media regarding a candidate's position, contributing to political candidates, and attending fund-raisers. In addition to traditional lobbying techniques, some groups engage in **grassroots lobbying**, which is the process of organizing the public to apply pressure on elected officials. **Reverse lobbying** occurs when elected officials reach out to interest groups to encourage them to engage in grassroots lobbying for issues that are important to the elected official.

Contributions to Candidates.   Interest groups are permitted to make political contributions to candidates in national elections through PACs. Candidates rely heavily on PAC contributions to fund their campaigns. In U.S. House elections, PAC contributions tend to favor incumbents, who typically receive roughly half their campaign funds through PAC contributions.

Issue Advocacy.   In a process often described as **issue advocacy**, interest groups spend resources to produce advertisements that influence the way people think about issues and in turn color the way voters think about candidates. Through the use of 527 groups, interest groups are permitted to advocate their causes and to link candidates to specific positions, but they are not permitted to specifically instruct voters to support a particular candidate.

Endorse and Rate Candidates.   Many interest groups assign scores to elected officials based on the officials' voting records, known as **candidate ratings**. The ratings are typically based on a 0–100 scale, with a low score signifying that the official usually votes against the group's desired outcome and a high score signifying that the official consistently supports the group's positions. See the Project Vote Smart website, at http://www.vote-smart.org/index.htm, for a list of interest-group ratings for elected officials. Other interest groups provide candidates with official **endorsements**, or formal statements of support for a candidate. Endorsements are intended as a voting cue, to let voters know that a candidate generally supports a group's policy positions.

C. RECENT CHANGES IN CAMPAIGN LAWS THAT INFLUENCE PARTIES AND INTEREST GROUPS

The **Bipartisan Campaign Reform Act of 2002 (BCRA)**, also known as the **McCain-Feingold campaign-finance reform** for its two primary sponsors, attempted to rid the system of the corrupting influence of unregulated big-dollar contributions. Among its many changes (see chapter 8 for a detailed discussion of the BCRA), the legislation banned **soft money**—unlimited contributions to political parties that were being used to fund loosely veiled political advertisements that did not expressly call on voters to support a specific candidate but instead painted one candidate in a favorable light or another candidate in an unfavorable light. The BCRA has led to a new development in the way that large contributions are influencing American elections. With the soft-money loophole closed, the role of 527 groups has substantially expanded, creating an avenue for mega-donors to spend millions of dollars to influence election results. In recent elections, wealthy donors like George Soros and Peter Lewis have been able to influence elections by contributing more than $20 million apiece to 527 groups in a single election cycle.

D. COMPARATIVE PERSPECTIVE

Campaign-finance laws and electoral procedures combine to create a unique situation for political groups in the United States. The general lack of public financing for candidates and the relatively long and expensive campaigns create a rich environment for group influence, as candidates look to organized interest groups to help fund their media-intensive campaigns. The nation's winner-take-all system, combined with single-member districts, promotes the formation and maintenance of two major political parties. Since there is no reward for second place in the American political system, minor parties that fail to win a majority vote receive no representation in government and have a difficult time building support. Likewise, because a state's electoral votes are generally

---

Box 7.1.   Skill Box: Follow the Law and Follow the Money

Note that the amount of money that interest groups can contribute directly to political campaigns is limited by the current campaign-finance laws. As shown in table 7.1, the single most active PAC in the 2004 election cycle (the National Association of Realtors) gave less than $4 million to candidates. On the other hand, contributors to 527 groups, which influence elections through loosely veiled issue advertisements rather than making direct contributions to political candidates, do not face similar restrictions. As shown in table 7.2, a single contributor in the 2004 election cycle, billionaire George Soros, spent more than $23 million.

**Table 7.1.   Top 10 PAC Contributors to Federal
Candidates, 2003–2004 (dollars)**

Political Action Committee (PAC)	Total Amount
National Assoc. of Realtors	3,787,083
Laborers Union	2,684,250
National Auto Dealers Assoc.	2,603,300
Int'l Brotherhood of Electrical Workers	2,369,500
National Beer Wholesalers Assoc.	2,314,000
National Assoc. of Home Builders	2,201,500
Assoc. of Trial Lawyers of America	2,181,499
United Parcel Service	2,142,679
SBC Communications	2,120,616
American Medical Assoc.	2,092,425

Source: Center for Responsive Politics, http://www.opensecrets.org/
pacs/topacs.asp?txt=A&Cycle=2004.

allocated exclusively to the winning candidate in the state, the Electoral College system also works against minor-party candidates. For example, Ross Perot, who won 19 percent of the popular vote in the 1992 presidential race, received no electoral votes and saw his party wither following the 1992 contest. The combined effect is a political system that is dominated by two large and centrist political parties and numerous interest groups that operate on the fringe of the electoral process and fulfill many of the roles that minor parties play in other Western democracies.

**Table 7.2.   Top 10 Individual Contributors to 527 Groups, 2004 Election
Cycle (dollars)**

Contributor	Total Contributions
George Soros (Soros Fund Management)	23,450,000
Peter Lewis (Peter B Lewis/Progressive Corp.)	22,997,220
Steven Bing (Shangri-La Entertainment)	13,852,031
Herb & Marion Sandler (Golden West Financial)	13,008,459
Bob Perry (Perry Homes)	8,085,199
Alex Spanos (AG Spanos Companies)	5,000,000
Dawn Arnall (Ameriquest Corp.)	5,000,000
Ted Waitt (Gateway Inc.)	5,000,000
Boone Pickens (BP Capital)	4,100,000
Jerry Perenchio (Chartwell Partners)	4,050,000

Source: Center for Responsive Politics, http://www.opensecrets.org/527s/527indivs.asp
?cycle=2004.

E. ENDURING STRUCTURAL AND INSTITUTIONAL QUESTIONS AND HOW TO RESEARCH THEM

Single-Member Districts and the Two-Party System

It is interesting to note that the U.S. Constitution does not specify the single-member, winner-take-all congressional districts that we have come to associate with congressional elections in the United States. In the early republic, congressional candidates from a particular party would often run for office as a ticket, with voters using a single ballot provided by the party to select all the party's candidates. The result was that if one party enjoyed a small majority of public support in a particular state, they would be allocated all the state's congressional seats and the loosing party would gain no representation. The problem was essentially the same as the dilemma that minor parties face today at the district level—second place results in no representation. To promote a more representative system, Congress passed legislation in 1842 that prohibited the

---

Sample Hypothesis

If the party ticket hampered party competition in the early republic, then as states moved to single-member districts, party competition should have increased within individual states.

Hints for Accomplishment

The research question explores the manner in which election rules can help or hinder party competition. While this idea that rules influence party competition is generally accepted, it is a particularly difficult question to research. Typically, this type of research either compares a single country's existing election rules against hypothetical rules, or it calls on the researcher to compare two or more countries that have different election rules. The problems associated with the first approach are obvious. For example, we could predict that should the United States adopt a proportional system of representation tomorrow, the Green Party would win roughly 3 percent of the seats in Congress, since that reflects their national support in recent elections. However, the Green Party might do far better than 3 percent of the vote in a proportional system, since voters who support the Green Party's positions but fear "wasting" or "throwing away" their vote might be in a position to support a minor party. Comparing countries with different election laws is also problematic, as there are reasons countries have adopted different sets of rules and these reasons might also relate to party competition. The historical approach suggested here is one way to address the influence of election laws in the United States.

use of at-large districts, though a few states continued the practice well into the twentieth century, and required members of Congress to represent specific geographic districts.

The Free-Rider Phenomenon and Interest-Group Formation

In 1965 Mancur Olson published a seminal work in the field of interest-group research, *The Logic of Collective Action*. In this work Olson explained the difficulty of interest-group formation and maintenance. The primary obstacle to interest-group formation, according to Olson, is a phenomenon he described as the **free-rider problem**—the tendency of potential members of an interest group not to join a group if they can receive the benefits that the group seeks without having to pay the price of membership. Olson went on to explain that small groups that pursue narrow material benefits for their group members (like lower taxes for a specific industry) were least likely to feel the negative effects of the free-rider problem. In contrast, groups that pursued nonmonetary goals for the benefit of the general public (like clean air or water) were most likely to face significant problems related to free-riding. Olson's work challenged the theory of

Sample Hypothesis

a. If the free-rider problem disproportionately works against broad-based interest groups (e.g., environmental groups), then donations from narrow material groups (e.g., business groups and labor groups) should dominate political contributions.
b. If the free-rider problem disproportionately works against broad-based interest groups, then these types of groups are likely to provide selective benefits to their members (like magazines and travel discounts) to overcome the free-rider problem, while narrow interest groups will not need to provide similar benefits.

Hints for Accomplishment

Testing the first hypothesis is a relatively straightforward exercise. The Center for Responsive Politics provides a user-friendly tool for exploring political contributions by groups. From their website (http://www.opensecrets.org), you can compare political contributions by group type and assess the strength of Olson's theory. Investigating the comparative incentives that groups use to attract and maintain members (the second hypothesis) requires a different approach. A comparative case-study approach is useful for this type of analysis. By conducting an in-depth analysis of two unlike groups (one broad-based, like an environmental group, and one narrow and material, like a business association), you can assess the organizational barriers that different types of groups face.

pluralism, which suggested that group formation was relatively easy and that existing groups were a mirror of the competing interests in society.

F. IDEA GENERATOR: STRUCTURAL QUESTIONS RELATED TO POLITICAL PARTIES AND INTEREST GROUPS

The following chart provides some general guidelines for developing a research plan.

Specific Issue	Hypotheses	Hints
Campaign Reforms		
Consequences of the McCain-Feingold campaign-finance reform (2002)	a. If the McCain-Feingold reforms benefited one political party more than the other, then we should see noticeable fund-raising disparities between the Democratic and the Republican parties. b. If the McCain-Feingold reforms reduced the flow of unregulated political contributions, then it should now be easier to identify sources of political contributions.	There have been numerous consequences of the McCain-Feingold campaign reforms, many of which were unintended. While the reform closed one loophole (i.e., the soft-money loophole) it left open an even larger campaign-finance loophole (the 527-group loophole). Tracking political contributions to parties and 527 groups using sites like www.opensecrets.org is a great way to explore the consequences of this important legislation.
The Regulation of Campaign-Finance Activities by the Political Parties at the State Level		
The political consequences of the nation's various campaign-finance laws regulating political parties at the state level	a. If a state places few or no restrictions on the finances of political parties, then the state will have well-financed political parties. b. If a state places heavy restrictions on the finances of political parties, then the	While national political elections are regulated by the Federal Election Commission, political parties that operate exclusively at the state level fall under state laws. Some states, like Virginia, have virtually no restrictions on how parties

(continued)

Specific Issue	Hypotheses	Hints
	electoral activity of interest groups will be relatively high in the state.	raise their funds or how they spend them. Other states, like Colorado, have clear limits regarding how much an individual can contribute to a state party and how much the state party can contribute to state candidates. The differences in state campaign-finance laws provide an opportunity to conduct a comparative analysis of the political impact of distinct campaign-finance systems.

State Laws Concerning Participation in Nominating Contests

The political consequences of the nation's various laws regulating participation in state-level primaries	a. If a state has a closed primary system, then the voters in the state are less likely to support moderate candidates. b. If a state has an open primary, then moderate candidates are likely to be favored by voters.	State law determines who is eligible to participate in a party's nomination process. Some states have *closed primaries*, which require voters to formally register as a party member in advance of the primary in order to participate. Other states have *open primaries*, which allow all registered voters to participate, regardless of party affiliation. And some states have *semi-open primaries*, which allow voters to declare their support of a party on the day of the primary. It is interesting to compare how presidential candidates fare in states that have different primary rules.

Interest Groups and Internal Revenue Service Tax Designations

How does a group's IRS tax	a. If an interest group chooses to organize	One way to investigate the influence of a group's tax

Specific Issue	Hypotheses	Hints
designation influence an interest group's level of political participation?	under a complex tax designation (e.g., maintain 501(c)3, 501(c)4, and 527 affiliates), then it can actively participate in the electoral process. b. If an interest group chooses a 501(c)3 tax status and maintains no affiliate organizations, then the group's electoral activities will be severely limited.	status on its political activities is to conduct a comparative case study of two groups that advocate for similar policy outcomes but have chosen different tax designations. An example would be to compare the political activity of an environmental group like the Sierra Club, which aggressively pursues its environmental objectives through affiliate groups that have different tax statuses, with a less politically active environmental group like the Chesapeake Bay Foundation which is a 501(c)(3) group. For information on Sierra Club's 501(c)(4) affiliate, go to http://www .sierraclub.org; for Sierra Club's 501(c)(3) affiliate, go to http://www .sierraclub.org/foundation; for Sierra Club's national 527 affiliate, go to http:// www.sierraclubvotes.org; and for the Chesapeake Bay Foundation, go to http://www.cbf.org.

Interest-Group Structure

Does a group's organizational structure influence the way it lobbies government?	a. If an interest group is composed of various local or state affiliates, then it will be better situated to pursue grassroots lobbying activities. b. If an interest group is organized at the	Some interest groups organize at the national level (adopting a unitary structure), while other groups choose to operate semi-autonomous state or local affiliates (adopting a federated structure). The political consequences of

(continued)

Specific Issue	Hypotheses	Hints
	national level, then it will be better situated to pursue traditional lobbying activities.	a group's organizational structure are not well understood. This type of inquiry is suited for a comparative case-study approach, comparing a small number of groups in a single issue area that maintain distinct organizational structures.

The Anti-Lobbying Act of 1919 and Reverse Lobbying

Specific Issue	Hypotheses	Hints
Do government officials avoid restrictions against direct lobbying by encouraging interest groups to lobby on their behalf in a process that is known as reverse lobbying?	a. If reverse lobbying is prevalent, then government officials should hold regular meetings with interest-group leaders to convey their policy objectives. b. If reverse lobbying is prevalent, then interest groups should engage in public-awareness campaigns in favor of major policy initiatives.	The Anti-Lobbying Act of 1919 bars governmental officials from making direct appeals to the general public in support of or in opposition to legislation. Nevertheless, government officials can, and do, encourage groups to engage in grassroots lobbying on behalf of their policy objectives. While this is not an easy subject to explore, as the connections are often hidden, it can be addressed by identifying the key policy goals of an administration and the activities of interest groups to promote those goals (e.g., Bill Clinton's health-care proposal in 1993, Newt Gingrich's Contract with America in 1994, or George W. Bush's energy plan in 2001).

2. Participants

A. WHO ARE THE POLITICAL PARTY AND INTEREST GROUP PARTICIPANTS AND WHY ARE THEY THERE?

The Democratic Party

The modern **Democratic Party** has roots that date back to Thomas Jefferson's Democratic-Republican Party, which Jefferson organized to oppose the Federalists of his era. Following the controversial election of 1824, when Andrew Jackson, a Democratic-Republican, won both the popular vote and the electoral vote only to lose the presidential election in the House of Representatives to John Quincy Adams, a new party emerged in support of Jackson. Jackson's Democratic Party helped him win the presidency in 1828 and again in 1832. In 1832, the Democratic Party held its first nominating convention and has held quadrennial nominating conventions ever since, making it the nation's oldest political party.

The policy positions of the Democratic Party have changed substantially over time. At one point, the Democratic Party was the party of states' rights, racial segregation, and limited federal powers. More recently, the party has advocated minority rights, workers' rights, social-welfare programs, environmental protection, and a host of programs that tend to concentrate power at the federal level. In ideological terms, the modern Democratic Party is a relatively moderate party that tends to favor more liberal public policies than the modern Republican Party. The modern party receives strong support from African Americans, the working class, single women, urbanites, and liberals.

The Republican Party

The **Republican Party** was born in 1854 out of frustration with the two dominant parties of the period (the Democratic Party and the Whig Party). In the mid-1850s a crisis emerged over the expansion of slavery in the Nebraska Territory, with neither of the mainstream parties taking a strong stance against expansion. The Republican Party was formed in large part in opposition to the slave economy. While John C. Frémont was the first presidential candidate to run as a Republican in 1856, Abraham Lincoln, who won the presidency in 1860 as a Republican, is often considered the father of the Republican Party.

Like the Democratic Party, the Republican Party has reinvented itself over time. Once the "Union party," hated in the American South, revered by freed slaves and northerners, the modern Republican Party now finds its greatest support in the South, generally supports states' rights, and has remarkably little support among African American voters. Today, the party is considered the more conservative of the nation's two dominant parties. Its priorities tend to favor military spending, an active foreign policy, economic growth, limited government control over the economy, and low taxes. The modern Republican Party has found support among evangelical Christians—especially in the South—voters in rural areas, conservatives, and the upper class.

Third Parties

While third parties rarely win elections in the United States, they are perennial players in the electoral process and often exert substantial indirect influence over the political system. They generally form out of frustration over the way the two dominant parties address a specific issue (e.g., slavery, prohibition, states' rights, environmental protection), or they form to support a specific candidate (e.g., Theodore Roosevelt's Bull Moose Party and Ross Perot's Independent Party). Third parties often act as **spoilers,** taking support away from one of the dominant parties and thereby facilitating an electoral victory for the less popular of the major parties. Ironically, third parties often deliver the election to the party that is least like the third party, as the third party takes disproportionate support away from the party that is most similar to itself. Other examples of significant third parties throughout the last century include the Green Party, the Libertarian Party, the American Independent Party, the States' Rights Democratic Party (often referred to as "Dixiecrats"), the Progressive Party, and the Socialist Party. Not all third parties fail to achieve major-party status: the Republican Party started as a third party during the 1850s.

Partisans in the Electorate

The extent to which people identify with a specific party is described as their **party identification.** Political observers tend to divide voters into three groups according to their level of party identification—partisans, independents, and leaners. **Partisans** are people who strongly identify with a specific party. **Independents** are people who do not consider themselves members of a specific party. Among independents, there are those who typically vote for members of one party (**independent leaners**) and those who generally do not favor candidates from a single party (**true independents**). In recent years the percentage of the public that clearly identifies with a single party (partisans) has dropped substantially, with independents (including leaners) now representing the largest voting bloc of the electorate.

Interest-Group Types

Interest groups can be divided into four broad categories. A group's classification is determined by the breadth of the issues it pursues and the nature of its objectives.

- *Ideological groups:* Groups that promote a specific worldview, rather than material benefits or single issues, are generally classified as **ideological groups**. This type of group exists across the political spectrum but tends to cluster on the left and right of the spectrum, rather than in the middle. Examples of conservative ideological groups include Focus on the Family, the Christian Coalition of America, the American Enterprise Institute, the John Birch Society, Eagle Forum, the Heritage Foundation, and the Cato Institute. Examples of liberal ideological groups include the Democratic Leadership Council, Americans for Democratic Action, MoveOn.org, the Campaign for America's Future, the National Committee for an Effective Congress, and People for the American Way.
- *Single-issue groups:* Groups that promote a specific issue (e.g., environmental protection, opposition to abortion, gun rights, reduced taxes, opposition to war, and gay rights) are generally classified as **single-issue groups**, or the more pejorative "special-interest groups." Like the broader ideological groups, single-issue groups tend to cluster on the left and the right of the ideological spectrum. Well-known conservative single-issue groups include the National Rifle Association, the National Right to Life Committee, and the National Taxpayers Union. Well-known liberal single-issue groups include Public Citizen, the National Association for the Advancement of Colored People (NAACP), Defenders of Wildlife, NARAL Pro-Choice America, and the National Organization for Women.
- *Labor groups:* **Labor groups** organize to promote the interests of workers through collective bargaining. In recent years, the size and influence of labor unions has generally decreased in the United States. Examples of prominent labor groups in the United States include the AFL-CIO, the Fraternal Order of Police, the Industrial Workers of the World, the Major League Baseball Players Association, the International Brotherhood of Teamsters, and the United Steelworkers of America.
- *Business groups:* **Business groups** are organized to protect the financial interests of a specific industry. Examples of business groups include the Semiconductor Industry Association, the National Association of Home Builders, the National Beer Wholesalers Association, the American Bankers Association, the National Automobile Dealers Association, the American Soybean Association, and the National Thoroughbred Racing Association.

Box 7.2.   Skill Box: Longitudinal Analysis

Longitudinal analysis allows a researcher to measure change over time. Table 7.3 tracks the partisan composition of the U.S. House of Representatives over a fifty-year period. Note that the Democratic Party dominated the House for more than a generation. Republicans, under the leadership of Newt Gingrich, gained control of the House following the 1994 **midterm elections** and retained power for more than a decade. Also note the dearth of third-party representation in the U.S. House. During the period shown in table 7.3, rarely was there more than one independent or third-party member represented in the House.

B. COMPARATIVE PERSPECTIVE

While much has been written about the polarization of the American electorate and differences between "**red states,**" that is, states that tend to elect Republican candidates, and "**blue states,**" that is, states that tend to elect Democratic candidates, Americans remain remarkably nonpartisan when compared with citizens in other Western democracies. For example, in Great Britain's multiparty system, the percentage of people who claim to be independents rarely exceeds 15 percent, while in the United States the figure now approaches 40 percent. The dif-

---

Box 7.3.   Skill Box: Analyzing Complex Graphs

The **party-unity score** is a key measure that political scientists use to assess party cohesion within Congress. The score is calculated by determining the number of votes in which the majority of one party votes against the majority of another party (often referred to as **party-line votes**). An individual member's party-unity score is calculated by identifying the percentage of votes in which the individual voted with his or her party during party-line votes. A score of 100 indicates that the member voted with his or her party in all party-line votes. The average party-unity score for Congress is a good indication of the level of party discipline that exists within a given Congress. Figures 7.1 and 7.2 show the percentage of members who voted with their party during party-line votes and suggests that party discipline has been on the rise for both Democrats and Republicans in recent years.

Table 7.3.   Partisan Composition of the U.S. House of Representatives, 1957–2007

Congress (Years)	Democrats	Republicans	Other
85th (1957–1959)	234	201	0
86th (1959–1961)	283	153	1
87th (1961–1963)	263	174	0
88th (1963–1965)	259	176	0
89th (1965–1967)	295	140	0
90th (1967–1969)	247	187	0
91st (1969–1971)	243	192	0
92nd (1971–1973)	255	180	0
93rd (1973–1975)	242	192	1
94th (1975–1977)	291	144	0
95th (1977–1979)	292	143	0
96th (1979–1981)	277	158	0
97th (1981–1983)	242	192	1
98th (1983–1985)	269	166	0
99th (1985–1987)	253	182	0
100th (1987–1989)	258	177	0
101st (1989–1991)	260	175	0
102nd (1991–1993)	267	167	1
103rd (1993–1995)	258	176	1
104th (1995–1997)	204	230	1
105th (1997–1999)	206	228	1
106th (1999–2001)	211	223	1
107th (2001–2003)	212	221	2
108th (2003–2005)	204	229	1
109th (2005–2007)	202	232	1
110th (2007–2009)	233	202	0

Source: Office of the Clerk, U.S. House of Representatives, http://clerk.house.gov/art_history/ house_history/partyDiv.html.

ference is most likely the consequence of the two-party system in the United States, which tends to present moderate conservatives and moderate liberals, but also tends to alienate the bulk of Americans who consider themselves centrists, as well those Americans who have political views outside the mainstream.

C. ENDURING QUESTIONS ABOUT POLITICAL-PARTY AND INTEREST-GROUP PARTICIPANTS AND HOW TO RESEARCH THEM

The Decline of Partisans in the United States

While partisanship within Congress approaches all-time highs (see figure 7.1), the number of voters in the Unites States who identify with a specific political

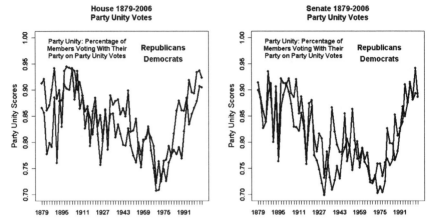

Figure 7.1.   House and Senate party-unity votes, 1879–2006.
Source: Reprinted from Nolan McCarty, Keith T. Poole, and Howard Rosenthal, *Polarized America: The Dance of Ideology and Unequal Riches* (Boston: MIT Press, 2006). Abstract available online, at http://polarizedamerica.com.

Sample Hypothesis

a. If a voter claims to be an independent, then that voter is less likely to vote.
b. If a voter claims to be an independent but leans toward one party, then that voter will vote like a partisan.
c. If the use of negative campaign advertisements continues to rise, then the number of independents will also rise.

Hints for Accomplishment

The hypotheses represent two distinct lines of inquiry. The first relates to the importance of independent status on voter behavior (hypotheses (a) and (b)). Essentially, these hypotheses ask if a researcher is able to make better predictions about a voter's political behavior (the likelihood of voting and voter preference) if the researcher considers the voter's independent status. This question requires individual-level data (polling data). The second line of inquiry (hypothesis (c)) asks what factors are responsible for the increase in self-professed independent voters. Here, independents are the dependent variable, and understanding the factors that have increased the number of independents in the United States is the major concern. Factors that are often considered when investigating this issue include the rise of negative advertisements, the rise of candidate-centered campaigns, the decline of political patronage, and the effects of campaign-finance reform.

party has decreased substantially in recent years. Political scientists generally refer to the decline in party loyalty among voters as **de-alignment**. Observers disagree about the importance of this apparent decline. Some scholars suggest that while a large percentage of voters refer to themselves as "independents," they still tend to vote along party lines. Other scholars point out that independents constitute the bulk of **swing voters**, voters who are not committed to a specific candidate or candidates from a single political party, and believe that understanding the behavior of independents is the key to deciphering election outcomes.

Understanding the Interest-Group Community

Interest groups do not operate in isolation but instead operate in loosely bound groupings often referred to as **issue networks**. While interest groups within an issue network might have common objectives, they often have different strategies for achieving their goals. Moreover, interest groups often compete for members and funding. Some observers suggest that each interest group fills a specific role, or a specific niche, within the larger interest-group community.

Sample Hypothesis

a. If one moderate interest group dominates an issue network, then it is likely that rival groups will engage in more aggressive tactics.
b. If several groups compete for influence within an issue network, then it will be difficult for groups to cooperate in pursuit of their common goals.

Hints for Accomplishment

The key to this line of inquiry is to understand the spectrum of groups that influence policy in a certain area and to investigate how the groups interact. For example, in the environmental-advocacy community, the tactics of moderate groups like the Sierra Club differ from those of less moderate groups like Green Peace. It is not just that the groups have chosen different tactics; the success of one group influences the options that are available to others. As groups seek new members and new sources of funds, they market their unique characteristics. Conducting comparative case studies of dissimilar groups within a single issue network is an effective way to conduct this type of analysis.

D. IDEA GENERATOR: ADDITIONAL QUESTIONS RELATED TO POLITICAL-PARTY AND INTEREST-GROUP PARTICIPANTS

The following chart provides some general guidelines for developing a research plan.

Specific Issue	Hypotheses	Hints
Interest-Group Influence		
Understanding the limits of interest-group influence over the political process	a. If an interest group has a large membership base, then it will rely heavily on grassroots lobbying to influence the political process. b. If an interest group has a small number of wealthy members, then it will rely on campaign contributions to influence the political process.	To a certain extent, a group's tactics are determined by the political tools that are at the interest group's disposal. An interesting way to explore these differences is to conduct a comparative case study of the lobbying efforts of two unlike groups. This type of analysis requires in-depth analysis of the political activities of unlike groups.
Interest-Group Lobbying		
Understanding the importance of access in interest-group lobbying	a. If a lobbyist's influence is derived from personal contacts, then the lobbyist is likely to have former experience as a congressional staffer or as an elected official. b. If a lobbyist's influence is derived from substantive expertise, then the lobbyist is likely to have an advanced degree.	While this is not an easy issue to study, public records and the Internet have made lobbying activity easier to explore in recent years. The lobbying database made available by the Center for Responsive Politics, at http://www.opensecrets.org/lobbyists/index.asp, enables researchers to assess individual lobbyists and specific lobbying firms. A follow-up visit to a firm's website is likely to provide profiles of individual lobbyists, including information regarding their educational and political backgrounds.
Interest Groups as Providers of Public Information		
Analyzing interest group information	a. If an interest group is a well-established and respected organization, then it will refrain from	Interest groups not only apply pressure on elected officials, but they also affect the political process

Specific Issue	Hypotheses	Hints
	spreading factually incorrect information. b. If an interest group was formed to influence a particular election, then it will be more likely to spread factually incorrect information.	by influencing what people know about politics and how people frame political questions. Some of the information they provide is factually correct and helps voters make informed decisions, but some of it is false. A great source of information for analyzing the quality of interest-group claims is the Annenberg Public Policy Center of the University of Pennsylvania, at http://www.factcheck.org.

Interest Groups and Political Parties as Cue Givers

Understanding the role of endorsements and party labels in voters' decision-making process	a. If a voter is aware of the endorsements of key interest groups, then he or she can make informed decisions about a candidate even if he or she has relatively little information about the candidate's policy preferences. b. If a voter is aware of a candidate's party label, then he or she can make informed decisions about a candidate even if he or she has relatively little information about the candidate's policy preferences.	Many studies have revealed that voters generally possess relatively little information about candidates. One school of thought suggests that voters overcome their information shortfall by taking cues from interest groups. One way to study this issue would be to conduct your own survey of likely voters in your school. Comparing the candidate preferences of fully informed voters, partially informed voters, and ill-informed voters should yield interesting results. For a sophisticated example of this type of analysis, see Arthur Lupia, "Shortcuts Versus Encyclopedias: Information and Voting

(continued)

Specific Issue	Hypotheses	Hints
		Behavior in California Insurance Reform Elections," *American Political Science Review* 88, no. 1 (1994): 63–76.

Partisanship in the Electorate

Specific Issue	Hypotheses	Hints
Red states versus blue states: is the nation as polarized as some experts suggest?	a. If a voter is from a rural area, then he or she is more likely to vote for Republicans. b. If a voter is from an urban area, then he or she is more likely to vote for Democrats. c. If a person is from the Northeast, then he or she is more likely to vote for Democrats. d. If a person is from the South, then he or she is more likely to vote for Republicans.	Some political analysts have argued that the nation is divided politically by geography. "Red states" are those that tend to vote for Republican candidates and are found in the rural South and the Mountain West region. "Blue states" are those that tend to support Democratic candidates and are found in the more urban Northeast and along the West Coast. Other political observers suggest that the differences between red and blue states have been grossly overstated.

Partisanship in Congress

Specific Issue	Hypotheses	Hints
Why has partisanship in Congress increased at the same time as party identification in the electorate has declined?	a. If a member of Congress represents *a safe district* (a congressional district drawn to favor the incumbent or the incumbent's party), then the member will engage in high levels of party-line voting. b. If a member of Congress represents a *marginal district* (a congressional district in which there is strong competition between	It has been argued that the partisanship of Congress does not represent the partisan divide in the general public but is caused by the homogeneous nature of congressional districts, which is due in part to sophisticated redistricting plans designed to secure a district for members of a specific party. There are several ways to explore this important topic. One straightforward way would

Specific Issue	Hypotheses	Hints
	candidates of different parties), then the member will be less likely to engage in high levels of party-line voting.	be to analyze the district composition of Congress's most partisan members. This could be done by looking at party-line voting scores of individual members of Congress and the voting record of the district. The appearance of a strong relationship between party-line voting and congressional composition would supply some support for the hypotheses listed here and would provide insights into the political consequences of congressional *gerrymandering*.

Party Loyalty

Specific Issue	Hypotheses	Hints
The sleeping giant: how the Hispanic vote will influence American electoral politics in the future	a. If Hispanics become loyal supporters of the Democratic Party, as African Americans did in the past, then the Democrats are likely to form a new majority coalition. b. If the Republican Party promotes a guest-worker program and amnesty for undocumented workers, then the Republicans can win support from Hispanic voters.	Hispanic Americans have surpassed African Americans as the nation's largest minority group, though their political influence remains relatively modest because of low voting rates. The future impact of the Hispanic vote remains one of the most interesting and debated topics in political science today. While predicting the future is risky business, a detailed analysis of previous voting blocs and careful consideration of how the parties are responding to issues of importance to Hispanic voters could supply meaningful support for this line of inquiry.

3. Context and Performance

A. HISTORICAL DEVELOPMENT OF POLITICAL PARTIES AND INTEREST GROUPS

The Birth and Evolution of Political Parties

At the time of the nation's founding, there was little support for the formation of traditional political parties, which were viewed as divisive factions and a threat to democratic governance. In George Washington's Farewell Address, the nation's first president warned of "the baneful effects of the spirit of party." Thomas Jefferson, one of the strongest opponents of parties, once wrote:

> I never submitted the whole system of my opinions to the creed of any party of men whatever in religion, in philosophy, in politics, or in anything else where I was capable of thinking for myself. Such an addiction is the last degradation of a free and moral agent. If I could not go to heaven but with a party, I would not go there at all.[4]

Jefferson was also a pragmatic politician who understood the benefit of collective action and the importance of winning elections. During his bid for the presidency, Jefferson, the man who would rather not go to heaven if it required belonging to a party, founded the nation's first national political party in 1800—the Democratic-Republicans (the forerunner of the Democratic Party).

For much of American history, the nation's political context has been divided between two competing parties. The modern divide between Democrats and Republicans has proved remarkably resilient, dominating the political context since the mid-1860s. While the parties live on, the influence of political parties over the electorate has declined. The period from 1874 to 1912 is generally considered the golden age of parties. In more recent years, voters have been far less loyal to parties. **Ticket-splitting** (voting for members of more than one party in a single election) has become a common phenomenon, and candidates have run more **candidate-centered campaigns**, that is, campaigns in which candidates emphasize their personal attributes rather than their party ties.

Occasionally, the nation undergoes what is often referred to as a critical election—a single election that has a durable and meaningful impact on the direction of the nation. This usually occurs when a minority party wins majority status and keeps control for an extended period of time. **Realignment** is the term used to describe the electorate's new party preference following a critical election. Several factors are believed to be responsible for realignments—scandals, dissatisfaction with the direction of the country or opposition to a major political issue, economic uncertainty, or simply the collapse of what had been a ruling coalition. While researchers do not always agree on which elections represent critical elections, the election of 1932 (which ushered in President Franklin Roosevelt and his New Deal) is generally considered the classic critical election.

The Interest-Group Explosion

In the *Federalist* No. 10, James Madison explained that one of the primary benefits of the proposed Constitution was that it would control the mischief of factions. Madison argued that the Constitution "would extend the sphere" of civil society, making it difficult for any particular faction or interest group to form a majority of the whole and to "invade the rights of other citizens." Madison believed that bigger was better, as it would reduce the destructive threat of factions. Madison's hopes were fulfilled, at least for the first fifty years of nationhood, as factions in the early republic tended to be localized and relatively small.

By the 1830s, however, communication and transportation networks were improving, essentially shrinking the nation and making possible the formation of national interest groups. Groups formed around issues such as workers' rights, temperance, abolition, women's rights, and education. By the late nineteenth century and early twentieth century, national groups were on the rise. Early labor groups included the Knights of Labor, the American Federation of Labor (AFL), the United Mine Workers, and the Industrial Workers of the World (known as the Wobblies). As labor groups organized for collective bargaining, business groups followed suit. First the railroad industry and then numerous other business groups, like the National Association of Manufacturers and the U.S. Chamber of Commerce, began sending their paid representatives to Washington.

By the mid- to late twentieth century, the number of interest groups on the national political scene had dramatically increased. Advances in technology like the facsimile machine, personal computers, photocopiers, printers, databases, and the Internet reduced the start-up costs for groups and made it easier than ever for people with common interests to identify each other and to form groups. At the same time, the nation was undergoing a period of intense social activism with issues like civil rights and environmental protection capturing the national attention. In addition, the size of the federal government, the scope of government regulations, and issues related to globalization increased the stakes for interest groups, providing further incentives for business interests and labor groups to press their issues on the national stage.

B. PARTIES AND INTEREST GROUPS AT WORK

By design, the American political system is fragmented to its core. The government is divided into local, state, and national levels; the national government is divided into three separate institutions with overlapping powers; and the legislative branch is further divided into two distinct bodies and hundreds of specialized committees. Throughout much of American history, political parties, and to a lesser extent interest groups, have served as the elastic bands that unite the otherwise disjointed political system.

While the Constitution says little about congressional leadership, other than the fact that House "shall choose their Speaker and other Officers," congressional leadership today is organized around a complex system of leaders based on party loyalty. Following the 2006 congressional elections, the Democratic Party regained majority status in the House and elected Nancy Pelosi as Speaker of the House, the first woman to hold this position. The House Democrats also selected a new majority leader and majority whip, while the minority party elected its own leadership team.

Leadership in the Senate, while also based on party, is far less concentrated than leadership in the House. The position of Senate majority leader, currently held by Democratic senator Harry Reid, is not specified in the Constitution and was not formalized until the early twentieth century. The Senate leaders have far fewer powers than party leaders in the House. The Senate's tradition of permitting **filibusters** (a filibuster is a stalling technique that enables a single senator to speak for as long as he or she wishes unless a supermajority of the Senate, 60 percent, cuts off debate) severely limits the power of party leaders in the Senate. Moreover, the Senate's informal rules and reliance on unanimous consent agreements maximizes each senator's influence and minimizes the role of party leadership.

Beyond the institutional leadership positions, parties also elect a separate group of leaders to coordinate their campaign activities. For the Democrats, former presidential candidate Howard Dean serves as chairman of the Democratic National Committee and is responsible for the party's national campaign strategy. Representative Chris Van Hollen and Senator Charles Schumer lead the party's elections strategies in their respective chambers. The chairman of the Republican National Committee is Mike Duncan, while Representative Tom Cole and Senator John Ensign lead the party's congressional campaign strategies. (See table 7.4.)

Interest groups also serve vital roles in the policy process and electoral process. Groups provide information to elected officials through sworn testimony and direct lobbying. They often help draft legislation and inform elected officials of the likely political consequences of supporting or opposing certain legislation. Interest groups serve as coalition builders, bringing together diverse groups that support or oppose legislative initiatives. And of course, interest groups provide monetary resources for political campaigns, as well as endorsements and ratings of elected officials. They are a primary conduit through which

Table 7.4. National Party Leaders, 2007

Republican Party Leaders		Democratic Party Leaders	
Campaign Leaders	*Floor Leaders*	*Campaign Leaders*	*Floor Leaders*
President (George W. Bush)			
Republican National Committee (Chairman, Mike Duncan)		**Democratic National Committee** (Chairman, Howard Dean)	
National Republican Congressional Committee (Chairman, Tom Cole)	**Republican Leader of the House** (Minority leader, John Boehner)	**Democratic Congressional Campaign Committee** (Chairman, Chris Van Hollen)	**Speaker of the House** (Speaker, Nancy Pelosi)
			Democratic Leader of the House (Majority leader, Steny Hoyer)
	Republican Whip of the House (Minority whip, Roy Blunt)		**Democratic Whip of the House** (Majority whip, James E. Clyburn)
National Republican Senatorial Committee (Chairman, John Ensign)	**Republican Leader of the Senate** (Minority leader, Mitch McConnell)	**Democratic Senatorial Campaign Committee** (Chairman, Charles Schumer)	**Democratic Leader of the Senate** (Majority leader, Harry Reid)
	Republican Whip of the Senate (Minority whip, Jon Kyle)		**Democratic Whip of the Senate** (Majority whip, Richard Durbin)

Box 7.4. Skill Box: Incumbency Advantage in Dollars and Percents

Note that interest groups, across the various sectors, disproportionately favor incumbents. This should not be surprising given the high reelection rate for incumbents in the United States (greater than 95 percent in recent House contests). Contributing PAC money to a **challenger** is risky business for an interest group, as challengers are unlikely to win and the contribution can alienate the interest group from future government officials. It is generally believed that interest groups give PAC contributions to gain access to elected officials. As table 7.5 suggests, the exceptions to the rule are ideological groups, which give a considerable amount to challengers and candidates in **open-seat** contests. For ideological groups, it is likely that access is less important than electing officials who share the group's ideological perspective.

Table 7.5. 2004 PAC Contributions to Incumbents, Challengers, and Open-Seat Candidates, by Sector

Sector	Total ($ millions)	To Incumbents (%)	To Challengers (%)	To Open Seats (%)
Agribusiness	17.1	83	4	13
Communications/ Electronics	18.2	90	2	8
Construction	12.0	83	6	12
Defense	8.1	94	2	4
Energy/Natural Resources	19.5	84	4	13
Finance/Insurance/ Real Estate	49.6	87	2	11
Health	31.7	85	3	12
Lawyers & Lobbyists	11.4	84	5	11
Transportation	18.5	87	2	11
Misc. Business	24.9	82	4	15
Labor	53.7	75	12	13
Ideology/Single-Issue	46.1	54	19	27

Source: Center for Responsive Politics, http://www.opensecrets.org/bigpicture/pac2cands.asp?cycle=2004.

information flows, educating both the public and elected officials about the likely consequences of public-policy decisions.

C. RED STATES VERSUS BLUE STATES RECONSIDERED

The American news media typically presents the results of the presidential election with a color-coded map similar to that shown in figure 7.2. States that are carried by the Republican candidate are typically colored red, while states won by the Democratic candidate are colored blue. The standard color-coded map is useful in that it provides a descriptive summary of each candidate's relative support, though it can also be quite misleading. For example, figure 7.3, which has been scaled according to each state's population, reveals that the support for the Democratic candidate in 2004 was far more robust than figure 7.2 suggests. Likewise, figure 7.4 reveals that within all states, whether they are "red states" or "blue states," there exists considerable support for both political parties. This map is particularly revealing, as it shows that partisanship is far less clear-cut than suggested by the typical election-night media report and that most of nation is neither completely red nor completely blue but a shade of purple.

Figure 7.2.   2004 presidential vote. The (contiguous 48) states are colored to indicate whether a majority of their voters voted for the Republican candidate (light states) or the Democratic candidate (dark states).
Source: Reprinted from Michael Gastner, Cosma Shalizi, and Mark Newman, "Maps and Cartograms of the 2004 U.S. Presidential Election Results," http://www-personal.umich.edu/~mejn/election.

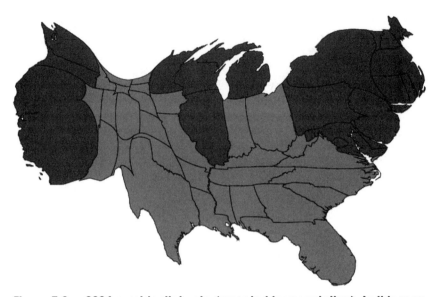

Figure 7.3.   2004 presidential vote (rescaled by population). In this map, the size of each state has been rescaled according to its population.
Source: Reprinted from Michael Gastner, Cosma Shalizi, and Mark Newman, "Maps and Cartograms of the 2004 U.S. Presidential Election Results," http://www-personal.umich.edu/~mejn/ election.

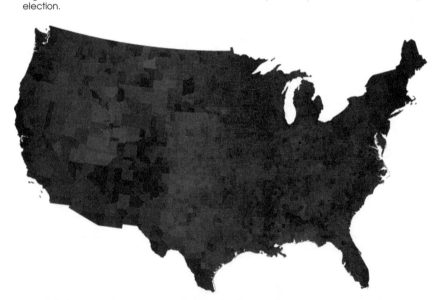

Figure 7.4.   2004 presidential vote (color coded at the county level). Instead of using just two colors, this map uses shades of gray to indicate percentages of voters at the county level.
Source: Reprinted from Michael Gastner, Cosma Shalizi, and Mark Newman, "Maps and Cartograms of the 2004 U.S. Presidential Election Results," http://www-personal.umich.edu/~mejn/election.

D. ENDURING CONTEXTUAL QUESTIONS ABOUT INTEREST GROUPS AND POLITICAL PARTIES AND HOW TO RESEARCH THEM

Exploring the Conditions That Promote the Formation of Third Parties

While the prevalence of minor parties is a constant in American politics, the appearance of prominent third parties in national politics remains relatively rare. Examples of third parties that have made a difference in national politics in recent years include the Green Party in 2000, Ross Perot's Independent Party in 1992, George Wallace's American Independent Party in 1968, Henry Wallace's Progressive Party in 1948, Robert La Follette's Progressive Party in 1928, and Teddy Roosevelt's Bull Moose Party in 1912. Exploring the conditions that promote the rise of influential third parties remains an important research topic.

Sample Hypothesis

a. If the two dominant parties adopt similar positions on divisive national issues (e.g., both parties support a war that is losing public support), then conditions become ripe for third parties.

b. If loyalty for the two dominant parties continues to decrease in the United States, then it becomes more likely that a third party will rise in prominence.

c. If an issue divides one of the two dominant parties, then there is an increased likelihood that a third party will spin off from the dominant parties.

Hints for Accomplishment

There are essentially two strategies for studying this issue. You can use past examples of third parties to asses the current conditions for third parties (i.e., are conditions ripe, and if so, what kind of third party are we likely to see in the near future?), or you can attempt to explain the factors that led to third parties in the past. The first approach is interesting, but difficult to support, as it requires making predictions about the future that are impossible to test. The second approach, while less topical, enables you to explore the determinants of third parties using empirical outcomes. In either case, make sure to understate your claims and that your assessment is consistent with the available information.

How Have Technological Changes Influenced Interest-Group Politics?

The difficulty of interest-group formation and maintenance has long been a topic of interest to political observers. James Madison, in the *Federalist* No. 10, argued that the difficulty of group formation in the early republic would help guard against the numerous problems associated with factions. Mancur Olson, in his classic work *The Logic of Collective Action* (1965), argued that the difficulty of group formation biased the political system in favor of narrow material interests (see the discussion of the free-rider problem above). The considerable technological advances of the last twenty years provide a sufficient reason to reassess the claims of Olson and the earlier thinking on interest-group formation.

Sample Hypothesis

a. If technology has eased the obstacles to group formation, then the number of interest groups should have substantially increased in recent years.
b. If technology has eased the obstacles to group maintenance, then established groups should have grown significantly in recent years.
c. If technology facilitates group membership, then the number of groups that individuals belong to should have increased in recent years.

Hints for Accomplishment

A quick look at the *Encyclopedia of Associations: National Organizations of the U.S.* provides a glimpse into the sheer number of interest groups at play in the United States. Exploring the growth of this publication over time (it is currently in its forty-third edition) is a useful way to gauge the "interest-group explosion" that has occurred in the United States. Relying exclusively on this publication, however, can be deceiving, as not all groups are equally powerful in a political sense. Another way to measure the growth of interest-group activity in recent years is to track the total number of registered lobbyists in the United States and the number and size of PACs. See the Center for Responsive Politics website (http://www.opensecrets.org and http://www.opensecrets.org/lobbyists/index.asp) for data in this area.

E. IDEA GENERATOR: ADDITIONAL CONTEXTUAL QUESTIONS RELATED TO INTEREST GROUPS AND POLITICAL PARTIES

The following chart provides some general guidelines for developing a research plan.

Specific Issue	Hypotheses	Hints
Critical Elections		
Understanding the determinants of critical elections	a. If a significant segment of the nation's voting population undergoes a substantial life change (e.g., baby	A critical election occurs when a single election has a durable and meaningful impact on the direction of the nation (e.g., a minority

Specific Issue	Hypotheses	Hints
	boomers approach retirement), then the chance of a critical election increases. b. If the electorate believes that the dominant party is not meaningfully addressing an important societal problem (e.g., the deficit), then the chance of a critical election increases. c. If the nation enters a war, then the chance of a critical election decreases.	party wins majority status and maintains control for an extended period of time). The factors that trigger this type of electoral change remain unclear. Studying the conditions surrounding previous critical elections enables researchers to predict the conditions that might lead to future critical elections.

Party Coalitions

Specific Issue	Hypotheses	Hints
The looming fight for Hispanic voters and the consequences for future majority coalitions in America	a. If the issue of immigration divides fiscal conservatives (those who desire a cheap source of labor) and national-security conservatives (those who favor closed borders) within the Republican Party, then the GOP will have difficulty achieving a majority coalition in future years. b. If the issue of immigration divides pro-labor Democrats (those who see immigrants as a threat to higher wages for workers) and pro-immigrant-rights Democrats (those who see immigrant rights as a civil rights issue), then the Democratic Party	Parties continually try to expand their coalition of supporters without alienating their existing base. This line of inquiry calls for speculation of future circumstances, by looking at recent trends and past precedents.

(continued)

Specific Issue	Hypotheses	Hints
	will find it difficult to retain control of Congress.	

Ticket-Splitting

Specific Issue	Hypotheses	Hints
Why are Americans increasingly willing to vote across party lines?	a. If the power of party identification is on the decline in the American electorate, then ticket-splitting should be on the rise. b. If candidates increasingly engage in candidate-centered campaigns, then ticket-splitting should continue to gain in prominence.	There are a number of ways to analyze ticket-splitting. One is to observe the cases in which members of different parties are elected from the same ballot (e.g., a congressional district voting for a Republican member of Congress and a Democratic candidate for president). This phenomenon can also be studied at the individual level, making use of polling data that asks a likely voter about his or her willingness to support candidates from different parties. It is generally understood that straight-ticket voting is on the decline in the United States, though the factors responsible for this decline are less well established.

Midterm Elections (i.e., elections in which there is no presidential contest and consequently no possibility of presidential *coattails*)

Specific Issue	Hypotheses	Hints
Why does the party of the president tend to lose seats in Congress during midterm elections?	a. If the president's approval rating is above 50 percent, then it is unlikely that the president's party will lose seats in the House during a midterm election. b. If a president's approval rating is below 50 percent, then it is likely that the	One of the most reliable trends in American electoral politics is that the president's party loses seats in the House in midterm elections. This happened consistently from 1950 to 1994. In 1998 and again in 2002, however, the president's party gained seats. There are many factors that

Specific Issue	Hypotheses	Hints
	president's party will lose seats in the House during a midterm election. c. If the House is controlled by the president's party, then it is likely that the president's party will lose seats in the House during a midterm election.	influence the loss of seats in House races; the hypotheses listed here represent only a few. Given the relatively small number of cases and the unique circumstances that surround each election, simple cross-tabulations and detailed analysis of particular elections is a useful way to explore this subject.

4. Secondary Sources That Will Help You Get Started

Maisel, Sandy L., and Charles Bassett, eds. *Political Parties & Elections in the United States: An Encyclopedia*. New York: Garland Publishers, 1991.

National Journal Group. *The Almanac of American Politics*. Washington, D.C.: National Journal, 2006.

Roberts, Robert North, and Scott John Hammond. *Encyclopedia of Presidential Campaigns, Slogans, Issues, and Platforms*. Westport, Conn.: Greenwood Press, 2004.

Sabato, Larry J., and Howard R. Ernst, eds. *Encyclopedia of American Political Parties and Elections*. New York: Facts On File, 2006.

Stanley, Harold, and Richard Niemi. *Vital Statistics on American Politics 2005–2006*. Washington, D.C.: CQ Press, 2005.

5. Original Research That Will Impress Your Professor

General

Campbell, Angus, Philip E. Converse, Warren E. Miller, and Donald E. Stokes. *The American Voter*. New York: Wiley, 1960.

Key, V. O., Jr. *Politics, Parties, and Pressure Groups*. 5th ed. New York: Crowell, 1964.

McCarty, Noland, Keith T. Poole, and Howard Rosenthal. *Polarized America: The Dance of Ideology and Unequal Riches*. Cambridge, Mass.: MIT Press, 2006.

Truman, David B. *The Governmental Process: Political Interests and Public Opinion*. New York: Alfred A. Knopf, 1951.

Political Parties

Aldrich, John Herbert. *Why Parties? The Origin and Transformation of Political Parties in America*. Chicago: University of Chicago Press, 1995.

Baumgartner, Frank, and Beth Leech. *Basic Interests*. Princeton, N.J.: Princeton University Press, 1998.

Chambers, William Nisbet, and Walter Dean Burnham, eds. *The American Party Systems: Stages of Political Development*. 2nd ed. New York: Oxford University Press, 1975.

Cotter, Cornelius P., and Bernard C. Hennessy. *Politics without Power: The National Party Committees*. New York: Atherton Press, 1964.

Cox, Gary, and Mathew McCubbins. *Legislative Leviathan: Party Government in the House*. Berkeley: University of California Press, 1994.

Fiorina, Morris P. *Culture War?* New York: Pearson Longman, 2005.

Fiorina, Morris P. *Divided Government*. Boston: Allyn and Bacon, 1996.

Maisel, L. Sandy, ed. *The Parties Respond*. 4th ed. Boulder, Colo.: Westview, 2002.

Mayhew, David R. *Placing Parties in American Politics*. Princeton, N.J.: Princeton University Press, 1986.

Milkis, Sidney M. *The President and the Parties: The Transformation of the American Party System since the New Deal*. New York: Oxford University Press, 1993.

Pomper, Gerald M. *Passions and Interests: Political Party Concepts of American Democracy*. Lawrence: University Press of Kansas, 1992.

Price, David E. *Bringing Back the Parties*. Washington, D.C.: CQ Press, 1984.

Ranney, Austin. *Curing the Mischief of Factions: Party Reform in America*. Berkeley: University of California Press, 1975.

Sabato, Larry J., and Bruce A. Larson. *The Party's Just Begun: Shaping Political Parties for America's Future*. 2nd ed. New York: Longman, 2002.

Schattschneider, E. E. *Party Government*. New York: Holt, Rinehart and Winston, 1942.

Wattenberg, Martin P. *The Rise of Candidate-Centered Politics*. Cambridge, Mass.: Harvard University Press, 1991.

Wattenberg, Martin P. *The Decline of American Political Parties, 1952–1996*. Cambridge, Mass.: Harvard University Press, 1998.

Interest Groups

Berry, Jeffrey M. *The Interest Group Society*. 4th ed. New York: Addison Wesley, 2001.

Cigler, Allan J., and Burdett A. Loomis, eds. *Interest Group Politics*. 6th ed. Washington, D.C.: CQ Press, 2002.

Grossman, Gene M., and Elhanan Helpman. *Special Interest Politics*. Cambridge, Mass.: MIT Press, 2001.

Hernson, Paul S., Ronald G. Shaiko, Clyde Wilcox, eds. *The Interest Group Connection*. 4th ed. Washington, D.C.: CQ Press, 2005.

Olson, Mancur, Jr. *The Logic of Collective Action: Public Good and the Theory of Groups*. Cambridge, Mass.: Harvard University Press, 1965.

Rosenthal, Alan. *The Third House: Lobbyists and Lobbying in the States*. 2nd ed. Washington, D.C.: CQ Press, 2001.

Walker, Jack. *Mobilizing Interest Groups in America*. Ann Arbor: University of Michigan Press, 1991.

Wright, John R. *Interest Groups and Congress: Lobbying, Contributions, and Influence.* New York: Longman, 2002.

6. Where to Find It

Where can I find the most respected academic polls related to political parties and American elections?
The American National Elections Studies (ANES) has been conducting comprehensive election studies since 1948. The ANES is a collaborative project between Stanford University, the University of Michigan, and the National Science Foundation. Data is available on the ANES website, at http://www.electionstudies.org.

Another rich source for high-quality survey research is the General Social Survey (GSS) of the National Opinion Research Center (NORC) at the University of Chicago, http://www.norc.uchicago.edu/projects/gensoc.asp.

Where can I find reliable information regarding interest-group and political-party spending in federal elections?
The Federal Election Commission website, http://www.fec.gov, is the federal government's official site for election results and campaign-spending information. The Center for Responsive Politics, at http://www.opensecrets.org, presents the Federal Election Commission data in a user-friendly format and is an excellent resource for investigating the influence of campaign contributions.

Where can I find information about the latest developments in lobbying and the campaign industry?
Campaigns and Elections Magazine, available online at http://www.campaignline.com, is the leading source of contemporary information regarding the campaign consulting industry. The Center for Responsive Politics maintains an excellent database with information about specific lobbyists and lobbying firms, at http://www.opensecrets.org/lobbyists/index.asp.

Where can I find information about the legal restrictions placed on political action committees?
The Federal Election Commission is responsible for regulating PACs, and the commission's website contains information regarding PACs, at http://www.fec.gov/ans/answers_pac.shtml.

Where can I find analysis regarding the truthfulness of claims made in political advertisements, including advertisements run by interest groups and political parties?

The Annenberg Public Policy Center of the University of Pennsylvania analyzes political advertisements. The center's analysis is available at http://www.factcheck .org.

Where can I find historical information regarding national party conventions?
See *National Party Conventions, 1831–2004* (Washington, D.C.: CQ Press, 2005).

Where can I find information about political candidates?
Project Vote Smart, http://www.votesmart.org, is a nonpartisan, not-for-profit organization that collects campaign-finance information, biographical information, and issue positions for a wide array of candidates.

Where can I find information about the Democratic Party?
You can find information on the Democratic Party on the websites of the Democratic National Committee, http://www.democrats.org; the Democratic Congressional Campaign Committee, http://www.dccc.org; and the Democratic Senatorial Campaign Committee, http://www.dscc.org.

Where can I find information about the Republican Party?
You can find information on the Republican Party on the websites of the Republican National Committee, http://www.gop.com; the National Republican Congressional Committee, http://www.nrcc.org; and the National Republican Senatorial Committee, http://www.nrsc.org. Links to state Republican Parties can be found at http://www.gop.com/connect/States.aspx.

Where can I find a list of third parties in the United States?
Politics1.com maintains an excellent list of third parties, at http://www.politics1 .com/parties.htm.

Where can I find comprehensive lists of national advocacy groups in the United States?
Kathi Carlisle Fountain maintains a list of advocacy groups, available at http:// www.vancouver.wsu.edu/fac/kfountain. While this list is not complete, it does contain major groups and provides useful links. You may also want to look at Kristy Swartout, ed., *Encyclopedia of Associations: National Associations of the United States*, 43rd ed. (Detroit, Mich.: Gale Research Company, 2006), which includes all not-for-profit membership organizations and contains information about more than twenty-two thousand groups.

Notes

1. The text of Washington's Farewell Address is available from the Avalon Project at Yale Law School, at http://www.yale.edu/lawweb/avalon/washing.htm.

2. See, e.g., *Tax-Exempt Status for Your Organization*, IRS Publication 557, available online at http://www.irs.gov/pub/irs-pdf/p557.pdf.

3. Federal Election Commission, "Quick Answers to PAC Questions," http://www.fec.gov/ans/answers_pac.shtml.

4. Thomas Jefferson to Francis Hopkinson, March 13, 1789. The text of the letter is available online at http://etext.virginia.edu/jefferson/quotations/jeff0800.htm.

CHAPTER 8

Elections and Voting Behavior

In the American political system, **elections** are the processes by which the **electorate**, the group of people qualified to vote, chooses public officials and influences the direction of public policy. By providing an essential check on political leaders and influencing the direction of public policies, elections serve a key function in democratic societies. Simply stated, without free and open elections, democratic governance is not possible. This chapter provides the essential tools necessary for exploring the health of the electoral process in United States and for assessing the state of democracy in America.

1. The Structure and Intention of Elections

A. CONSTITUTIONAL AND LEGAL BASIS

Articles I and II of the U.S. Constitution outline the qualifications and selection methods for the U.S. House of Representatives, the U.S. Senate, and the president (the selection of federal judges is done by appointment, rather than election, and is discussed in chapter 4).

Structure

The electoral system in the U.S. is a **representative democracy** (a political system in which voters select political representatives to make public policy decisions and to perform essential governmental services).

Citizen Qualifications for Voting

Article 1, Section 4 of the U.S. Constitution permits the states to establish their own qualifications for voting, called **suffrage requirements**. Initially, states generally limited voting to white male property owners. The Fourteenth and Fifteenth Amendments to the Constitution (ratified in 1868 and 1870, respectively) granted voting rights to former slaves. The Nineteenth Amendment (1920) extended voting rights to women. The Supreme Court banned white-only primaries in 1944 (*Smith v. Allwright*), and the 1965 Voting Rights Act added further protections for African American voters. The Twenty-third Amendment (1961) permitted residents of the District of Columbia to vote in presidential elections; the Twenty-fourth Amendment (1964) banned the use of poll taxes; and the Twenty-sixth Amendment (1971) lowered the voting age from twenty-one to eighteen.

Elections

U.S. House members are elected for two-year terms. Though the Constitution does not require **single-member legislative districts**, districts in which a single elected official represents a specific geographic region in the legislature, Congress passed legislation in 1842 requiring House members to represent distinct geographic districts. Two Supreme Court cases (*Baker v. Carr*, in 1962, and *Reynolds v. Sims*, in 1964) established that congressional districts must, to the extent possible, have equal populations. Each state, through the **apportionment** process, is allocated a number of House seats according to the results of the decennial census. The redrawing of congressional district lines following the decennial census is known as **redistricting** and is the responsibility of the states.

U.S. Senators are elected for six-year terms and represent their entire state. Each state elects two senators. While the Constitution originally called on state legislatures to select senators, the Seventeenth Amendment (1913) established the popular vote as the selection mechanism for U.S. Senators.

Presidents are elected to four-year terms and, following passage of the Twenty-second Amendment (1951), are prohibited from being "elected to the office of the President more than twice." Presidential selection is achieved through the **Electoral College**, which allocates to each state a number of electors equal to their total number of members in Congress (both the House and the Senate) and allocates three electors to the District of Columbia (538 total electors). In most states, the winner of the popular vote in that state wins that state's entire electoral vote. The exceptions to the winner-take-all rule are Maine and Nebraska, which allocate their electoral votes by congressional districts. The candidate who receives a majority of electoral votes (270) wins the presidency. If no candidate wins an absolute majority, the election moves to the House of Representatives, where each state's coalition is given a single vote. The first candidate to receive a majority vote in the House of Representatives becomes president.

The vice presidency was originally awarded to the person who received the second-highest number of electoral votes. In the case of a tie for second place, the Senate chose the vice president. As a result of the Twelfth Amendment (1804), the Electoral College votes for president and vice president take place separately, allowing the president and vice president to run as a ticket and guarding against the election of a president from one party and a vice president from a different party, which happened in the 1796 presidential election.

B. GOALS AND INTENTIONS

Select Government Officials

One of the most basic functions of elections is to fill important posts with qualified officials. The electoral component of representative democracy is designed to promote the selection of highly qualified officials. James Madison, in the *Federalist* No. 10, explained that elections are intended to "refine and enlarge the public views, by passing them through the medium of a chosen body of citizens." He went on to say that if the electoral process functions properly, it will produce officials "whose wisdom may best discern the true interest of their country, and whose patriotism and love of justice, will be least likely to sacrifice it to temporary or partial considerations."

Provide Checks and Accountability

Elections not only give citizens a direct hand in selecting their representatives to government, but they also enable citizens the power to remove government officials from office. While reelection rates remain remarkably high in the United States, the threat of being voted out of office helps keep elected officials in check and responsive to the desires of their constituents. In the *Federalist* No. 51, James Madison explained the founders' intentions: "In framing a government which is to be administered by men over men, the great difficulty lies in this: You must first enable the government to control the governed; and in the second place, oblige it to control itself. A dependence on the people is no doubt the primary control on the government."

Affirm Popular Sovereignty and Foster Political Legitimacy

The principle of popular sovereignty asserts that the source of all legitimate political power is derived from the consent of the governed. As Thomas Jefferson famously wrote in the Declaration of Independence, "Governments are instituted among men, deriving their just powers from the consent of the governed." Elections are uniquely capable of linking government officials to the will of the public, and by doing so they affirm popular sovereignty and provide legitimacy to the political system. Even people who strongly disagree with government policies generally follow those policies because they respect the legitimacy of the democratic process that brought about the policies.

Influence Public Policy

Elections also enable the public to influence the policy process. Political parties and candidates identify specific policy positions that they favor and campaign on these policies, or **platforms**. Parties and elected officials will claim an electoral **mandate** based on electoral results—that is, assert that the voters have expressed their preference for the candidate's or party's stated policy positions. The public can also influence public policy less directly through retrospective and prospective voting. **Retrospective voting** refers to a voter's decision to reward or punish a candidate or a candidate's party for decisions since the last election (e.g., voting incumbents out of office because of a tax increase or a downturn in the economy). **Prospective voting** refers to a voter's decision to punish or reward a candidate or a candidate's party because of the voters' perception of the direction of the country. If voters believe that the country is headed in the right direction, they are likely to reward incumbents. Challengers benefit when voters perceive the country to be headed in the wrong direction. In either case, voters are able to indirectly influence the direction of public policy through the electoral system.

C. RULES GOVERNING THE FUNDING OF POLITICAL CAMPAIGNS

Because of the potentially corrupting influence of campaign contributions, political reformers have long attempted to rid the electoral system of unlimited campaign spending. Early examples of campaign-finance reform include

- **the Civil Service Reform Act of 1883** (also known as the **Pendleton Civil Service Act**), which prohibited solicitation of political contributions from federal employees;
- **the Tillman Act of 1907**, which barred registered corporations from contributing to political campaigns;
- **the Federal Corrupt Practices Acts of 1910, 1911, and 1925**, which established spending limits and disclosure requirements and represented the nation's first attempt at comprehensive campaign-finance reform;

- **the Hatch Act of 1939**, which regulated primaries and put additional restrictions on the political activities of federal employees; and
- **the Taft-Hartley Act of 1947**, which banned contributions from unions and corporations in primary and general elections.

The modern period of campaign-finance reform began with the passage of the **Federal Election Campaign Act of 1971 (FECA)**. This landmark legislation created a system of public funding for presidential campaigns and limited the amount of money that federal candidates could spend on their own campaigns, as well as the amount that individuals, interest groups, and political parties could contribute to federal candidates. It required that interest groups contribute through regulated **political action committees (PACs)**. The **Federal Election Commission** was established in 1975 to enforce and administer FECA. In 1976, the Supreme Court ruled in *Buckley v. Valeo* that FECA could not limit the amount of money that a candidate could spend on his or her own campaign, equating campaign spending with political speech, which is protected by the First Amendment. However, the court upheld the contribution limits from individuals and interest groups, as well as the public-financing component of FECA.

The **Bipartisan Campaign Reform Act of 2002 (BCRA)** was the most recent attempt to limit the influence of campaign spending in American elections. This legislation, also known as the **McCain-Feingold campaign-finance reform**, named for its two primary sponsors, attempted to rid the system of the corrupting influence of unregulated big-dollar contributions. The legislation banned **soft-money contributions**—unlimited contributions to political parties that were being used to fund loosely veiled political advertisements that did not expressly call on voters to support a specific candidate but instead painted one candidate in a favorable light or another candidate in an unfavorable light. In addition, the legislation increased individual contribution limits from $1,000 to $2,000 and increased PAC contribution limits from $2,000 to $5,000. Since the passage of the bill, the federal courts have upheld all the major components of the BCRA.

In the wake of the BCRA, a new development has emerged in the way that large contributions are influencing American elections. So-called **527 groups**, groups that are not directly associated with political parties or candidates but that spend unregulated amounts of money to influence elections, have exploded onto the political scene. Much like soft-money contributions prior to the BCRA, 527 groups create an avenue for mega-donors, like George Soros and Peter Lewis, to spend millions of dollars to influence election results. The most famous of these groups is MoveOn.org, which supports Democratic candidates, though the Republicans have 527 groups of their own, such as Swift Boat Veterans for Truth.

D. COMPARATIVE PERSPECTIVE

The election season in the United States is generally longer than in other Western democracies, and elections are far more expensive in the United States than in other democracies. No other nation uses anything like the Electoral College, few countries have single-member legislative districts, and most democratic nations have more than two dominant political parties. Most democratic nations either elect their chief executive through direct elections or use a parliamentary system. Another major difference between elections in the United States and elsewhere in the world is the timing of elections. Elections in the United States happen at set intervals (four years for the president, six years for the Senate, and two years for the House). In many parliamentary systems, elections do not happen at regular intervals; the chief executive can call for new elections or the parliament can demand elections through a vote of no confidence.

E. ENDURING STRUCTURAL QUESTIONS AND HOW TO RESEARCH THEM

The Consequences of Campaign-Finance Reform

Political observers have long bemoaned the manner in which elections are funded in the United States. Critics of the nation's private funding system have argued

---

Sample Hypothesis

a. If the McCain-Feingold act has been successful, then special-interest groups should no longer be able to funnel unlimited amounts of money into the political process.
b. If the McCain-Feingold act has been successful, then it should be easier to track the sources of campaign spending.

Hints for Accomplishment

Go to the Center for Responsive Politics website, at http://www.opensecrets.org, and explore campaign fund-raising trends leading up to the McCain-Feingold act in 2002 and after passage of the act. Note that while "soft money" has been effectively banned from the system, "hard money" contributions have substantially increased since 2002 (see figure 8.1). Moreover, interest groups have found a new loophole (527 groups) through which to funnel unregulated campaign spending (see the information on 527 groups at http://www.opensecrets.org/527s/index.asp).

that the system drives up the cost of elections, gives disproportionate influence to interest groups, lacks adequate disclosure requirements, benefits incumbents, and corrodes public confidence in the electoral process. Passage of the BCRA (the McCain-Feingold act) was the latest attempt to rid the system of the corrupting influence of unregulated political contributions. But did it work?

Box 8.1.   Skill Box: Analyzing Fund-Raising by Party over Time

Note that the Republican Party has traditionally raised more hard-money contributions than the Democratic Party (see figure 8.1), while the Democrats have been more competitive in raising soft-money contributions (see figure 8.2). Since the elimination of the soft-money loophole, both parties have increased their hard-money fund-raising, and the Republican advantage in raising hard money has been substantially narrowed. With Democrats regaining control of the House and Senate following the 2006 election, the comparative fund-raising power of the Democratic Party should continue to rise.

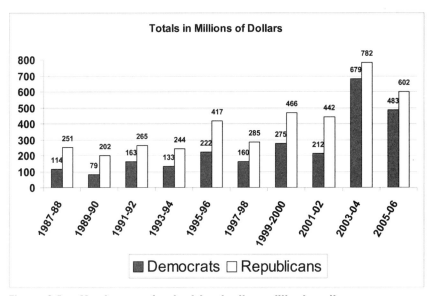

Figure 8.1.   Hard-money fund-raising by the political parties.
Source: Reprinted from the Center for Responsive Politics, http://www.opensecrets.org/bigpicture/ptytots.asp?cycle=2004.

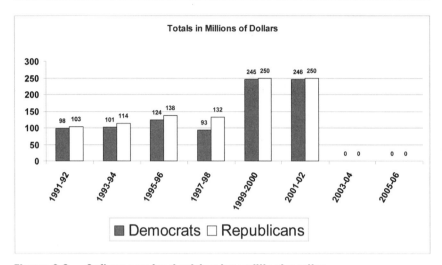

Figure 8.2.   Soft-money fund-raising by political parties.
Source: Reprinted from the Center for Responsive Politics, http://www.opensecrets.org/bigpicture/
ptytots.asp?cycle=2004.

Sample Hypothesis

a. If a state is closely divided along party lines, but controlled by a single party, then there is likely to be a high degree of gerrymandering.
b. If a state is closely divided along party lines and government control is divided between the parties, then there should be a low degree of gerrymandering.
c. If a state is dominated by one party, then gerrymandering will be used to protect incumbents and friends of the party leadership.

Hints for Accomplishment

Note that the logic of gerrymandering changes depending on the situation of a particular state. If possible, a party will use redistricting to secure its position within the state. However, in situations of **divided government**, when control of the government is divided between two parties, partisan redistricting becomes problematic, as one party will block the actions of the other. In situations where one party dominates the political scene, officials might feel less of a need to engage in gerrymandering and may base their redistricting plans on secondary concerns. This research topic lends itself to comparative case-study analysis. You can compare a single state's redistricting plans at different periods of time or two different states that are facing different partisan pressures. In either case, detailed analysis can reveal how district maps reflect the specific circumstances of a state. Be cautious in stating any causal claims, as comparative analysis is ill suited for establishing causality.

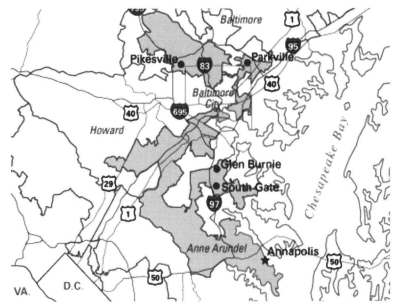

Figure 8.3.   The face of gerrymandering: Maryland's Third Congressional District.
Source: Reprinted from *The National Atlas of the United States* (produced by the U.S. Department of the Interior), http://nationalatlas.gov/printable/congress.html#md.

Exploring the Electoral Effects of Redistricting and Gerrymandering

Every ten years, following the decennial census, state governments redraw their congressional districts. The contentious process protects against **malapportionment**, which is the tendency of some legislative districts to represent more people than other legislative districts because of population shifts over time, but it also creates opportunities to draw political boundaries for political advantage—often referred to as **gerrymandering**. The tensions that sometimes arise between the competing interests of a party and individual elected officials within the party, as well as considerable tensions between the parties, can lead to interesting research questions.

Note that gerrymandering is the work of the majority party in a state. When a state is controlled by a single party, as is the case in Maryland, where the Democratic Party is in control, gerrymandering can take on outlandish configurations, as figure 8.3 illustrates.

F. IDEA GENERATOR: A SAMPLE OF ADDITIONAL STRUCTURAL QUESTIONS RELATED TO ELECTIONS

The following chart provides some general guidelines for developing a research plan.

Specific Issue	Hypotheses	Hints

Money and Elections

The source and nature of political contributions to candidates	a. If a state has loose contribution laws, or no contribution limits at all (e.g., Virginia), then candidates for state office will receive fewer, but larger, political contributions. b. If a state has "clean election laws," laws that provide matching funds in exchange for abiding by fund-raising limits (e.g., Maine), then candidates for state office will receive more, but smaller, contributions.	The laws that govern elections and political contributions for state office vary substantially from state to state. (See the National Association of Secretaries of State website, at http://www .nass.org, for links to each state.)

Presidential Selection

Likely consequences of electoral-college reform	a. If the Electoral College was replaced with a direct vote, then cities and urban areas would gain political influence. b. If the Electoral College was replaced with a direct vote, then presidential elections would become more expensive. c. If the Electoral College was replaced with a direct vote, then third parties would gain influence.	This is a common "what if" question that requires a researcher to speculate about the future. To meaningfully address this issue, you might want to compare the U.S. system with systems in other countries, or you might want to compare it with the selection of chief executives in large states. You might also want to explore the likely consequences of different Electoral-College plans, as there are several. (See the Center for Voting and Democracy website, at http://www.fairvote .org/e_college/reform .htm, for information on various reform options.)

Specific Issue	Hypotheses	Hints

Voter Registration

Do differences in voter registration requirements influence voter participation?	a. If a state permits "same day registration," then it will have higher voter participation rates. b. If a state closes registration early in the election season, then it will have lower voter participation rates.	Numerous studies have shown that voter registration requirements are one of the greatest obstacles to voter participation. Registered voters vote, and unregistered voters do not. Since states determine their own registration requirements, cross-state comparisons are a useful way to explore this issue.

Candidate Selection

Presidential primaries and caucuses	a. If a state makes use of *a closed primary* (a primary only open to party members), then the state will favor ideologically extreme candidates. b. If a state makes use of an *open primary* (a primary in which all voters are permitted to participate regardless of party affiliation), then the state will favor moderate candidates.	States determine their own method for selecting delegates to the national party conventions. Some states have open systems that encourage widespread participation, while others try to limit participation to the party faithful. Limiting your analysis to a single election and two politically similar states that use different selection mechanisms is one way to explore this issue.

Reelection

The effects of term limits	a. If a state has term limits, then more women and members of minority groups will fill elected positions. b. If a state has term limits, then the state will provide more generous pay to its elected officials.	Several states have adopted term limits for their state representatives and governors. In addition to limiting the number of years an official can hold office, term limits can have interesting, and often unintended, consequences in the governmental process. Comparing term-limit

(continued)

Specific Issue	Hypotheses	Hints
		states with non-term-limit states can yield unexpected results. For information about term-limit states, see U.S. Term Limits, http://www .termlimits.org.

Reapportionment

Specific Issue	Hypotheses	Hints
The electoral impact of re-apportionment trends	a. If reapportionment trends continue in the same direction, then the Republican Party will increase its strength in the Electoral College. b. If reapportionment trends continue in the same direction, then the Hispanic vote will play a greater role in determining future presidential elections.	Every ten years, following the decennial census, the nation's 435 congressional seats are reallocated to account for population shifts (reapportionment). In recent years, southern states, many of which are GOP strongholds, have gained seats, while states in the Northeast, traditionally the Democratic Party's geographic base, have been losing seats. This line of inquiry allows you to assess how this trend might affect presidential elections in the future.

2. Participants

A. WHO ARE THE PARTICIPANTS AND WHY ARE THEY THERE?

Incumbents and Challengers

Incumbents are current officeholders, while **challengers** are the candidates who seek to unseat incumbents. Incumbents are reelected at remarkably high rates in the United States (reelection rates in the U.S. House are as high as 98 percent, and reelection rates in the U.S. Senate regularly exceed 85 percent). The **incumbency advantage**—the advantage that incumbents have over challengers because of the benefits of holding office—is attributed to several factors, including higher name recognition, generous travel allowances, **war chests** (campaign funds from previous campaigns), flexible schedules, large professional staffs, generous office budgets, free mail, media coverage, and preferred treatment among campaign contributors. Many congressional districts are drawn to favor an incumbent or an incumbent's party, creating "**safe districts**," and the number of competitive districts, or "**marginal districts**," has decreased in recent years. The power of incumbency can lead to low-quality challengers, often described as **sacrificial lambs**, since they have little chance of winning. An **open-seat election** is an election with no incumbent in the race and consequently no incumbency advantage. Open-seat elections tend to be the most competitive and attract the most campaign contributions.

The Campaign Consulting Industry

Campaign consulting has become a multibillion-dollar industry in the United States. **Campaign consultants** are the paid professionals who help candidates develop a campaign message, raise funds, target voters, deliver the message, and get out the vote. The industry consists of professional campaign consultants who participate in all aspects of political campaigns: general strategy, message development, polling, media relations, direct mail, web design, targeting, voter mobilization, and fund-raising. Beyond the paid consultants, most campaigns have a **campaign manager**, the person who oversees the day-to-day operations of the campaign; a **campaign press secretary**, the person who interacts with the media; and a **campaign finance chair**, the person who is responsible for the day-to-day fund-raising operation and compliance with fund-raising laws. Most of the money raised in political campaigns is spent on paid media in the form of campaign advertisements.

Voters and Nonvoters

Roughly 300 million people reside within the United States, though less than 125 million voted in the 2004 elections. Many nonvoters are ineligible because they have not reached the voting age of eighteen, are not legal citizens of the United States, or have been convicted of a felony in a state that limits political participation by convicted felons. Another substantial group of nonvoters are those who are legally eligible to vote but are not permitted to vote because they failed to register in their particular state. There are several groups who are consistently underrepresented at the polls—namely, young voters, Hispanic voters, poor voters, and voters with low levels of education. A state's registration laws and voting procedures are also believed to influence voting rates, with states that use same-day registration (i.e., that allow voters to register on the day of the election) and states that have mail-in voting (i.e., that allow or require people to vote by mail) experiencing higher levels of voter participation than states with more restrictive voting laws.

Partisans, Party Leaners, and Independents

Political observers tend to divide voters into three groups according to their level of party identification (see chapter 7 for a discussion of trends in party identification). **Partisans** are people who strongly identify with a specific party. **Independents** are people who do not consider themselves members of a specific party. Among independents, there are those who typically vote for members of one party (**independent leaners**).

Ideologues: Conservatives, Moderates, and Liberals

Conservatives are considered to be on the right of the political spectrum and tend to support Republican candidates in the United States. They believe in individual liberty and tend to favor military and police spending over social policies and environmental programs. Conservatives tend to favor low taxes and limited government control of the economy. **Liberals** are considered to be on the left of the political spectrum and tend to support Democratic candidates in the United States. They believe in social responsibility and that the government has a leading role to play in promoting social well-being and social justice. Liberals tend to favor spending on public education, environmental programs, and social programs over military and police spending. **Moderates** hold an ideological perspective that is considered to be in the middle of the political spectrum and in the United States have less predicable partisan associations than true conservatives and liberals. Moderates generally make up the bulk of **swing voters**, that is, voters who can be persuaded to vote for candidates from either political party, and consequently receive a great deal of attention in competitive general-election campaigns.

Voting Blocs

Pollsters, and the candidates to whom pollsters report, tend to organize the public into voting blocs. Winning the votes of these subgroups is often considered the key to winning elections. In recent years, African American voters have overwhelmingly supported Democratic candidates and consequently receive a great deal of "**get out the vote**" attention—campaign activities that are designed to increase the chances that a candidate's supporters vote on Election Day—from the Democratic Party. Hispanics, who now surpass African Americans as the nation's largest minority group, continue to vote at relatively low rates in the United States and have less predicable party loyalty than African Americans. In a trend referred to as the **gender gap**, women voters, who now constitute a majority of the electorate, tend to favor Democratic candidates more than men do. Evangelical Christian voters have become the grassroots force of the Republican Party, especially in the South. **NASCAR dads** are a group of conservative married men who tend to support the

Republican Party. **Soccer moms** are married women with children, who tend to be more conservative than single women but less conservative than their male counterparts. Soccer moms have been identified as a key swing vote in recent elections. Other voting blocs are associated popular personalities, like **Lou Dobbs Democrats**, working-class Democrats who take a hard-line stance on immigration; **Ron Paul Republicans**, Republicans with a libertarian bent that does not fit well with the mainstream Republican Party; **Reagan Democrats**, Democrats who supported Republican candidate Ronald Reagan for president; and **Obamacans**, Republicans who supported Democratic candidate Barack Obama for president.

B. COMPARATIVE PERSPECTIVE

There are several significant differences between electoral participation in the United States and in other Western democracies. First, voting rates in the United States, which tend to peak between 50 to 60 percent in presidential election years, are far lower than in other countries, which tend to have less restrictive voter registration requirements and greater incentives for voting—for example, **compulsory voting**, which requires nonvoters to pay a penalty for failing to vote. Outside the United States, Western democracies tend to have election rates that regularly reach 70 to 90 percent. Other factors that tend to distinguish electoral politics in

Sample Hypothesis

a. If incumbents are members of the party of a popular president, then their reelection rates will be higher than those for members of the opposing party.
b. If incumbents are members of the party of an unpopular president, then their reelection rates will be lower than those for members of the opposing party.
c. If incumbents are involved in a political scandal, then their reelection rates will be low.
d. If incumbents face challengers with high name recognition, then their reelection rates will be low.

Hints for Accomplishment

There are two basic strategies for exploring these issues. You can explore the issue by explaining the aggregate-level data (e.g., the factors that caused the reelection rate in the U.S. Senate to dip to below 56 percent in 1980). Or you can explore a specific election cycle, or even a specific race, to investigate the issue. Since reelection rates in the House are remarkably high, it is often useful to look at the small number of incumbents who lost their reelection contests in a specific year. What distinguished the failed incumbents from the vast majority of incumbents who won reelection?

Box 8.2.   Skill Box: Reelection Rates over Time (House and Senate)

There is a great deal of information that can be derived from figures 8.4 and 8.5. Note that the House reelection rates have remained stable and high, suggesting that changing national conditions have had little effect on House races in general. The Senate reelection rates, on the other hand, have fluctuated considerably, but have leveled off at a high level over the last decade. What factors might help explain the fluctuation in the Senate? Why are reelection rates higher in the House than in the Senate?

United States from other Western democracies include the nation's highly developed campaign-consulting industry, the two-party system, weak party identification among voters, drawn-out campaign seasons, the frequency of elections, the reliance on private funding for campaigns, and the expensive media markets.

C. ENDURING QUESTIONS ABOUT THE PARTICIPANTS AND HOW TO RESEARCH THEM

Exploring the Reelection Connection: The Power of Incumbency

As we discussed earlier, not all candidates are created equal. Those who currently occupy an elected position (i.e., incumbents) have a substantial electoral advantage over those who challenge incumbents. The advantage is associated with several factors that come with holding elective office, including name recognition, travel allowances, flexible schedules, gerrymandering, paid staffs, free mail, access

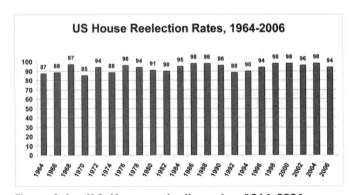

Figure 8.4.   U.S. House reelection rates, 1964–2006.
Source: Reprinted from the Center for Responsive Politics, http://www.opensecrets.org/bigpicture/reelect.asp?cycle=2006.

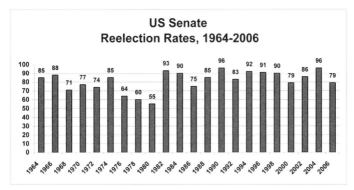

Figure 8.5.   U.S. Senate reelection rates, 1964–2006.
Source: Reprinted from the Center for Responsive Politics, http://www
.opensecrets.org/bigpicture/reelect.asp?Cycle=2006&chamb=S.

to free media coverage, and preferred treatment among campaign contributors. In recent years incumbents have been reelected at remarkably high rates—as high as 98 percent in recent U.S. House elections. While the reelection rate for U.S. Senate and gubernatorial contests is lower than that for House races, incumbents running for reelection in these contests typically experience reelection rates that exceed 80 percent.

Sample Hypothesis

a. If attention is focused on married voters, then we will find that support of Republican candidates among women is similar to Republican support among men.
b. If attention is focused on college graduates, then we will find that support of Republican candidates among women is similar to Republican support among men.
c. If attention is focused on religious voters, then we will find that support of Republican candidates among women is similar to Republican support among men.

Hints for Accomplishment

This type of analysis allows you to isolate the influence of gender by controlling for the influence of additional factors (e.g., marital status, education, and religion). If the gender gap decreases, or is eliminated altogether, when the analysis focuses on specific subgroups, this would challenge the traditional way of thinking about gender differences. It would suggest that the gender gap is in part due to the fact that women disproportionately fall into subgroups that tend to support Democrats more than Republicans, and that gender itself might have little to do with perceived differences. To conduct this type of analysis, you would need to have access to polling data and the ability to organize your findings into contingency tables.

The Source and Nature of the "Gender Gap"

The gender gap first gained attention in the 1980s, when men favored the Republican presidential candidate, Ronald Reagan, more than women did. The general trend of men favoring Republican candidates more than women do, and women favoring Democratic candidates more than men do, has persisted since the 1980s. While the general trend is well established, there are several aspects of the trend that are less well understood.

D. IDEA GENERATOR: A SAMPLE OF ADDITIONAL QUESTIONS RELATED TO ELECTORAL PARTICIPANTS

The following chart provides some general guidelines for developing a research plan.

Specific Issue	Hypotheses	Hints
Candidates		
Deciding to run for office	a. If an election is for an open seat, then the race will attract high-quality candidates. b. If an incumbent is running for reelection and has a substantial war chest, then the race will attract low-quality challengers or no challengers at all.	Political aspirants are aware that their chances of unseating an incumbent are small—and a well-financed incumbent even smaller. Given this knowledge, we should expect high-quality challengers to behave in a predictable manner—selecting contests in which there is no incumbent.
Challengers and campaign spending	a. If a candidate is an unknown challenger, then the candidate's campaign spending should have a substantial impact on the race. b. If a candidate is an unknown challenger, then the candidate's early campaign fund-raising should have a substantial impact on the race.	Unknown challengers use campaign funds to establish name recognition and credibility. It is difficult to determine whether challengers win votes because they raise a substantial amount of money, or whether they are able to raise money for the same reason they win votes—because they are popular. Claiming a direct causal relationship can be tricky.

Specific Issue	Hypotheses	Hints
Incumbents and campaign spending	a. If an incumbent is interested in a leadership position within a party, he or she will contribute money to the campaigns of other members of the party. b. If an incumbent faces a weak challenger, then the incumbent will refrain from spending large amounts of money on his or her own campaign.	It is widely believed that elected officials spend campaign funds in a rational manner (i.e., in a manner that promotes their political objectives of reelection and increased influence). If this is the case, it should be possible to identify predicable spending trends.
Does race matter?	a. If a congressional district is a *majority-minority congressional district* (in which a majority of the population is composed of a group that makes up a minority of the total U.S. population), then the district is likely to elect a representative who is a member of a minority group. b. If a majority of the population in a congressional district is white, then the district will be more likely to elect a white representative.	Members of minority groups remain underrepresented in almost every level of government. Exploring the conditions that foster minority representation can produce interesting results.
Name recognition (celebrities, billionaires, widows, generals, and members of famous families)	a. If an incumbent faces a challenger with high name recognition, then the incumbent is less likely to win reelection. b. If an incumbent faces a challenger who is independently wealthy,	It is believed that one of the key sources of the incumbency advantage is name recognition. Celebrities, spouses of elected officials and celebrities, military leaders, and members of famous

(*continued*)

Specific Issue	Hypotheses	Hints
	then the incumbent is less likely to win reelection.	families often have name recognition that rivals that of elected officials. Likewise, wealthy challengers can afford to buy name recognition through campaign spending, thereby reducing the incumbency advantage.
Does character matter? (Scandal, character, and image)	a. If an incumbent is embroiled in an ongoing scandal, then the incumbent will be more likely to face an opponent in the primary. b. If an incumbent is embroiled in an ongoing scandal, then the incumbent is more likely to face a high-quality challenger in the general election.	It is generally held that scandals are one of the few factors that make incumbents vulnerable to challengers. Consequently, it is likely that the presence of a scandal may attract high-quality challengers who sense the incumbent's vulnerability. Conducting an in-depth case study of the impact of a scandal on challengers can be a useful research strategy.

The Influence Industry

Specific Issue	Hypotheses	Hints
Who gives to campaigns and why?	a. If a person is politically aware and wealthy, then that person will be more likely to contribute to a political campaign. b. If a person is politically aware but is not wealthy, then that person will be more likely to volunteer for a political campaign.	Who contributes to campaigns and the manner in which they contribute is an important and little-understood issue. It helps explain the GOP's traditional fund-raising advantage over Democrats and the GOP's working-class evangelical base, as well as the Democratic Party's traditional reliance on labor-union support.
How mega-donors exert influence over	a. If regulations restrict large contributions in one area of campaign	From funding partisan presses to creating PACs to making soft-money

Specific Issue	Hypotheses	Hints
the election process	finance, then large donors will find alternative ways to influence the electoral process. b. If a person is a large money donor, then that person will tend to support candidates of one specific party.	contributions and now contributing unlimited sums to 527 groups, large-money donors have a long tradition in American electoral politics. This issue can be studied from a historical perspective, by studying specific large donors or by focusing on a specific attempt to regulate large donors and the subsequent loopholes that emerged.

Voters

Specific Issue	Hypotheses	Hints
Identifying the causes of nonvoting	a. If a person has a college degree, then that person is more likely to vote. b. If a person's parents are registered voters, then that person is more likely to vote.	Through the use of polling data, political scientists can identify the characteristics of voters and nonvoters. These findings can be used to inform predictions about elections and the likely consequences of electoral reform.
The sleeping giant: the Hispanic vote	a. If Hispanic Americans become loyal supporters of the Democratic Party, as African Americans did in the past, then the Democrats will be able to form a new majority coalition. b. If the Republican Party promotes a guest worker program and amnesty for undocumented workers, then the Republican Party can win support from Hispanic voters.	Hispanic Americans have surpassed African Americans as the nation's largest minority group, though their political influence remains relatively modest due to low voting rates. The future impact of the Hispanic vote remains one of the most interesting and debated topics in political science today.

(continued)

Specific Issue	Hypotheses	Hints
Voter competence: do voters know enough to make informed decisions?	a. If a voter has a low level of information about candidates, then that voter is more likely to support a candidate who does not share his or her policy preferences. b. If a voter watches a great deal of entertainment-based television, rather than news coverage, then that voter is more likely to form opinions about a candidate based on image rather than policy preferences.	Whether voters are sufficiently competent to make educated electoral decisions remains an important research question. Related questions concern how voters learn about politics (newspapers, television, the Internet) and the types of information shortcuts they use to make up for their information deficiencies.

3. Context and Performance

A. HISTORICAL DEVELOPMENT OF CAMPAIGN COVERAGE AND POLLING

Media and Elections: The Ever-Changing Relationship

The news media is the primary vehicle through which political information flows to the electorate and has consequently been influential from the outset of American democracy. The debates between the **Federalists**, who supported ratification of the U.S. Constitution, and the **Anti-Federalists**, who opposed ratification of the U.S. Constitution, played out in partisan political newspapers in the late 1780s. By the mid-1830s, the inexpensive "**penny presses**" greatly increased the availability of electoral information. By the late 1890s, publishers like William Randolph Hearst were introducing a new breed of journalism, referred to as **yellow journalism**, which sensationalized the news to win greater readership. In 1928, elections were first broadcast on commercial radio stations, and in 1948 election results were first covered by television broadcasters.

By 1952, television coverage had taken center stage, with presidential hopefuls airing the first televised campaign commercials. The nation viewed the first face-to-face general-election presidential debates on television in 1960. The 1980s saw the birth of cable news coverage and the increased popularity of conservative AM radio programs. Throughout the 1990s elections entered the Internet age, with candidates, interest groups, and news organizations disseminating electoral information online. The latest developments in the way elections are covered on the Internet include the development of blogs, the use of social networking sites (e.g., MySpace and Facebook), and the use of streaming media sites (e.g., YouTube).

When it comes to conveying information to voters, candidates are no longer at the mercy of the **free media**, that is, campaign coverage that is derived from news organizations. With sufficient funding, candidates can purchase media spots known as **paid media**. The campaign can make use of advertisements to promote the virtues of a candidate and the merit of the candidate's policy preferences (**positive advertisements**), or the campaign can make use of advertisements that seek to portray the candidate's opponent in a negative light (**negative advertisements**). The bulk of a candidate's campaign funds are spent on media buys, with a substantial amount of these funds being used to purchase negative ads. Candidates have a wide array of media venues through which they can deliver their messages (broadcast television, cable television, print media, radio, and the Internet).

Measuring Public Opinion: Polls, Polls, and More Polls

A dominant contextual factor in any election is the public mood, and the most reliable way to measure public sentiment is through **public-opinion polling**, which entails surveying a small number of people to estimate the opinions of a larger population. As early as the nineteenth century, newspapers attempted to scoop their competitors by predicting election results. They used an unscientific and unreliable method that consisted of interviewing people as they left their voting places. In 1916, the popular *Literary Digest* magazine conducted an ambitious mail survey using names and addresses of millions of Americans garnered from telephone books. The *Digest* correctly predicted the presidential winner from 1920 to 1932, but failed to predict Franklin D. Roosevelt's landslide victory in 1936. Because phones were more likely to be owned by upper-class and middle-class people through the 1930s, the *Digest's* reliance on sampling from phone books overrepresented wealthy voters and consequently overestimated the support for Alfred Landon, the more conservative candidate.

Box 8.3.   Skill Box: Become a Sophisticated Poll Watcher

Poll results receive widespread media coverage but are rarely questioned by the general public. Polling "literacy" is an important skill for anyone desiring to effectively make use of poll results. Fortunately, reputable pollsters and newspapers provide readers with information regarding how their polls were conducted, thus alerting readers to potential limitations. The following checklist of factors indicates some of the important things to consider when analyzing poll results.

- *Defining the population:* Determine who is being sampled. Is the population appropriate to your interests? A sample of "eligible voters" (those who are legally permitted to vote) will tell you something about opinions but may not tell you as much as a sample of "likely voters" (those people who are likely to vote on Election Day). This latter group would be of most interest to a candidate facing an election, but is often difficult to identify. Different polling places use different techniques to identify likely voters (some simply ask people if they plan to vote, while others ask respondents if they have voted in recent contests).
- *Randomness:* A sample is random only if everyone's opinion has an equal chance of being counted. Be wary of samples selected from incomplete or selective listings. Media outlets are increasingly relying on Web-based and Internet surveys that are cheap to conduct but provide questionable results. These types of polls exclude people without computers and people who do not visit the media outlets' websites, and cannot be relied on to provide reliable results.
- *Accuracy:* Assuming a random sample, polling accuracy is based on the fixed laws of statistics. For a single population, samples of the same size have the same potential for error. The 3 percent error for a sample of 1,500 participants increases to more than 6 percent for a sample of 300 participants. When interpreting a survey, keep in mind that while the polling company is likely to report its result as a single number (e.g., 52 percent of the public supports a candidate), what the poll actually tells us is that assuming a 3 percent margin of error, somewhere between 49 percent and 55 percent of the population is likely to support the candidate.
- *Bias:* Pay attention to the actual wording of the question and check for obvious bias. For example, questions beginning with "Do you agree with most Americans that . . ." are leading questions and encourage sup-

port, while questions asking respondents to agree with views of unpopular groups or individuals discourage support. Also evaluate who funded the poll. Polls funded by interest groups often make use of questionable methods or report only the most favorable results.

- **Timing:** Look at the date of the poll and consider the major intervening events that might have altered opinions. Also consider the time it takes to conduct a good poll. Instant overnight analyses can require major shortcuts. On the other hand, the longer it takes to complete a poll, the more likely that intervening events could have affected the results.

- **Robo-polls:** Conducting high-quality polls takes time and money. To cut corners, some polling firms are conducting inexpensive polls that make use of automated calling machines. The response rate for these types of polls is generally very low (who wants to push buttons while being prompted by a recording), and they are generally less accurate than polls conducted by live interviewers.

- **Straw polls:** Do not be misled by "straw polls" (nonscientific polls that do not make use of random sampling techniques). Examples of such polls include filling out a ballot at the state fair or answering questions at the mall. Generally speaking, these polls cannot be relied on to produce meaningful results.

Today, major polling outfits use scientific random-sampling techniques that are designed to minimize the chance of biased results. Nevertheless, the lessons of the 2000 and 2004 elections reveal that polling remains an imperfect science, as early exit polls in those elections incorrectly predicted the defeat of George W. Bush. In the future, as more and more people make use of cell phones and Internet-based communication devices, and those with traditional "land lines" are increasingly reluctant to participate in surveys because of frustration with telemarketers, it is likely that pollsters will have to find new ways to measure public sentiment.

B. ELECTIONS AT WORK: CONTEXTUAL FACTORS THAT MATTER

Political scientists are quite good at predicting election results using contextual information. Table 8.1, created for a U.S. House contest, indicates several contextual factors that might influence an election and specifies which type of candidate (incumbent or challenger) would be likely to benefit from each situation.

Table 8.1. U.S. House Contests: Important Contextual Factors

Factor	Incumbent	Challenger	Comments
Incumbent has served several terms	+	–	The longer an incumbent serves in office, the greater the cumulative benefits of incumbency are and the less likely the incumbent is to be defeated by a challenger in the general election.
The district was drawn as a safe district	+	–	The existence of safe districts, those in which the electorate has a clear preference for one party, makes it difficult for a challenger from a different party to unseat an incumbent.
Strong economic conditions	+	–	In a process known as retrospective voting, voters tend to reward incumbents during good economic times.
Perception the country is headed in the right direction	+	–	In a process known as prospective voting, voters tend to reward incumbents when they believe the economy is headed in the right direction.
Popular war effort	+	–	In a process referred to as **rallying around the flag**, voters tend to support the status quo during the initial period of a military campaign.
First-term incumbent	–	+	Incumbents are often viewed as vulnerable at the end of their first term. The out-of-power party often targets these races to defeat an incumbent before the incumbent becomes entrenched.
District does not strongly favor the	–	+	In marginal districts, or swing districts, the electorate's partisan predisposition

Factor	Incumbent	Challenger	Comments
incumbent's party			does not strongly favor one party over the other.
Weak economic conditions	–	+	During an economic downturn or recession, the electorate might decide to punish an incumbent by voting for a challenger.
Perception the country is headed in the wrong direction	–	+	When the public senses the economy is heading in the wrong direction or simply not growing fast enough, the electorate might decide to pursue new leadership by voting for a challenger.
Unpopular war effort	–	+	Unpopular military efforts can also draw the ire of voters and benefit challengers.
Scandal	–	+	Incumbents who are plagued by allegations of extramarital affairs, bribery, or abuse of power are vulnerable to challengers.
Well-known challenger	–	+	Challengers who enter a race with name recognition, or who are able to buy name recognition, have an advantage over less well-known challengers.
Midterm election and incumbent is member of the president's party	–	+	The president's party tends to lose seats in Congress during midterm elections, particularly in midterm elections during a president's second term.
Incumbent is a member of the president's party and the president is unpopular or plagued by scandal	–	+	If the president is unpopular, but not up for reelection, voters might chose to punish the president by voting against members of the president's party.

C. ENDURING CONTEXTUAL QUESTIONS AND HOW TO RESEARCH THEM

Understanding the Effects of Presidential Coattails and Midterm Elections

All elections take place within the context of the presidential election cycle. During presidential election years, candidates who are members of the same party of a popular presidential candidate tend to gain electoral support in a process that is

---

Sample Hypothesis

a. If the strength of the incumbency advantage is increasing in congressional elections, then the effects of presidential coattails and midterm elections should become less pronounced.
b. If presidents actively campaign for members of Congress during midterm elections, then the trend of the president's party losing congressional seats in the off years should decrease.

Hints for Accomplishment

Winning and losing seats because of the effects of coattails and midterm elections has been a fairly stable phenomenon in electoral politics. However, in recent years the trend has been far weaker and less reliable than in previous years. For example, Bill Clinton's Democratic Party lost seats when he won the presidency in 1992, a phenomenon that repeated itself in 2000, when George W. Bush won the presidency though his party lost seats in Congress. During the final midterm election of Clinton's presidency (1998), when Clinton was embroiled in the Monica Lewinsky scandal, his party bucked historical trends and gained seats in the House. Rather than "disprove" the trends associated with coattails and midterm elections, the recent cases require detailed analysis—analysis that places elections in a historical context and gives due weight to specific circumstances.

Box 8.4.   Skill Box: Presidential Coattails over Time

When analyzing table 8.2, think about the additional contextual factors that can reduce or magnify the effects of coattails and midterm elections (economic conditions, war, scandal, etc.). Also be cognizant of the long-term trends such as partisan **realignment**, which is a durable change in the public's partisan preferences, candidate-centered elections, incumbency advantage, and the advent of the 24-hour cable news and Internet news cycle.

Table 8.2.   Gain or Loss of President's Party in Congress

President/Year	Presidential Election Years House	Senate	Year	Nonpresidential Election Years House	Senate
Johnson (D): 1964	+38	+2	1966	−47	−4
Nixon (R): 1968	+7	+5	1970	−12	+2
Nixon (R): 1972	+13	−2	Ford (R): 1974	−48	−5
Carter (D): 1976	+2	0	1978	−15	−3
Reagan (R): 1980	+33	+12	1982	−26	+1
Reagan (R): 1984	+15	−2	1986	−5	−8
G. Bush (R): 1988	−3	−1	1990	−9	−1
Clinton (D): 1992	−10	0	1994	−52	−9
Clinton (D): 1996	+10	−2	1998	+5	0
G. W. Bush (R): 2000	−2	−4	2002	+6	+2
G. W. Bush (R): 2004	+3	+4	2006	−30	−6

Source: Adapted by the authors from Karen O'Conner and Larry J. Sabato, *American Government: Continuity and Change*, 2006 ed. (New York: Pearson Education, 2006), 486.

known as "riding the president's **coattails**." During **midterm elections**, elections in which there is no presidential contest and consequently no possibility of coattails, the president's party tends to lose seats in government, a trend that generally increases if the president is unpopular. With the changing nature of elections and party loyalty in the United States, one would expect the trends associated with coattails and off-year (midterm) elections to change in predicable ways.

Sample Hypothesis

a. If Internet bloggers are influencing the way mainstream media covers campaigns, then breaking campaign stories in the mainstream press should have been covered by Internet bloggers prior to appearing on traditional media outlets.

b. If cable news has a conservative bias, then cable-news watchers should vote for more conservative candidates than network-news watchers.

Hints for Accomplishment

The media's influence on electoral politics can lead researchers in numerous directions. For example, are people who receive their information from the Internet more or less informed than people who rely on more traditional news providers? Do late-night comedy shows (like the *Daily Show* on Comedy Central) provide meaningful political information? Are the late-night comedy shows biased in any particular direction? How does news provided by the Internet component of a mainstream news organization differ from the news provided by the organization's parent provider? How can you evaluate the electoral influence of online blogs?

How the Modern Media Affects Elections

The broadcast and cable media have replaced radio and print as the primary means through which people acquire campaign information. As television news continues to evolve, developing more specialized programming and merging with Internet-based news providers, the influence of the news media will also continue to change, leading to interesting hypotheses.

D. IDEA GENERATOR: A SAMPLE OF ADDITIONAL CONTEXTUAL QUESTIONS RELATED TO ELECTIONS

The following chart provides some general guidelines for developing a research plan.

Specific Issue	Hypotheses	Hints
Money and Elections		
How the political context influences political contributions	a. If a race has an incumbent running for reelection, then PACs will tend to support the incumbent. b. If the contest is for a competitive open seat, then PACs will tend to support both candidates. c. If a candidate running for reelection serves on an influential committee within the legislative body, then the candidate will raise substantial funds from groups with business before the committee.	The context of a specific election can have a significant influence on the source and nature of campaign contributions. Has the national mood turned against the president and the president's party? Are scandals hurting a party's ability to raise funds? Is control of Congress up for grabs? Is the race for an open seat? Did the candidate win key endorsements? Is the seat considered a safe seat? All these factors, and others, should influence campaign fund-raising in a predicable manner.
Economic Conditions		
How do economic conditions influence the vote?	a. If a voter's personal economic situation is his or her dominant electoral consideration, then that voter will	While most scholars agree that economic conditions influence electoral decisions, scholars debate whether national

Specific Issue	Hypotheses	Hints
	support incumbents during times of personal prosperity. b. If national economic conditions are a voter's dominant electoral consideration, then that voter will support incumbents during times of national prosperity.	conditions, personal conditions, past economic trends, or the perception regarding the future direction of the economy has the greatest impact on voters. This line of inquiry allows you to explore this persistent controversy in the literature.

4. Secondary Sources That Will Help You Get Started

The Almanac of American Politics. Washington, D.C.: National Journal, 2006.

Herrnson, Paul S., Colton Campbell, Marni Ezra, and Stephen K. Medvic, eds. *Guide to Political Campaigns in America.* Washington, D.C.: CQ Press, 2005.

Maisel, Sandy L., and Charles Bassett, eds. *Political Parties & Elections in the United States: An Encyclopedia.* New York: Garland, 1991.

Moore, John L., Jon P. Preimesberger, and David R. Tarr, eds. *Congressional Quarterly's Guide to U.S. Elections.* Washington, D.C.: CQ Press, 2001.

Sabato, Larry J., and Howard R. Ernst, eds. *Encyclopedia of American Political Parties and Elections.* New York: Facts On File, 2006.

5. Original Research That Will Impress Your Professor

Ansolabehere, Stephen, and Shanto Iyengar. *Going Negative: How Political Ads Shrink and Polarize the Electorate.* New York: Free Press, 1997.

Bartels, Larry M. *Presidential Primaries and the Dynamics of Public Choice.* Princeton, N.J.: Princeton University Press, 1988.

Butler, David, and Bruce Cain. *Congressional Redistricting: Comparative and Theoretical Perspectives.* New York: Macmillan, 1992.

Burnham, Walter Dean. *Critical Elections and the Mainsprings of American Politics.* New York: W. W. Norton, 1970.

Campbell, Angus, Philip E. Converse, Warren E. Miller, and Donald E. Stokes. *The American Voter.* New York: Wiley, 1960.

Ceaser, James W. *Reforming the Reformers: A Critical Analysis of the Presidential Selection Process.* Cambridge, Mass.: Ballinger, 1982.

Fiorina, Morris P. *Retrospective Voting in American National Elections.* New Haven, Conn.: Yale University Press, 1981.

Herrnson, Paul S. *Congressional Elections: Campaigning at Home and in Washington.* 4th ed. Washington, D.C.: CQ Press, 2003.

Holbrook, Thomas M. *Campaigns Matter?* Thousand Oaks, Calif.: Sage, 1996.

Jacobson, Gary C. *The Politics of Congressional Elections,* 5th ed. New York: Harper-Collins, 2000.

Nie, Norman H., Sidney Verba, and John R. Petrocik. *The Changing American Voter.* Cambridge, Mass.: Harvard University Press, 1980.

Niemi, Richard G., and Herbert F. Weisberg, eds. *Classics in Voting Behavior.* Washington, D.C.: CQ Press, 1993.

Niemi, Richard G., and Herbert F. Weisberg, eds. *Controversies in Voting Behavior.* Washington, D.C.: CQ Press, 2001.

Patterson, Thomas E. *The Vanishing Voter: Public Involvement in an Age of Uncertainty.* New York: Vintage, 2003.

Sabato, Larry J,. and Glenn R. Simpson. *Dirty Little Secrets: The Persistence of Corruption in American Politics.* New York: Random House, 1996.

Teixeira, Ruy. *The Disappearing American Voter.* Washington, D.C.: Brookings Institution, 1992.

Thurber, James A., and Candice J. Nelson. *Campaign Warriors: Political Consultants in Elections.* Washington, D.C.: Brookings Institution, 2000.

Weisberg, Herbert F. *Democracy's Feast: Elections in America.* Chatham, N.J.: Chatham House, 1995.

6. Where to Find It

Where can I find the most respected and sophisticated academic polls related to American elections?

The American National Elections Studies (ANES) has been conducting comprehensive election studies since 1948. The ANES is a collaborative project between Stanford University and the University of Michigan, with additional funding provided by the National Science Foundation. Data is available on the ANES website, at http://www.electionstudies.org.

Another rich source for high-quality survey research is the National Opinion Research Center (NORC) at the University of Chicago. Their General Social Survey (GSS), available at http://www.norc.uchicago.edu/projects/gensoc.asp, rivals the ANES data.

Where can I find information about the latest developments in the campaign industry?

Campaigns and Elections Magazine, available online at http://www.campaignline.com, is the leading source of contemporary information regarding the campaign consulting industry.

Where can I find reliable information regarding campaign spending in federal elections?
The Federal Election Commission website, http://www.fec.gov, is the federal government's official site for election results and campaign-spending information. Unfortunately the website is poorly designed and difficult to search. The Center for Responsive Politics, at http://www.opensecrets.org, presents the Federal Election Commission data in a user-friendly format and is an excellent resource for investigating the influence of campaign contributions.

Where can I find recent media polls related to elections?
The nation's oldest and most respected commercial poll is the Gallup Poll (http://www.galluppoll.com). For two high-quality commercial sites that offer a broad array of media polls, see PollingReport.com, at http://www.pollingreport .com, and RealClearPolitics, at http://www.realclearpolitics.com/polls.

Where can I find quality information about political candidates?
Project Vote Smart, http://www.votesmart.org, is a nonpartisan, not-for-profit organization that collects campaign-finance information, biographical information, and issue positions for a wide array of candidates.

Where can I find analysis of the truthfulness of campaign advertisements?
The Annenberg Public Policy Center of the University of Pennsylvania analyzes the truthfulness of claims made in political advertisements. The center's analysis is available at http://www.factcheck.org.

7. Taking Action—Acting and Influencing

Voter registration requirements remain one of the chief obstacles to voting in the United States. When nonvoters are asked why they do not vote, the leading reason remains their failure to register, or failure to register in time to meet their state's specific registration deadline. One way to combat chronic low voting rates in the United States is to sponsor a voter registration drive in your area. With the National Voter Registration Form, conducting a voter registration drive has never been easier. The form, along with instructions and mailing addresses for each state, is available online from the U.S. Election Assistance Commission, at http://www.eac.gov/voter (click on "Register to Vote").

Glossary

academic journals. Scholarly journals published by professional associations and affiliated with major universities.

academic press. A publisher that is associated with a university and that publishes scholarly works.

advise and consent. The constitutional requirement that the president submit specified nominations and treaties to the Senate for approval.

American federalism. A division of power between the federal government and state governments in which each derives power directly from the people and both remain sovereign in their separate spheres.

amicus curiae briefs. Unsolicited statements presented by interested parties ("friends of the court") advocating a particular ruling by the court.

Annapolis Convention (1786). A meeting to discuss ways to strengthen the national political system, which in turn led to the Philadelphia Convention of 1787.

antecedent variable. A third factor that comes prior to the independent and dependent variables and is responsible for fluctuations in both variables.

Anti-Federalists. Those opposed to ratification of the U.S. Constitution.

apportionment. The allocation of congressional seats to the states on the basis of population figures from the national census.

appropriating committee. A congressional committee (one in the House and one in the Senate) with the power to approve the spending of funds.

Articles of Confederation (1781–1788). Ratified in 1781, the Articles of Confederation served as the nation's first governing document until they were replaced by the Constitution in 1788.

authorizing committee. A specialized policy committee in Congress that approves programs and legislation but does not authorize the use of funds.

beat. The relatively permanent assignment of a journalist to cover a particular institution, issue, or person.

bias. A misrepresentation of reality.

bicameral legislature. A legislature that is divided into two separate chambers.

bicameralism. The practice of having legislative bodies with two chambers.

biennial legislative sessions. Legislative sessions held every other year.

Bill of Rights. The first ten amendments to the U.S. Constitution.

Bipartisan Campaign Reform Act of 2002. Also known as the McCain-Feingold campaign-finance reform, this act attempted to rid the electoral system of the corrupting influence of soft-money contributions.

block grants. Broad federal grants that are awarded to states with few or no restrictions.

blue state. A state that tends to elect Democratic candidates. States in the Northeast and on the West Coast tend to be blue states.

Boston Massacre (1770). On March 5, 1770, British troops fired on a group of colonists in Boston, killing five in what became known as the Boston Massacre.

Boston Tea Party (1773). Protesting British taxation, the Sons of Liberty, dressed as Mohawk Indians, seized British tea and dumped it into Boston Harbor.

bought coalition. A group of decision makers who are persuaded to support a position through favors or revisions to the proposal.

brief. A legal document outlining one side's arguments in a case. The term may be misleading, since briefs can be hundreds of pages long.

broad constructionism. A judicial philosophy that holds that constitutional interpretation should be based not only on constitutional language and an appreciation for the framers in designing its provisions but also on ideas that have evolved about civil rights and social justice.

Buckley v. Valeo **(1976).** A Supreme Court case in which the court ruled that limits on candidate spending are unconstitutional but that limits on campaign contributions to candidates are constitutional.

business groups. Interest groups organized to protect the financial interests of a specific industry.

campaign consultants. The paid professionals who help candidates develop a campaign message, raise funds, target voters, and deliver the message.

campaign finance chair. The person in a campaign who is responsible for the day-to-day fund-raising operation and compliance with fund-raising laws.

campaign manager. The person who oversees the day-to-day operations of the campaign.

campaign press secretary. The person in a campaign who is responsible for media relations.

candidate-centered campaigns. Campaigns in which candidates emphasize their personal attributes rather than their party ties.

candidate ratings. Scores based on candidates' voting records.

categorical grants. Federal grants that are awarded to states and require the states to spend resources for specific purposes.

causal relationship. A relationship in which changes in the independent variable are known to cause changes in the dependent variable.

challenger. A candidate who seeks to unseat an incumbent.

checks and balances. The constitutional power each branch of government has to limit the freedom of action of another branch. *See also* "separation of powers."

chief diplomat. The president's role as manager of U.S. relations with other countries.

chief economist. The president's role in overseeing governmental spending, taxation, and job creation.

chief executive. The president's role as the administrator of the federal government.

chief legislator. The extraconstitutional role of the president in defining problems worthy of legislative action and suggesting the preferred solution.

chief of state. The president's role as the symbolic leader of the country, representing the United States at official events and embodying national goals and aspirations.

city council. The legislature of a municipality.

city manager. A nonpartisan executive authority created to manage the daily operations of a municipal government.

civic journalism. The commitment of a media outlet to involve itself in the civic and political life of a community by facilitating dialogue and encouraging involvement.

civil liberties. A special category of personal freedoms that governments should not abridge without a compelling government interest.

civil rights. Protection from arbitrary discrimination based on classifications such as race, sex, national origin, age, or sexual orientation.

Civil Service Reform Act of 1883. A campaign finance act that prohibited the solicitation of political contributions from federal employees.

Civil War Amendments. A series of constitutional amendments enacted following the Civil War: the Thirteenth Amendment (1865) barred slavery, the Fourteenth Amendment (1868) extended legal rights to all citizens, and the Fifteenth Amendment (1870) barred states from denying voting rights because of race, color, or previous condition of servitude.

classified charter. A standard charter provided by the state to local jurisdictions on the basis of their population size.

closed primary. A party's nominating contest in which voters must formally register as a party member in advance of the primary in order to participate.

coattails. During presidential election years, candidates who are members of the winning presidential candidate's party tend to gain support from the general public.

Coercive Acts (1774). King George III's response to the Boston Tea Party, which included sending additional troops to the New World and a blockade on Boston Harbor. The Coercive Acts, as they were called in Britain, were referred to by the colonists as the Intolerable Acts.

commander in chief. The president's role in managing and utilizing the U.S. armed services.

commerce clause. Article 1, Section 8, Clause 3 of the U.S. Constitution, which grants Congress the power to regulate commerce among the states.

Committees of Correspondence. Created to establish channels of communication between colonial leaders, particularly leaders who were discontent with British rule.

common carrier. Any organization that operates communications circuits used by other people and whose usage must be monitored to avoid interference.

Common Sense (1776). Thomas Paine's influential pamphlet arguing that the time had come for the colonists to sever their ties with England and that all forms of monarchical rule were unjust.

common-interest community. A form of private government that includes homeowners' associations, condominium associations, and housing cooperatives.

commute a sentence. To cancel part or all of a criminal's sentence (but keep the conviction).

comparative analysis. In-depth analysis of a small number of cases that can yield rich detail and can be used to explore causal relationships.

compulsory voting. Requires nonvoters to pay a penalty for failing to vote.

concurrent powers. Governmental powers granted to both state and national governments.

confederated federalism. A system of government in which the federal government derives its authority from the state governments.

confederated system. A political arrangement in which strong state governments have sovereignty over the federal government.

confirmation. The constitutionally required approval of a presidential appointment by the Senate.

Connecticut Compromise. A proposal put forth at the Constitutional Convention that resolved differences between the Virginia and New Jersey plans by allocating political representation in the lower branch of the national legislature (the House) according to population and allocating political representation in the upper chamber (the Senate) equally to all states.

conservatives. Those who adhere to an ideological perspective that is considered to be on the right of the political spectrum and in the United States tends to correspond with Republican Party policies.

constituents. Those who elect a person to office or to whom an appointed official is accountable.

constitution. A document that defines the structure and legal authority of a government.

Constitutional Convention (1787). At this meeting, also known as the Philadelphia Convention, fifty-five delegates from twelve states drafted the U.S. Constitution and developed a mechanism for ratifying the new governing document.

contingency table. A straightforward mechanism for assessing whether changes in an independent variable have an observable impact on a dependent variable, typically constructed by calculating the frequency of cases that satisfy the criteria of both the independent variable and the dependent variable.

cooperative federalism (1933–1964). Also known as "marble cake" federalism. During this period of time, the federal government began to dominate the federal-state relationship.

county. A political subunit within states.

county commission. The legislative branch of county government.

county executive. The chief executive in a county.

creative federalism (1965–1980). A period of time during which the federal government's role in funding state projects dramatically increased, federal regulations increased, and the use of categorical grants and matching grants increased.

critical election. A single election that has a durable and meaningful impact on the direction of the nation.

crossover press. A publisher that attempts to achieve the rigor of academic presses but markets its books to a wider audience.

de-alignment. A gradual decline in partisanship among voters.

Declaration of Independence (1776). The Declaration of Independence served as a formal declaration that the British government had violated its responsibilities to colonies and that the newly created states had officially severed their ties from England.

delegate. One who represents the views of constituents, no matter what he or she might prefer. *See also* "trustee."

Democratic Party. The more liberal of the two dominant political parties in the United States, the Democratic Party supports minority rights, workers' rights, social-welfare programs, environmental protection, and a host of programs that tend to concentrate power at the federal level, and receives strong support from African Americans, the working class, single women, urbanites, and liberals.

dependent variable. The variable that is presumed to be affected by the independent variable(s).

descriptive analysis. Analysis that describes the characteristics of individual variables and tends to make use of summary statistics.

devolution. A systematic attempt to return power from the federal government to the state and local governments.

Dillon's Rule. A court ruling that established that municipal corporations derive their power and rights wholly from the state legislatures.

direct democracy. A political system in which government actions are controlled directly by the people.

discretion. The legal ability of federal officials to employ experience and personal judgment in executing policies.

divided government. A situation in which one coequal branch of government is controlled by one party and the other branch (or branches) is controlled by the opposing party. This term usually refers to the partisan split between the president and Congress.

divine right. The governing principle that political leaders receive their authority from a divine source rather than from the consent of the governed.

***Dred Scott v. Sandford* (1857).** A Supreme Court case that established that Congress lacked the authority to bar slavery in new territories.

dual federalism (1834–1933). Also known as "layer cake" federalism, a period in which Chief Justice Roger B. Taney and subsequent courts attempted to rein in the powers of the federal government.

Duverger's Law. The tendency of political systems that make use of winner-take-all single-member districts to produce two-party systems.

Eighteenth Amendment (1919). Prohibits the manufacturing, sale, and importation of intoxicating liquors in all states.

election. The process by which the electorate chooses public officials and influences the direction of public policy.

Electoral College. The collective name for individuals (electors) chosen by majority vote in each state to cast that state's ballots for president.

electorate. Those qualified to vote.

embed. Allowing the media to become part of an event in the attempt to more realistically cover it.

empirical analysis. Emphasizes the collection of hard data on observable events (e.g., votes in Congress, dollars spent in campaigns, opinions collected from a survey, decisions made by judges).

endorsement. A formal statement of support for a candidate.

ex post facto law. A law that makes some action taken in the past illegal and punishable at the time the law is enacted.

experiential research. Involves working in a political realm, keeping close track of one's experiences, and attempting to develop generalizations based on political experiences.

explanatory analysis. Describes relationships between variables and tends to make use of explanatory statistics.

express powers. Specific powers enumerated in the Constitution.

factions. The founders' word for organized interest groups and political parties.

Federal Corrupt Practices Act. A campaign-finance law that strengthened disclosure requirements and established campaign spending limits.

Federal Election Campaign Act (FECA) (1971). Limited the amount of money that an individual can contribute to federal campaigns, as well as the amount that political action committees and political parties can contribute to individual candidates.

Federal Election Commission. Created by Congress in 1975 to administer the Federal Election Campaign Act of 1971.

Federal Reserve Board. An appointed national regulatory commission that sets interest rates for federal borrowing and thereby sends signals to the investment community.

federalism. The relationship between the federal government and state governments.

Federalist Papers. Eighty-five essays written in support of ratification of the U.S. Constitution.

Federalists. Those in favor of ratification of the U.S. Constitution.

Fifteenth Amendment (1870). The third and final Civil War Amendment, this amendment prohibited states from denying voting rights because of a person's race, color, or previous condition of servitude.

filibuster. A stalling technique that enables a single senator speak for as long as he or she wishes unless a supermajority of the Senate, 60 percent, cuts off debate.

First Continental Congress (1774). An early meeting in Philadelphia among colonial leaders, which produced the Declaration of Rights and Resolves sent to England.

501(c)(3) groups. Not-for-profit and charitable organizations.

501(c)(4) groups. Civic leagues and social-welfare organizations.

501(c)(5) groups. Labor unions.

501(c)(6) groups. Trade or professional associations.

527 groups. Political groups that are not directly associated with political parties or specific candidates but that spend unregulated amounts of money influencing elections.

floor leaders. Party leaders within the House and Senate.

founding era (1763–1791). The period of time between the conclusion of the French and Indian War and the ratification of the Bill of Rights.

Fourteenth Amendment (1868). The second of the Civil War Amendments, this amendment extended legal rights to all citizens.

framers of the U.S. Constitution. The fifty-five delegates who attended the Constitutional Convention.

free media. Campaign coverage that is derived from news organizations.

free-rider problem. An interest-group theory that claims that potential members of an interest group will choose not to join a group if they can receive the benefits that the group seeks without having to pay the price of membership.

French and Indian War. A costly seven-year global struggle that lasted from 1756 to 1763 in which Britain and its North American colonists defeated France and its Native American allies.

frequency distribution. A listing of the values of a variable along with the number of cases or percentage of cases for each value.

gender gap. The difference in support for a candidate between men and women.

general charter. A standard charter provided by the state that is granted to all jurisdictions.

gerrymandering. Drawing legislative district boundaries for the purpose of creating political advantage for a political party or a particular group.

get out the vote. Campaign activities that are designed to increase the chances that a candidate's supporters vote on Election Day.

Gibbons v. Ogden **(1824).** A Supreme Court case that established that Congress has broad powers over interstate commerce.

grassroots lobbying. The process of organizing the public to apply pressure on elected officials.

Great Society programs. A series of federal initiatives by President Lyndon B. Johnson's administration that were designed to confront racial discrimination and end poverty in the United States.

Home rule. A concept that allows an individual community to draft and amend its own charter, so long as the charter meets the general requirements determined by the state.

hypothesis. A theory of how variables are related to each other.

ideological groups. Groups that promote a specific worldview rather than material benefits or single issues.

impeachment. The formal bringing of charges against a government official that could lead to that official's removal from office.

implied powers. Powers not specifically described in the Constitution but implied from the enumerated powers.

impressionistic research. Uses the arguments and interpretations of others to interpret the political world.

incumbency advantage. The electoral advantage that incumbents have over challengers because of the considerable benefits derived from holding office.

incumbent. Current officeholder.

independent. A person who is not a member of a specific political party.

independent leaners. People who do not consider themselves members of a specific party but who typically vote for candidates from one party.

independent variable. A variable that is presumed to affect the dependent variable.

initiative. A mechanism that enables citizens, by collecting a sufficient number of signatures on a petition, to place a statute or constitutional amendment on the ballot for the voters to adopt or reject.

interest groups. Voluntary associations, typically outside government, that are composed of individuals who share policy objectives and who work collectively in pursuit of their shared objectives.

intervening variable. A third variable that comes between the independent variable and the dependent variable and is responsible for fluctuations in the dependent variable.

issue advocacy. Interest groups spend resources to produce advertisements that influence the way people think about issues and in turn color the way voters think about candidates.

issue networks. Loosely bound networks of like-minded interest groups.

judicial review. The authority of the federal courts to consider the constitutionality of laws enacted by Congress and the actions taken by officials in the executive branch.

labor groups. Groups organized to promote the interests of workers through collective bargaining.

legislative referendum. A mechanism that enables voters to accept or reject a measure that is referred to them by the state legislature or other governmental body.

legitimacy. The public perception that an individual is the rightful occupant of a position of power or the feeling that the political process deserves public respect.

liberal. One who adheres to an ideological perspective that is considered to be on the left of the political spectrum and in the United States tends to correspond with Democratic Party policies.

line-item veto. The power of the chief executive to void part of a bill that has been passed by the legislature.

literature review. An analysis of the existing body of knowledge on a certain topic.

lobbying. The process by which interest groups attempt to influence key policymakers and promote policy objectives.

lobbyist. A paid representative of an interest group who is responsible for promoting the group's policy objectives to key policymakers.

Lou Dobbs Democrats. A voting bloc of working-class Democrats who take a hard-line stance on immigration.

Magna Carta. Sometimes referred to as the "Great Charter of Freedoms," the Magna Carta was imposed on King John of England by disgruntled English barons in 1215. It forced the king to accept legal procedures and to acknowledge that even the king was subject to the law.

majority party. The party that controls a majority of the seats in a legislative body.

majority-minority district. A legislative district in which a majority of the population is composed of a group that makes up a minority of the total U.S. population.

malapportionment. Occurs when some legislative districts represent more people than do other legislative districts.

mandate. The assertion that voters have expressed their preference for a candidate's or party's stated policy positions.

marginal district. Congressional district in which there is strong competition between candidates of different parties.

Marshall Court. The Supreme Court under Chief Justice John Marshall.

mass media. Newspapers, television networks, radio stations, and other vehicles of communication having the ability to connect with the vast majority of the population.

matching grants. Federal grants that are awarded to a state only if the state agrees to match the federal funds with additional state resources.

mayor. The chief executive of a municipality.

McCain-Feingold campaign-finance reform. *See* "Bipartisan Campaign Reform Act of 2002."

***McCulloch v. Maryland* (1819).** A Supreme Court case that established that the states do not have the right to tax the federal government.

mean. A statistical measure calculated by summing the values of a variable and dividing by the total number of cases.

measures of association. Statistical procedures used to independently gauge the strength of relationships between two variables.

media. The generalized term for all commercial communications that attempt to reach a mass audience with newsworthy information or entertainment.

median. The value below which 50 percent of the cases fall, and above which 50 percent of the cases fall.

midterm election. An election in which there is no presidential contest and consequently no opportunity to ride the president's coattails (also referred to as an off-year election).

minority party. A party that controls some seats in a legislative body, but less than a majority.

Missouri Plan. A complex judicial selection plan for state judges that makes use of a nominating committee, gubernatorial selection, and a popular vote.

mode. The most frequently occurring value for a variable.

moderate. One who adheres to an ideological perspective that is considered in the middle of the political spectrum and in the United States has less predicable partisan association than the conservative and liberal perspectives.

Mount Vernon Conference (1785). A conference between Virginia and Maryland officials regarding control of the Potomac River. The conference led to an invitation to all states to meet in Annapolis to discuss weaknesses in the Articles of Confederation.

multiparty system. A system in which several parties are represented in government.

multivariate statistical analysis. Sophisticated statistical procedures that enable a researcher to estimate the combined influence of several independent variables on a single independent variable and to estimate the individual impact of each independent variable while controlling for the impact of the other independent variables.

NASCAR dads. A group of conservative men who tend to support the Republican Party.

national party leader. The president's informal status as the spokesperson, fund-raiser, and agenda setter for his or her party.

natural coalition. A group of decision makers who are persuaded to support a position because it is aligned with their personal ideologies or the interests of their constituents.

naturalization. Becoming a legal citizen of a country by going through the specified procedure.

necessary and proper clause. Article 1, Section 8 of the U.S. Constitution states that Congress shall have the power to enact all laws that are "necessary and proper" for performing its enumerated powers.

negative advertisements. Advertisements that seek to portray a political opponent in a negative light.

New Deal. A series of federal government programs enacted by President Franklin D. Roosevelt's administration that were designed to create jobs and alleviate economic hardships felt during the Great Depression.

new federalism (1980–2001). Beginning with the presidency of Ronald Reagan, this period of federalism saw a systematic attempt to return power from the federal government to the state and local governments.

New Jersey Plan. A proposal put forth at the Constitutional Convention that would have created a unicameral legislature and allocated equal congressional representation to all states.

news hook. The character of a news event on which one hangs the story. This is often an individual who the media feel is newsworthy.

Nineteenth Amendment (1920). Granted women the right to vote in all states.

nonconnected committees. Political action committees that are not connected to corporations, labor unions, membership organizations, or trade associations and are permitted to solicit contributions from the general public.

off-year election. *See* "midterm election."

Obamacans. Republicans who supported Democratic presidential candidate Barack Obama.

omnibus legislation. Legislation that includes a wide variety of policy concerns having little to do with each other and that is designed to attract support more for its components than its overall intention.

open primary. A party's nominating contest in which all registered voters, regardless of party affiliation, are allowed to participate.

open-seat contest. An election with no incumbent in the race.

operational definition. A statement expressing the manner in which a variable is measured.

opinion piece. A written work in which the writer typically considers several sides of an argument before forming an opinion based on informed logic.

optional charter. A charter provided by the state that a jurisdiction can select through a direct vote of the citizens.

paid media. Media advertisements that are purchased with a candidate's campaign funds.

pardon. To cancel a criminal's conviction.

parliamentary system. A governmental system in which voters cast votes for their preferred party, seats within the parliament are allocated to the respective parties according to the proportion of votes the party received in the election, and the prime minister is selected by the ruling party or a coalition of minor parties in the parliament.

parole. The release of a criminal prior to the full completion of a sentence.

partisan. A person with a strong preference for a specific party.

partisan press. Media outlets that openly and consistently favor one party over the other.

party boss. A person who leads a party machine.

party identification. The extent to which people identify with a specific party.

party-line voting. In the context of elections, refers to voting for candidates of a single party. In the context of the legislature, refers to votes in which the majority (or more) of one party votes against the majority (or more) of the other party.

party machine. Party leaders who dominated urban politics and sometimes the politics of an entire state.

party platforms. Formal policy statements adopted at the parties' quadrennial conventions that discuss the parties' policy objectives in general terms.

party-unity score. A key measure that political scientists use to assess party cohesion within Congress.

Pendleton Civil Service Act (1883). Legislation that began establishing procedures that emphasized merit as the basis for employment and dismissal from federal jobs.

penny presses. Mid-nineteenth-century newspapers that cost only a penny.

Philadelphia Convention (1787). *See* "Constitutional Convention."

plagiarism. Making use of someone else's words or ideas without clear and complete credit being given to the original source.

platform. The specified policy positions that a political party and candidate favor.

***Plessey v. Ferguson* (1896).** A Supreme Court case that upheld state laws that provided separate but equal accommodations for blacks and whites.

pluralist system. A system in which numerous groups compete for influence within the political system.

political action committee (PAC). A group that accepts contributions and makes expenditures for the purpose of electing or defeating candidates for public office.

political party. In the United States, political parties are loosely bound coalitions that work to gain and maintain positions of authority through the electoral process.

popular referendum. A mechanism that enables citizens, by collecting a sufficient number of signatures on a petition, to force a popular vote on a measure that was previously enacted by the state legislature.

popular sovereignty. The governing principle that all legitimate governmental authority is derived from the consent of the governed.

positive advertisements. Advisements that promote the virtues of a candidate or the merits of a candidate's policy preferences.

power of the purse. The power of a government entity to determine how public funds are expended.

precedent. The decision or guideline established in a case that will be used by the courts in determining future decisions.

presidential system. A governmental system in which the chief executive (president) is elected nationally.

primary data. Data collected specifically for a study.

prior restraint. Stopping someone from doing something (in this case publishing a story) before the action takes place.

proportional representation. A system of representation that allocates legislative seats to political parties in proportion to the percentage of the vote the parties received in an election.

prospective voting. A voter's decision to punish or reward a candidate or political parties because of the voter's perception of the direction of the country.

public-opinion polling. Surveying a small number of people to estimate the opinions of a larger population.

qualitative data. Impressions of the political world based on the arguments and interpretations of others.

quantitative analysis. Analysis that makes use of a large number of cases and statistical procedures that are designed specifically for testing causal relationships.

question time. The weekly event at which the prime minister faces the parliament to answer questions from its members.

rallying around the flag. The tendency of voters to prefer the status quo when the country first enters a military campaign.

Reagan Democrats. Democrats who supported Republican candidate Ronald Reagan for president.

realignment. A durable change in the public's partisan preferences.

red state. A state that tends to elect Republican candidates. States in the rural South, as well as the Mountain states, tend to be red states.

redistricting. The process of redrawing constituency boundaries for elected officials. For Congress, redistricting is usually done by state legislatures.

reliability. Concerns whether empirical data would yield the same results if collected on separate occasions or by different observers.

representation. The process of taking into account the interests of others (often constituents) and fighting for those interests.

representative democracy. A political system in which voters elect political representatives to make public-policy decisions and to perform essential governmental services.

Republican Party. The more conservative of the two dominant political parties in the United States, the Republican Party favors military spending, an active foreign policy, economic growth, limited government control over the economy, and low taxes, and its receives strong support among evangelical Christians—especially in the South—the upper class, voters in rural areas, and conservatives.

reserved powers. Those powers specifically resting with the states.

retrospective voting. A voter's decision to reward or punish a candidate or a political party for decisions since the last election.

reverse lobbying. Occurs when an elected official reaches out to interest groups to encourage them to lobby for issues that are important to the elected official.

Ron Paul Republicans. A voting bloc of Republicans with a libertarian bent that does not fit well with the mainstream Republican Party.

rule of law. The concept that no person or group of people is above the law.

sacrificial lamb. A low-quality challenger that has little chance of winning an election.

safe district. A congressional district that is drawn to favor the incumbent or the incumbent's party.

salutary neglect. The period in which Parliament chose not to strictly enforce British authority in the New World; it ended following the French and Indian War.

Second Continental Congress (1775). An early meeting of colonial leaders in which delegates produced the Olive Branch Petition, which called for Britain to halt military actions against the colonists.

secondary data. Data adapted from a different study.

seminal works. Leading works on a given academic subject.

semi-open primary. A party's nominating contest in which voters can participate by declaring their support for that party on the day of the primary.

seniority system. The process of choosing congressional committee chairs on the basis of their length of service on the committee.

separate segregated funds (SSFs). A type of political action committee that is established and administered by corporations, labor unions, membership organizations, or trade associations.

separation of powers. The allocation of governmental powers among the three branches of government so that each is a check on another. The creation of separate political institutions with overlapping powers is designed to foster competition among political actors and reduce the chance of tyranny.

Seventeenth Amendment (1913). Takes the Senate selection process away from the state and grants it to the citizens.

Shays' Rebellion (1786). A rebellion led by Massachusetts farmer Daniel Shays, in which Shays and his small band of supporters attempted to forcibly halt foreclosures on farms by closing the state courts in Massachusetts.

single case study. In-depth analysis of a specific case that yields a great deal of detail but few general trends.

single-issue groups. Interest groups that promote a specific issue (e.g., environmental protection, opposition to abortion, gun rights, reduced taxes, opposition to war, gay rights).

single-member districts. Districts in which a single elected official represents that specific geographic region in the legislature.

Sixteenth Amendment (1913). Grants the federal government the power impose an income tax.

Soccer moms. Married women with children who tend to be more conservative than single women and who are seen as important swing voters.

social contract theory. The political theory put forward by John Locke that legitimate government authority is derived from the consent of free people.

soft money. Unlimited contributions to political parties generally used to fund loosely veiled political advertisements that do not expressly call on voters to support a specific candidate but instead paint one candidate in a favorable light or another candidate in an unfavorable light. Soft-money was banned by the Bipartisan Campaign Reform Act of 2002.

Sons of Liberty. A group of colonial radicals who opposed British authority and who helped organize the colonial resistance effort.

special districts. Political subunits created by state governments or local governments (county, town, or municipality) to meet a specific need of the community.

spin. The attempt to portray potentially negative events in the most positive light so that they do not "spin out of control."

spoiler. A minor party that takes support away from one of the dominant parties, resulting in an electoral victory for the less popular of the major parties.

spoils system. A comprehensive method of distributing jobs and government benefits to supporters of a particular party or candidate while discriminating against individuals who either remain neutral or support the opposition.

spurious claims. Claims that a causal relationship exists when in fact one does not exist.

Stamp Act (1765). One of several unpopular taxes that Parliament imposed on the colonists following the French and Indian War.

Stamp Act Congress (1765). The first national meeting of colonial leaders, convened for the purpose of formally petitioning British authorities with colonial grievances.

standing. The legal right to bring a case before the court based on one's status as a harmed party.

State of the Union address. The president's annual speech to Congress and the country outlining his evaluation of contemporary issues and plans for future policies.

state-centered federalism (1787–1834). The initial period of American federalism in which the states retained a great deal of autonomy, though the influence of the federal government was on the rise.

strict constructionism. A judicial philosophy that holds that constitutional interpretation should be limited to the language of the Constitution and to the interpretation of the framers' intentions.

suffrage requirements. The necessary qualifications for voting.

Sugar Act (1764). One of several unpopular taxes that Parliament imposed on the colonists following the French and Indian War.

sunset provision. An explicit statement in a law indicating that it will expire on a particular date unless it is formally renewed.

supremacy clause. Article VI of the U.S. Constitution states that the Constitution, federal laws, and treaties are "the supreme Law of the Land; and the Judges in every State shall be bound thereby."

swing voters. Voters who are not committed to a specific candidate or candidates from a single political party and can thus be persuaded to vote for candidates from either political party.

tabloid stories. Stories that emphasize lurid and often exaggerated personal information about newsworthy people.

Tammany Hall. The name for New York's political machine.

Tenth Amendment. Part of the Bill of Rights, this amendment states that "the powers not delegated to the United States by the Constitution, nor prohibited by it to the States, are reserved to the States respectively, or to the people."

term limits. Legal limits on the number of terms an elected official can serve in the same office.

The Tea Act (1773). One of several unpopular taxes that Parliament imposed on the colonists following the French and Indian War.

third party. A party other than the two dominant parties in a two-party system.

Thirteenth Amendment (1865). The first of the Civil War Amendments, this important constitutional amendment barred slavery in the United States.

three-fifths compromise. A constitutional compromise that counted slaves as three-fifths of a person when calculating a state's population for the purpose of allocating both seats in the House of Representatives and electors in the Electoral College.

ticket-splitting. Voting for members of more than one party in a single election.

Tillman Act of 1907. A campaign-finance law that barred registered corporations from contributing to political campaigns.

town. Depending on the state, it is either a political subunit smaller than a county or a small municipality.

Townshend Acts (1767). A series of unpopular taxes that Parliament imposed on the colonists following the French and Indian War.

trade press. A publisher that produces works for the general public and that often lacks the rigor of academic studies.

true independents. People who do not consider themselves members of a specific party and who do not typically favor candidates from one party.

trustee. One uses his or her individual judgment in looking out for the interests of others. *See also* "delegate."

two-party system. A system in which two major political parties dominate the political environment.

unfunded mandates. Federal requirements that bring additional costs to state governments but provide no federal funding source.

unicameral legislature. A legislative body that is not divided into upper and lower chambers but instead contains a single legislative chamber.

unit of analysis. The item on which one collects data in research (people, countries, articles, paragraphs, etc.).

unitary federalism. A political arrangement in which a strong national government has sovereignty over lower levels of government.

validity. Concerns whether empirical data truly measures the concept in question.

variable. A characteristic of people and phenomena that varies.

veto power. The power of the chief executive to void a bill that has been passed by the legislature.

Virginia Plan. A proposal put forth at the Constitutional Convention that would have allocated congressional representation according to each state's population.

vote of no confidence. A vote in the parliament indicating that the majority of members disagree with the prime minister, which leads to elections to select a new parliament (and presumably, a new prime minister).

voting cue. An information shortcut that helps voters make informed decisions with limited information.

war chest. Accumulated campaign funds that are carried over from one election to the next.

War Powers Resolution (1973). An act of Congress designed to limit military actions initiated by the president by requiring consultation with Congress and congressional approval.

winner-take-all system. An electoral system (also known as "first past the post") in which a candidate wins an election by receiving at least one more vote than all other candidates.

writ of certiorari. An order from a higher court demanding that a lower court send up the record of a specified case for review.

yellow journalism. A new breed of journalism introduced in the 1800s that sensationalized the news to win greater readership.

Index

About the Authors

Stephen E. Frantzich is professor of political science at the U.S. Naval Academy, where he has taught for thirty-one years. His sixteen books, focusing on technology and politics, and civic engagement, have utilized a wide variety of research methods. He has served as a consultant to the U.S. Congress, the German Bundestag, the Center for Civic Education, C-SPAN, and the Dirksen Congressional Center. When not writing books, he runs Books for International Goodwill (http://www.big-books.org), an organization designed to recycle books for use in developing countries.

Howard R. Ernst is associate professor of political science at the U.S. Naval Academy and senior scholar at University of Virginia's Center for Politics. His research and teaching interests include environmental politics, electoral politics, and American political development. His publications include *Dangerous Democracy? The Battle over Ballot Initiative in America* (2001), *Chesapeake Bay Blues: Science, Politics, and the Struggle to Save the Bay* (2003), and the *Encyclopedia of American Parties and Elections* (2007).